LIVES OF THE BIGAMISTS

Diálogos

A SERIES OF COURSE ADOPTION BOOKS ON LATIN AMERICA

Independence in Spanish America: Civil Wars, Revolutions, and Underdevelopment
(Revised edition)
Jay Kinsbruner, Queens College

Heroes on Horseback: A Life and Times of the Last Gaucho Caudillos
John Chasteen, University of North Carolina at Chapel Hill

The Life and Death of Carolina Maria de Jesus
Robert M. Levine, University of Miami,
and José Carlos Sebe Bom Meihy, University of São Paulo

The Countryside in Colonial Latin America
Edited by Louisa Schell Hoberman, University of Texas at Austin,
and Susan Migden Socolow, Emory University

¡Que vivan los tamales! Food and the Making of Mexican Identity
Jeffrey M. Pilcher, The Citadel

The Faces of Honor: Sex, Shame, and Violence in Colonial Latin America
Edited by Lyman L. Johnson, University of North Carolina at Charlotte,
and Sonya Lipsett-Rivera, Carleton University

The Century of U.S. Capitalism in Latin America
Thomas F. O'Brien, University of Houston

Tangled Destinies: Latin America and the United States
Don Coerver, TCU, and Linda Hall, University of New Mexico

Everyday Life and Politics in Nineteenth Century Mexico: Men, Women, and War
Mark Wasserman, Rutgers, The State University of New Jersey

Lives of the Bigamists: Marriage, Family, and Community in Colonial Mexico
Richard Boyer, Simon Fraser University

Series advisory editor:
Lyman L. Johnson, University of North Carolina at Charlotte

Lives of the
BIGAMISTS

Marriage, Family, and

Community in Colonial Mexico

RICHARD BOYER

Abridged **DIÁLOGOS** *edition*

University of New Mexico Press

Albuquerque

For My Family

Josette, Nicholas, Thomas, and Christophe

The Library of Congress has cataloged the unabridged
edition as follows:

Boyer, Richard E.
    Lives of the bigamists : marriage, family, and community in
colonial Mexico / Richard Boyer.
       p. cm.
    Includes bibliographical references and index.
    ISBN 0-8263-1571-2
    1. Bigamy—Mexico—History. 2. Marriage—Mexico—History.
3. Family—Mexico—History. I. Title
HQ561.B69 1995
364. 1'83'0972—dc20   94-38576
                                                        CIP

Design: *Mina Yamashita*

Contents

Preface to the Diálogos Edition

PREPARING A NEW EDITION of *Lives of the Bigamists* to fit the Diálogos series proved to be a more daunting task than simply scissoring away "superfluous" detail. My goal was to retain the essential character of the original work and yet cut enough material to make the book of manageable size for university and college courses. To begin I simplified the notes, removing a good deal of discursive interaction with archival documents and the secondary literature. Throughout I tried to shorten discussions of points by trimming detail and examples. But that wasn't enough. I finally had to select a whole section of the book that could be excised without disrupting its core focus on domestic life. I decided on chapter 5 of the original, "The Flow of Information," because its discussion of how people kept track of one another would have been the hardest to condense and because it is a systematic treatment of behaviors already hinted at in the other chapters. Readers interested in how gossip and ordinary conversations between people led to denunciations can best consult the original 1995 edition. I used the opportunity to prepare this edition to correct a number of small errors and also, at times, to recast sentences that seemed less clear than they did when I originally wrote them.

My warmest thanks to the Diálogos series editor, Lyman Johnson, for his advice and counsel mixed in with a few jokes. Our friendship goes all the way back to graduate school, but we passed some particularly fine moments in some of Seville's finest bars in the spring of 1999. Thanks also to David Holtby for expertly seeing the project through with patience and in good humor. As usual, my wife Josette Salles read and reread the manuscript and caught her usual number of glitches. I'm sure that she's tired of my bigamists by now, but was kind enough not to say so.

Acknowledgments to the 1995 Edition

THE TWO HUNDRED or so bigamists of this book have been fascinating companions over the years. Collectively, I view them as representative of colonial Mexico's plebeian world; individually, I see them as fashioning their worlds in distinctive ways. Trying to understand them has been a demanding task and, on taking leave of them now, I am all too aware that much about them can never be recovered.

But I have tried. And where I have faltered, it will not be for lack of encouragement and support from friends and colleagues. I hope that they will understand that the brief listing that follows, probably with too many omissions, cannot show how deeply I appreciate their comments, advice, and suggestions. Without implying that any of them is responsible for the book's errors and shortcomings, I warmly thank Asunción Lavrin, Solange Alberro, Cathy Duke, Sergio Ortega Noriega, Leda Torres, Murdo MacLeod, Dolores Enciso, William Monter, Patricia Seed, Jean-Pierre Dedieu, William French, James Lockhart, Michelle McFarlane, Doris Ladd, Douglas Cole, Brad Benedict, Jorge García, David Barnhill, Steve Stern, María Urquidi, the late Richard Sullivan, Hugh M. Hamill, Jr., Steve Peterson, Ben Metcalfe, and former students, now colleagues, Jennifer Asp and Jacqueline Holler.

I owe special thanks to several colleagues who read and commented on the entire manuscript: Michael Fellman, Edward Ingram, and Woodrow Borah fought their way through the thicket of a preliminary draft—more preliminary than I realized when I passed it to them—and managed to express their enthusiasm even as they pointed out that much remained to be done. Lyman Johnson, Jacqueline Holler, Philip Amos, and Ann Twinam took the time to make painstakingly detailed comments on a subsequent draft. Paul Edward Dutton gave invaluable suggestions for a late and all-important shift in the structure of the manuscript, and William

B. Taylor for final revisions. My wife Josette Salles read various versions
as I wrote and rewrote them. Her concern that I moderate my fascination
for the particular with a more developed framing of it led to a great deal
of cutting and revising, a decidedly ego-bruising business, but the result, I
hope, is a more reasonable balance between trees and forest.

I acknowledge with gratitude the financial support of the Social Sciences
and Research Council of Canada which allowed me to carry out most of the
archival research for this project. Travel grants and a President's Research
Grant from Simon Fraser University supported supplementary research. My
thanks go to the University of Nebraska Press and to the Universidad Nacional
Autónoma de México for allowing me to publish, in somewhat different
form, parts of essays that appeared in Asunción Lavrin, ed., *Sexuality and
Marriage in Colonial Latin America*, and in Ricardo Sánchez, Eric Van
Young, and Gisela von Wobeser, eds. *La ciudad y el campo en la historia de
México: Memoria de la VII Reunión de Historiadores Mexicanos y Norteamericanos*.
I am also grateful to the Huntington Library for granting permission to quote
from a document in their Mexican Inquisition collection.

When reading Inquisition records at the Archivo General de la Nación
during a year's residence in Mexico, the director, Leonor Ortiz Monasterio,
and the staff of that remarkable institution extended many professional
courtesies for which I thank them. At my home institution, Simon Fraser
University, my work was assisted by the attentive assistance of the inter-
library loans office of the W. A. C. Benett library. In my own department
of history, while juggling the demands of teaching, committee work, and
the work to complete this project, Joan MacDonald, Maylene Leong,
Joanna Koczwarski, and Jennifer Alexander helped in dozens of ways.
Anita Mahony, the word processing expert in the office of the office of the
Dean of Arts, formatted the completed manuscript. Finally, my special
thanks to David Holtby, *patrón editorial* of the University of New Mexico
Press, for taking an active interest in the project and guiding it through to
publication.

—January 1994
Simon Fraser University

Lives of the Bigamists

Introduction

THIS BOOK IS ABOUT family, marriage, and community in colonial Mexico from the mid-sixteenth to the mid-eighteenth century. It treats individuals as actors and protagonists, mostly in the ordinary situations of everyday living, by looking at their actions and their representations. It also treats them as social beings whose networks reach outward from the hearth to circles of relatives, neighbors, friends, work associates, and clienteles. These were the "friends and relatives" of the masses who for hundreds of years remained at the center of Catholic social and ritual life.[1] Charity, just as protection from one's enemies, came from the close circles of conviviality and support that enclosed daily routines.[2] It is my view that these close personal associations, more than the formal institutions of church and state, shaped daily life in colonial Mexico.

As a group, the people I shall be discussing come mostly from the laboring classes, though they did not see themselves in terms of social class. I have therefore used other terminology—plebeians, lower orders, ordinary people, and the like—to speak of them collectively. This reflects more accurately, I think, that the lower orders linked themselves with personal ties to families and clienteles, to neighbors in villages and barrios, or to associates in work places. Yet, in a sense, using the social class framework is an appropriate approach for introducing the bigamists, for it helps group them as to how they made their livings, how well they lived, and where they stood in a hierarchical society. As we shall see, they were mainly not upper class—not administrators, professionals, large merchants, or estate owners, but people selling their labor, working seasonally and short-term, and wandering the countryside to find work, escape debt, or peddle a few goods. That they exercised considerable initiative and some choice in day-to-day existence must not obscure their overall place in their society. They were lower-class people— more dependent on employers, masters, and patrons than reliant on their own tools, land, and capital to earn a living. In this they were gradually, but more rapidly from the second half of the eighteenth century, being drawn into larger systems and more complex divisions of labor as wage laborers and consumers rather than producers.[3]

If the protagonists of this book were "ordinary" in falling outside of elite status, they were also ordinary in patterns of childhood, marriage, work, and associations. Their behaviors and values place them well within the mainstream of Hispanic society. The webs of their connections to their society, dense and complicated even from incomplete references in the surviving documents, were remarkable only in their daily, ordinary quality. Thus, to cite the occupations of bigamists and witnesses, running into the hundreds, could serve as a credible sample of the working population of New Spain. I am, of course, speaking mainly but not exclusively of the Hispanic rather than the Indian world, for Indians, while the majority of the population, did not fall under the jurisdiction of the Holy Office. Indians therefore appear in Inquisition records in supporting roles— as wives or husbands, fellow workers, *compadres*, or informants—rather than as the main actors in the story lines of the cases. Nevertheless, the Indian presence shows us how they were both integral and marginal to Hispanic society. They and other humble types give us our view of those at the top of the social-class pyramid—wealthy merchants, mine owners, owners of rural estates (*hacendados*), and magistrates—who figure mainly as bosses, patrons, or judges.

The bigamists and their cohorts in this book reflect Hispanic values as they worked on farms and ranches, in mines, and in shops, doing skilled as well as repetitive and routine tasks. They depended on the patronage of upper-class benefactors or patrons, and moved from job to job and from place to place eking out a living and standing up for their honor as best they could. They did so in an environment possessed of a fundamental contradiction between what has been called "patrician society" and "plebeian culture"[4] that amounted to the lack of correspondence between attitudes and reality, between the supposed and actual frameworks for work. The ideal, in New Spain just as in eighteenth-century England, insisted that workers were not free but "servants," that men and women without a master must be seen as vagabonds and idlers. Yet only a portion of workers could be absorbed into the cozy master-servant relationship of mutual reciprocities. The rest of them moved from place to place, taking up one job after another. Some accepted itinerancy as a way of life; some continued to search for the elusive "good" master to take them in. The lower orders of New Spain, too hispanized to accept peasant manual labor as an ideal, but with too few patrons to go around, took on a picaresque mode, living as "free" men and women moving around and looking to take advantage of situations. But they also wanted to settle down and make a life, and everyday contingencies—accidents, ailments, insults, robberies, job offers, chance meetings—also determined the directions their lives took.

I saw the chance to follow the dramas of ordinary folk when I began to read bigamy files compiled by the Mexican Tribunal of the Holy Office of the Inquisition. It intrigued me that there were so many of them, and it appealed to me that they carry little of the emotional baggage of cases dealing with major heresy. In fact, the cases have a mundane feel, documenting in great detail commonplace activities of people in everyday settings. And such a range of people: women as well as men, mulattos (African-Spanish) and *mestizos* (Indian-Spanish) as well as Spaniards, idlers as well as workers, newcomers as well as old hands. Nearly all of them managed in a plebeian world, nearly all stand out as individuals. As they speak of their comings and goings, we hear about the places they lived in, the events they saw and heard about, the people they knew, and the conversations they engaged in. This, if not the full picture, was the stuff of their lives.

Bigamy files, of course, center on marriages of people because this is what the Inquisition wanted to know about. They can therefore be used to learn about marriage and domestic life. But not only in a narrow way, and not only from the normative standpoint of the judges and the court, for the viewpoints of the men and women who married and lived together also appear. Moreover, their testimonies and stories seldom confine themselves to marriage in a restricted sense, for talk about marriage naturally merges with talk about life more generally. I characterize this more ample view in my subtitle by referring to the *family* and *community* of bigamists. We learn about their wider associations not only from their own statements, but from the references to and testimony of family members, neighbors, and acquaintances of the accused.

From this testimony we shall see muleteers, shepherds, carpenters, servants, and street vendors portraying themselves as the protagonists of their life stories. I have stressed the agency or self-direction they assigned to themselves and, along with what they said, have paid attention to how they spoke. In this, as Carlo Ginzburg reminds us, a concern for "philology is . . . related to a kind of respect for the dead" and the best defense against falling into anachronism.[5] Attention to detail and process thus underscores the complexity of life and reminds us that representations of it in words (in our own as well as in those of our sources) are reductions. But perhaps that tendency can be countered; perhaps we can open up as well as tidy up an exceedingly disparate world and live with a picture of it as a place of complexity and contradiction.

The bigamists of this book, unlike, for example, the European cases of Emmanuel Le Roy Ladurie's Occitan villagers or Carlo Ginzburg's Friulian miller, do not belong to a single community in time and space.[6] Yet they do belong to a coherent Hispanic world of early modern times, from the 1500s to the 1700s. That world, which encompassed Spain and the Indies, had its patterns of values, beliefs, and customs imbedded in the culture. Within that complex, or set of patterns, there was variation and evolution, but at the level of family and private life beliefs and behaviors showed little change during the three centuries of Spanish rule in the Indies. To look at individuals and the ordinary details of their lives, therefore, calls for a periodization stressing continuity and the strength of tradition— more a composition of themes and variations than a linear sequence.

Although scattered in space and time, the subjects of this book spent a good part of their lives in colonial New Spain. In this they can be seen as men and women of the New World. Some of them started in Spain or Portugal, however. For those who began their lives in the Old World, the Indies loomed large. It beckoned the troubled, restless, and ambitious as a refuge and an opportunity; it was a place to make a new life. For those Hispanics "native" to the Indies—many of them the mestizos, mulattos, and *zambos* produced by the coupling of European and African migrants with each other and with the native populations—the New World was a vast space in which to range freely, a place where one might choose or fall into a new life. Whether one crossed the ocean by sail, or mountain and plain by mule, one could distance oneself from an old life.

If the scale of life possibilities in the Indies became extended, it nevertheless remained at the individual level confined to networks of human associations. Cities and towns where Hispanic populations concentrated can be viewed as small, compact societies, aloof from the larger Indian populations of the so-called suburbs and surrounding villages.[7] Both humble and middling types were "subsumed," using one scholar's term, in personalistic clusters revolving around kin, work, or patronage.[8] They labored with their hands, owned little real or personal property, and exercised scant power. A few with grander pretenses claimed the honorific *don* or *doña* (*after* getting to the Indies) to assume a rank and preferment in the colony they could not have claimed at home.

The use of Inquisition documents to flesh out individual lives and the societies that shaped them needs no justification here. As early as 1956, French scholar Pierre Chaunu wrote of their incomparable intimacy and detail for the study of manners and social psychology.[9] At about the same time Julio Caro Baroja was mining Inquisition records to develop arresting and poignant sketches of Jews and *converso*s in Spanish society.[10] The records of the Mexican tribunal are among the most complete of any inquisitorial court. In the past, scholars have used them to study the institution of the Inquisition as a religious and political force in colonial society. Yet Richard E. Greenleaf, for example, the leading modern authority on the Mexican Inquisition, has always stressed the personal and intimate details to be found in Inquisition records: "Kinship and family life show through the procedural apparatus and patterns of speech and behavior reveal the folk culture. The colloquial language of humble people paints vibrant pictures of lower-echelon Spanish and mestizo society. Glimpses of daily life, devotion, and recreation emerge from the documents."[11]

How best to use such records? In the field of social history, Colonial historian James Lockhart notes, historians have "concentrated on fleshed-out portrayals of individual cases and skeletal, aggregate statistics of numerous cases, while rarely adopting the procedure of looking at a moderate number of cases in as much detail as possible."[12] This project attempts the latter with the study of 216 bigamy files that concern people who lived from the sixteenth to the eighteenth century. Let's examine them in global fashion at this point. Known birth dates (n = 182) range from 1498 to 1765, first marriages (n = 186) from 1521 to 1777, and second marriages (n = 179) from 1525 to 1787. Birth dates are mostly approximations; I have calculated them from declarations of age by accused persons, from attributions of age by witnesses, or from the notary's estimates. Of the three approaches, I give precedence to the first unless other information in the document provides reason not to. Marriage dates are more accurate, frequently confirmed by entries copied from parish registers.[13] See the appendix for a listing of all known dates.

It would be impossible to discover how many people in colonial Mexico became bigamists. Some did so without knowing it themselves. We do know, however, that it was one of the most frequently investigated crimes tried by the Inquisition. The indexes in Mexico's national archive list a total of 2,305 cases, a figure that combines trial records (*procesos*) as well as denunciations or accusations that did not go to trial.[14] Although index entries do not necessarily document actual instances of bigamy,[15] they track the moment when individuals were catalogued as suspects, usually shortly after a second marriage. Dates of second marriages in my sample can therefore be compared with the index to show the chronological distribution of my sample in terms of all known cases. Denunciations followed second marriages by about four years, which tells us that bigamists who were caught were detected quickly, but not immediately.

Table 1. Second Marriages (sample) v. All Bigamy Investigations Grouped by Century

CENTURY	2nd MARRIAGE DATES	BIGAMY INDEX NO. AND %	NO. AND %
XVI	(1535–1600)	56 (31%)	345 (15%)
XVII	(1601–1700)	39 (22%)	684 (30%)
XVIII	(1701–1789)	84 (47%)	1,276 (55%)
Totals		179 (100%)	2,305 (100%)

Source: Richard Boyer, *Lives of the Bigamists: Marriage, Family, and Community in Colonial Mexico* (Albuquerque: University of New Mexico Press, 1995), appendix A, and Enciso Rojas, "El delito de bigamia," 80–83. Note the growth in the number of entries in the index is proportional to the growth in population. In 1789 the Inquisition lost jurisdiction over bigamy.

The sample weights the sixteenth century more heavily in number of cases than the indexes (16 percent more), although the seventeenth and eighteenth, with heftier files from the institutionally mature period, include more information about each case.

Men committed the crime of bigamy far more than women, who were more closely supervised and controlled within Hispanic society. My sample has a total of thirty-five women (16 percent), eleven (12.8 percent) of whom lived in the eighteenth century. This latter figure may be compared with a total of eighty-six women out of the total of 554 bigamy entries (15.5 percent) listed in the index for the entire eighteenth century.[16]

As for race, a fluid category that also points to *calidad* or overall reputation, the breakdown for the sample is given in table 2. A subset of those racial groupings from the eighteenth century can be set beside all of their cohorts, comparably clustered, for the same period (table 3).

Table 2. Bigamists by Race: Entire Sample (n = 210/216)

Spaniard	120 (57%)
Indian	4 (2%)
Mulatto	52 (25%)
Mestizo	34 (16%)
Total	210 (100%)

Source: Appendix. The category "Spaniard" includes 89 peninsular Spaniards, 22 creoles (Spaniards born in New Spain), and 9 "other" Europeans; "Mulatto" includes 2 blacks, 8 slaves (black or mulatto), and 5 zambos, an Afro-Indian mixture.

Table 3. Bigamists in the Eighteenth Century, by Race

	Sample (n = 85/86)	Index (n = 396/554)
Spaniard	31 (36.5%)	172 (43.4%)
Indian	3 (3.5%)	2 (0.5%)
Black	5 (6%)	8 (2%)
Casta	46 (54%)	214 (54%)
Totals	85 (100%)	396 (99.9%)

Source: Appendix, and Enciso, "El delito de bigamia," 101–4. I have combined my own breakdown of ethnic-racial types in order to match up better with Enciso. The category "Spaniard" includes peninsular Spaniards (n = 14) and creoles (n = 17); "Indias"; "Black" includes 4 slaves; "Casta" includes 22 mestizos, 20 mulattos, and 4 Afro-Indian mestizos. Enciso's category "Spaniard" combines peninsulars and creoles (n = 163) to which I have added 9 "other" Europeans; "Mestizo" includes all people of mixed race.

In chronology, sex, and race-calidad, my sample approximates the overall activity of the Inquisition with regard to bigamy and makes reference to a broad range of types in the non-Indian population (totaling perhaps half a million people in the middle of the seventeenth century) who fell under the jurisdiction of the Inquisition.[17] Nevertheless, even though "Indians" could not be brought to the Inquisition's dock, many of them, as we have mentioned, appear in the depositions in supporting roles as godparents, bystanders, observers, co-workers, or servants. As for the sample being racially "representative," even though designations found in the index can be refined from material in the files themselves, one careful assessment concludes that bigamy occurred within the racial-ethnic groups in proportion to the numbers of these groups in the population at large.[18] So, in those terms, the archive as a whole reflects the non-Indian population.

This book, largely a report drawn from archival materials, is something of a hybrid, for it ranges widely in time, place, and theme. Yet it remains centered on daily life and the circumstances and details that together make up a kind of pointillist picture of it.[19] In the text I have tried to keep visible the way people speak in their depositions, especially their habit to "quote" past conversations as dialogue rather than as third-person summaries. In this way readers may attend to the mental world of individuals more than to the court as an institution in its work of collecting and evaluating testimony. Consonant with a legal system based on Roman law, judges presumed guilt, sought confessions, and effected reconciliations even though, as we shall see, they also tried to understand motives and states of mind.

In general, then, I take the testimony in the files seriously, as reflective of what people thought and did. Even though the notaries' recording of it almost always shifted the words of witnesses from the first to the third person, that shift is mostly formulaic and predictably delimited. So much so that it might invite "decoding" the words back to direct speech by returning pronouns, possessives, and verb tenses to forms compatible with the speaker as self-referent.[20] Let a brief excerpt from a transcript serve as an example. On June 22, 1684, Alonso de Guizábal, a mestizo, appeared before the tribunal of the Inquisition in Mexico City for his first hearing (*audiencia de oficio*). As recorded by the notary, Alonso's response to the request that he give his life history is as follows:

> Dixo q toda su vida la ha gastado y ocupado desde el dho Pueblo de S Xptoval yendo y biniendo a las ciu^des de Goathemala y San Salvador y S. Miguel con la requa de Antt° Botello, español, vezino de dho pueblo y esso responde.[21]

A literal translation of the above would read:

> He said that he has spent and worked all his life out of the said pueblo of San Christóbal, going and coming to the cities of Guatemala, San Salvador, and San Miguel with the mule team of Antonio Botello, a Spaniard and vecino of the said pueblo and that is his answer.

A plausible reconstruction, in English, of what Alonso actually said might read as follows:

> I've spent my whole life in pueblo San Christóbal and from there worked with Antonio Botello's mule team—he's a Spaniard and vecino of San Christóbal—coming and going to the cities of Guatemala, San Salvador, and San Miguel.

But we cannot know this. For one thing this is a translation. True, it seems safe enough to drop d[i]cho or "said" that twice modifies pueblo that without a doubt represents the court's language, not Alonso's. More uncertain is the combination "gastado y ocupado" (spent and worked) that suggests a possible elision of two fully-realized clauses that I have opened up a bit. On the other hand, the more common "yendo y viniendo" (coming and going) rings as more likely words that Alonso might have joined. But the point is that even in such a brief and simple example much is left to guesswork. I have therefore not transposed the records back to direct speech, but nevertheless remain confident that just below the surface of notarial convention (possibly with some elisions at times) lie the individual voices of bigamists and their cohorts.

For this edition I have removed archival citation in the notes and instead direct readers to the database of bigamists in the appendix. This furthers the logic of the original edition to cite the archival file as a whole rather than a sub-file or a folio number. The reason for this is to simplify what would otherwise become a very cluttered text, for often a single sentence establishing "simple" aspects of a narrative such as the timing and place of an event will draw from several parts of the file. For quotations, however, I indicate in the text the part of the subdocument that it comes from (for example, the autobiographical statement of the accused, a deposition from a particular witness, or a response to one of the prosecutor's charges) and the date. It is important to bring this information into the text because the voices in the records should be seen as connected to the court as interlocutor. However nuanced their observations, however opinionated their judgments, witness-observers spoke within a context of subordination that called for a shaping of their material.

I have organized my discussion of bigamists as a kind of collective ethnography with parts of the stories of individuals distributed in the thematic chapters. In this way we may follow them as a group through the life cycle, albeit mostly a truncated one, because their stories, as far as the files go, stop when they are caught and punished in middle age or before. To divide a life into "stages" is a narrative convenience, and does not create absolute compartments. It also reflects the way people talked about themselves, moving forward and backward in time with the help of hindsight and remembered anticipations to recall rites of passage and moments of change. This comes through most clearly in chapter 2, a discussion of early socialization and training, mostly as reconstructed from the autobiographical sketches bigamists gave in the dock. Bigamists, as everyone else, became oriented to life and work as children and dependents in households. This stage ends as they take their leave and exert more independence in the wider world. The patterns set in the formative years often anticipate a long trajectory stretching well beyond them. Chapters 3 and 4 deal with the domestic worlds created by bigamists as they married and set up their own households, not once but at least twice. Because the Inquisition wanted to know why, we can learn something of how marriages began as well as how they failed. Before we take up the life cycle of bigamists, a chapter on bigamy and the Inquisition places that crime broadly in the context of the tribunal's work and then narrowly exemplifies it by following a single case through the eyes of the tribunal to illustrate how a bigamy file was created.

CHAPTER ONE

Bigamy and the Inquisition

ON A JULY DAY in 1762 Paula Salazar married Andrés González.[1] She was in her early twenties, he was thirty-four; both were mulattos. The marriage took place in Escuintla, Paula's hometown, an isolated pueblo in the Pacific coast province of Soconusco at the southeast edge of New Spain. Andrés, an outsider, had come into the district only a year or two before to work as a farm laborer. Before that, he lived and worked on a sugar hacienda in the district of Verapaz (northern Guatemala) named San Gerónimo where he had a wife, Manuela, and five children. No one from Escuintla knew any of this, of course, and the marriage took place routinely. As such, no one except those in the family and the locale would have found it remarkable or memorable. Yet it became notorious when locals discovered that Andrés was a bigamist. The Holy Office of the Inquisition arrested and tried him and the file their officials compiled on Andrés forms a record that survives to our own time. This file and others like it stand as the primary documentation for this book.

The story of Andrés's second marriage begins in 1760 or 1761 when he left San Gerónimo to look for work on "the south coast," a reference to coastal Soconusco. For "more than a year" he held agricultural jobs (possibly on *cacao* plantations), met Paula, and married her. But like all practicing Catholics, Andrés knew marriage to be a sacrament that forms a permanent bond between a man and a woman. So Andrés risked imprisonment, punishment, and infamy, and we cannot help but wonder why. Our best clue comes from Andrés's brief reply to the prosecutor's indictment (read to him on December 19, 1768) which, in a formulaic way, associates bigamists with "the heretics and Mohammedans who consider having a plurality of wives licit." Andrés rejected this association. Instead he presented himself as having been "carried away by sensual love" and so had "solicited" Paula. In conventional terms, then, the story is this: a man leaves home to find work; he falls in love with a young woman; and, probably to have sexual relations with her, marries her. In doing this, let us note, Andrés rejects only part of the Christian model of marriage—its permanence for as long as one's spouse lives—but for the rest dutifully follows procedures set out by the Council of Trent as filtered by local customs. In this he behaved in an ordinary way and against a more complex backdrop (barely hinted at in the documentation) than we can now reconstruct: perceptions of economic and work conditions in two adjacent regions, judgments about society's rules about sex and marriage, and private aspirations and emotions.

Wisely or unwisely Andrés threw himself into a new life. He later recalled with the utmost precision how long it lasted: "from the day before San Pedro [June 29, a week or so before the actual marriage] until the ninth of September." Then he briefly returned to San Gerónimo, the scene of his old life, to check on "a house, some cattle, and some mules." He wanted to sell the livestock and other property, it seems, and to help him he "employed" a "black" from Escuintla, Ignacio Figarroa. As a man of few resources, Andrés's plan is understandable. But why bring Ignacio, a man with a family connection to Paula?[2] We have no way of knowing but the answer, I think, lies in conventions of patronage. Andrés would have been expected to pick a partner from "family," and this overrode whatever unease he might have had that Ignacio, more than someone without a family connection, might note and denounce his marital irregularity. In fact Ignacio did overhear Andrés and some acquaintances talking about Manuela and, on reaching the next settlement, San Mateo Zalamá,[3] a pueblo near San Gerónimo, denounced Andrés to the deputy alcalde mayor of Verapaz province, "captain of infantry" don Jacinto de León. On November 10, 1762, don Jacinto wrote out the denunciation (no notary was available), arrested Andrés, and ordered his sergeant to take him (together with Ignacio "in case he is needed") to doctor don Juan

Falla, commissioner of the Inquisition in Guatemala City.

Thus another bigamist fell into the hands of the Holy Office of the Inquisition. And although Andrés's crime was a minor one, compared, for example, with major heresy, and a man of the lowest ranks of society, the tribunal took great care with his case. Before we follow it further, however, I should like to set the context for it (and for the other bigamy cases used in this study) by showing how the policing of bigamy fit more generally into the work of the Inquisition.

The Inquisition and Bigamy

The Spanish or "modern" Inquisition differed from its medieval predecessor in being an agent of the crown rather than of the papacy. Pope Sixtus IV granted royal jurisdiction over it to Ferdinand and Isabella in 1478 (for Castile) and in 1481 (for Aragón). By 1482 the earliest tribunals (in Seville, Córdoba, Valencia, and Zaragoza) had begun to uncover so-called crypto-Jews, New Christian converts accused of secretly practicing Jewish rites.[4] The creation and early work of these tribunals should be seen, as Edward Peters points out, as part of a mid-fifteenth-century shift in Spanish attitude: from "religious anti-Semitism" to "ethnic anti-Semitism."[5] The former had been concerned only with religious Jews and had welcomed conversos as converts; the latter suspected conversos as well as Jews. In fact even sincere conversos who were prominent in their communities became targets of Inquisitorial prosecution, envied and suspected because of their success, within the logic of local politics.[6] By 1560, this attitude dominated the Spanish outlook, serving as the base of popular support for no fewer than twenty-three tribunals set up to deal with suspect conversos.[7]

These tribunals had considerable success. By the early sixteenth century crypto-Jews had been controlled as, by mid-century, had *moriscos* (crypto-muslims), *luteranos* (Protestants), and *alumbrados* (mystics), the other groups deemed major heretics. Later, at the end of the sixteenth and early in the seventeenth century, the Inquisition launched a major effort against moriscos in Valencia, Zaragoza, and Granada. At the beginning, therefore, the Inquisition worked mainly to uproot major heresies, a task it continued to do later in special campaigns in the regions. For the rest, it went after

Old Christians accused of lesser offenses such as blasphemy, heretical opinions, superstition, bigamy, and the like. This more mundane work involved not the presumption of heresy, but the conviction that the faithful needed instruction, correction, and discipline. In the century and a half from 1540 to 1700, lesser offenses made up nearly sixty percent of the Inquisition's caseload.[8]

An Inquisition came to New Spain immediately after the conquest. For the first ten years friars manned it, and from 1532 to 1571 Mexican bishops (sometimes also friars) directed it. In 1571 the Tribunal of the Holy Office was formally established.[9] The timing matters. It means that the Inquisition in its fully institutionalized form came to the Indies only after completing its project to extirpate major heresies in Spain. By then it had been embarked for a generation on its post-Tridentine mission, "the consolidation of the dogmas and moral teachings of the Counter-Reformation."[10] Yet from the 1530s the Inquisition in New Spain had gone through a cycle similar to the Spanish tribunals, beginning with the policing of "major heresy" in the Indian population and shifting to the enforcement of the Counter-Reformation in the Hispanic population. But if comparable, the shift in New Spain came about for different reasons for, from the first, many judged the Inquisition too harsh and too demanding and therefore an inappropriate way to deal with idolatry and paganism. So began the campaign to remove Indians from Inquisitorial jurisdiction as reports of excessive severity by friars acting as inquisitors in Oaxaca and the Yucatan circulated.[11] It reached a kind of crescendo in 1539 when Bishop Zumárraga "relaxed," or released, don Carlos Ometoczin of Texcoco to secular authorities to be burned at the stake as a "heretical dogmatizer," a punishment considered too harsh by the Inquisitor General in Spain.[12]

Perhaps Indians needed to be exempt from the long arm of the Inquisition. But no one doubted that the Inquisition should deal with the Hispanic population. In fact the reason for setting up tribunals in the New World had been the same as that for founding them in Spain: the fear of crypto-Jews. In particular the crown came to believe that Portuguese Jews had come to the Indies in large numbers. But even so, right from the first the tribunal concerned itself with minor offenses more than major heresies. In 1572, for example, the first full year of work for the tribunal under Inquisitor General Pedro Moya de Contreras, ninety-three cases of "heretical propositions" and forty-four of bigamy came to light.[13] So from the mid-sixteenth century the Inquisition in both the Old and New Worlds dealt mainly with correcting practices and opinions rooted in tradition and in popular culture. In doing so it delved into matters of sex, morals, and popular beliefs about magic and superstition.[14] These concerns touched not just particular groups but the entire Hispanic population, perhaps twenty percent of the total.[15]

Inquisitorial Procedures

The Supreme Council of the Holy Office in Madrid set Inquisition trial procedures and gave direction to all tribunals. Moya de Contreras, having been inquisitor of Murcia, came to New Spain fully experienced in inquisitorial procedures but also carried with him detailed instructions for the founding of a new tribunal.[16] So the unifying force of central direction lay on all tribunals, but even so they varied to some degree depending on place, time, kind of case, and the quality (and qualities) of the officials in charge of individual tribunals.[17]

At a deeper level, the assumptions and procedures used by all inquisitorial tribunals came out of Roman and common law as church canonists applied it.[18] In this the Inquisition shared a common legal tradition with secular jurisdictions, especially that of criminal law. Both, for example, took confession to be the "perfect proof" because accused persons confirmed their guilt directly. More importantly, confession unburdened the conscience, for just as crime was sin, so the court-imposed remedy was "voluntary submission to penitence."[19] Inquisitorial courts made this link more firmly than secular courts because heresy, lodged as it was in the inner world of thoughts and intent, could best be corrected through confession and penitence.

Inquisitorial trials moved through three stages: the indictment, a collecting of evidence leading to a formal accusation (*sumario*); the trial proper (*prueba*); and the sentence (*sentencia*). Indictments started with denunciations. The Inquisition wanted these to be "voluntary" and "spontaneous," but edicts of faith, read in churches and posted on church doors, reminded people of what they should denounce in themselves and in others. The edicts were primers that listed errors, gave examples of suspicious behavior, and urged the faithful to examine their consciences.[20] They threatened curses, damnation, and infamy for those who pushed aside this call for personal and collective self-examination.

The threats were so fearful, says Jaime Contreras, that they "could have transformed anyone into the inquisitor of his neighbor."[21] But more frightening than threats of damnation and excommunication was the atmosphere of fault-finding, betrayal, and petty acts of vengeance encouraged by the edicts in communities.[22] Mexico's first inquisitor, don Pedro Moya de Contreras, underscored the benefits of such an atmosphere in a letter dated May 24, 1572, six months after he read the first edict in the cathedral of Mexico City. "If they censor and denounce each other with very Christian zeal," he wrote, "they will live and speak decently without the need for punishments."[23] So Moya anticipated a self-sustaining inquisitorial system taking hold in New Spain. If the punishments helped, habits of Christian watchfulness mattered more, for these carried the threat of punishment. The edict of grace combined the two nicely by giving the faithful a period of "grace," usually thirty days, to denounce themselves in, thereby to avoid a public penance.[24] Moya's first edict, however, allowed only a grace period of six days and thus he used it more as stick than carrot.[25] For New Spain in general, however, the edicts had a spotty impact because they were read irregularly, were incomprehensible to many, and were often not accompanied by inquisitorial visits.[26] By the eighteenth century the populace had learned to use the tribunal largely for individual ends with a seemingly endless stream of tattling. Reports of witchcraft or superstition seemed an ever more tedious waste of time to the inquisitors, "the despicable prattle of some silly women of the lowliest rank," as one of them complained in 1786.[27]

Once judges received a denunciation along with supporting testimony, they voted on whether to complete the proceso by bringing the case to trial. A "yes" vote meant issuing the order to confine the suspect incommunicado in the secret prison. Formal imprisonment presumed guilt, and often extended detentions already made to prevent flight. Formal indictment and the trial itself were meant to extract a confession and, through penance, effect reconciliation. This last came in an auto de fe, the public ritual that culminated and dramatized the process. From the first, autos de fe were enormously popular. For example, in Moya's first auto de fe in 1574, a huge crowd of both Spaniards and Indians gathered in the main plaza. From seven in the morning until six in the afternoon they listened to the sentences being read out. In particular the important cases, wrote inquisitors Moya and Bonilla, excited "much attention and applause of the people and surprise that there should be such crimes in this land where they had expected not even the shadow of heresy to rest."[28]

The pattern of denunciations, investigations, trials, and autos de fe date from 1484 when, one year after fray Tomás de Torquemada was appointed Inquisitor General of Castile and Aragon, he modeled tribunal procedures on those of the medieval inquisition.[29] By the 1560s—in time to be well imbedded in procedures carried to Mexico in 1571—the Inquisition's Supreme Council in Madrid had standardized and elaborated the ceremony of the auto de fe for maximum public impact. It remained the model for all subsequent trials for the next 250 years.[30]

The Mexican tribunal had a structure and mandate identical to its counterparts in Spain and Portugal but had to deal with a vastly larger territory. It also depended on less principled men to carry out its work. Irregularities therefore resulted, especially in areas distant from tribunal headquarters in Mexico City, but also routinely, especially in the life of prisoners.[31] Yet the Inquisition also policed itself and, on the whole, followed its standardized procedures well enough to produce orderly files.

Inquisition files can be divided into "legal" and "personal" materials. The former include dispatches to commission investigations and to collect testimony; orders to arrest, transport, and jail an accused person; queries and reprimands because of delays or improperly collected evidence; prosecutors' arraignments and consultations (*consultas-de-fe*) in which the judges, theological advisors, and a representative of the local bishop expressed opinions on guilt or innocence; and verdicts indicating penalties to be imposed. Personal materials show up in "life histories" of accused persons; depositions from a sometimes very large number of witnesses; the defendant's responses to the prosecutor's arraignment and to excerpts from witnesses' depositions; and inventories of a prisoner's possessions.

The present study relies mainly on the personal material. Legal and bureaucratic materials of a file can sometimes provide supplementary information and suggest a broader, perhaps more skeptical view of testimony, but they nevertheless represent the voice of the court, not the voices of individuals. From the latter, one glimpses the circumstances, connections, and projects of ordinary people. Personal testimony occurs for three reasons: the inquisitors encouraged it; the procedures of trials allowed for it; and the witnesses spoke with less inhibition than one might expect.

First consider the inquisitors who elicited testimony. They acted primarily as churchmen and only secondarily as judges. Within the ethos of the confessional they worked to reconcile sinners, not merely to punish them. So they drew out a broad range of testimony to probe states of mind, sense of motive, degree of intent, and surrounding circumstances. "With the bare enumeration of our mortal sins," summarized the Council of Trent, "we should not be satisfied; that enumeration we should accompany with the relation of such circumstances as considerably aggravate or extenuate their malice."[32] Such were the theological grounds for drawing out the accused person's point of view, a process that went far beyond comparable probings of contemporary judges in secular courts.[33]

Second consider the trial. Witnesses replied to open-ended questions and said whatever they wanted with no apparent interruptions. More importantly for our purposes, notaries took great care in writing down testimony. They did so because they were instructed to and because the work of the court depended on accurate, complete transcripts. To edit testimony, therefore, would have been audacious, irresponsible, and irreverent. However banal the settings and details described by witnesses, theologians and judges needed to sift through all of it. Moreover testimony had to be read back and ratified as accurate by the witness and by two attesters (a type of witness), and this ratification process put the work of notaries under constant review. Professional, moral, and procedural reasons held notaries to high standards.

Last consider the witnesses who spoke of their lives. As mentioned above, notaries almost always transposed testimony into the third person. The documents that make up an Inquisition file, therefore, are usually not verbatim transcripts. Yet, except for the transposition of tense done in a formulaic way, I have taken them to be essentially that. Recorded testimony comes in a meandering, unstructured shape; remembered dialogues crop up here and there. The "garrulous, faithful memory of the illiterate," in Pierre Goubert's phrase, catches past events and conversations with detail and verve.[34] People casually repeat bits of rough language showing it to be commonplace in verbal exchanges. Thus Juan de Lizarzaburo recalled his wife shouting "be gone Jewish dog" (*anda, perro judío*). As if to underscore the peculiar phrases that came from witnesses, notaries occasionally put in a notation such as "this is the way he said it."[35]

The Ordeal of Andrés González

Having looked briefly at the Inquisition and its procedures, let us now return to Andrés González. His case gives a picture of the Mexican tribunal at work and thus shows us how it created its files. Andrés, to summarize, has been denounced, arrested, and sent to the commissioner of the Inquisition in Guatemala City. A constable locks him in a jail on November 10, 1762, and he does not reappear until December 17 when the commissioner, doctor don Juan Falla, interrogates him.[36] Don Juan's questions follow a standard pattern to establish Andrés's identity and offense. For the first they elicit his age, parents' names, civil status, and place of birth; for the second they extract his admission that he has been arrested "for the crime of marrying two times" and record the information he gives about his wives, children, and marriages (places, dates, names of witnesses, *padrinos*, and officiating priests). The commissioner also asks Andrés why he married a second time. The interview ends with the notary entering into the record a physical description of Andrés: "very tall, with white skin and curly hair, and he lacks most of his upper teeth." Following the interview don Juan returned Andrés to the custody of the constable Joseph de Amaia.

The inquiry proceeded slowly as the inquisitors in Mexico City wrote repeatedly to their representatives in this distant province asking them to provide the evidence they would need to judge the case.[37] They needed, for example, certified copies of the entry in the parish registers in which Andrés's first and second marriages were recorded. They also needed the depositions of witnesses to the marriages and statements from Andrés's wives. To secure this material friar Juan Infante, vicar of the Dominican friary in Guatemala City, was sent to San Gerónimo, the sugar hacienda where Andrés had first married and lived. His instructions are of interest because they show us in ideal form how agents of the inquisition collected the evidence to be used for trials.

> Ask each witness if he knows or presumes why he has been called. If he does not know, you will ask if he knows Andrés González, if he knows that he is married to Manuela López, if he saw them marry, [and if so] which vicar joined their hands, when it [the marriage] was contracted, how long they lived together, how many children they had, what are their names, [and] why the said Andrés González was imprisoned in Zalama. To each question *you will write whatever reply the witness gives* [emphasis added]; you will also ask for a personal description of Andrés González and will close the examination saying: "Is this the truth by the oath you have made?"

Friar Juan did as he was told but his diligence was not up to the standards expected by the inquisitors in Mexico City. In a letter dated July 27, 1764, Inquisitor Vizente wrote that "we find fault with these dispatches, for no authentic copy in judicial form was taken of the entry in the marriage register [and] also missing are the dispatches relative to the second marriage." The evidence collection process continued for five years as friars tried to track down witnesses and take depositions and Mexico City urged haste but also insisted that judicial standards be maintained.

Meanwhile, desperate to resolve his case, Andrés broke out of jail, traveled to Mexico City, and surrendered to the Holy Office. In a hearing two days later, he explained that "seeing that it has been five years since he was put in jail without a determination of his case he took it as more convenient to come and present himself to this Holy Tribunal to be punished for his crime so that afterwards he can help his children who are in great need."

The judges placed Andrés in the secret prison, listed his possessions and described his person (*cala y cata*), and set his board at one-and-a-half *reales* per day. Finally, the preamble to Andrés's trial was to begin. On December 13, 1768, they summoned him for the first of the requisite three formal hearings (audiencias de oficio), each of which ended with the stern admonition (*monición*) to search his conscience and reveal the whole truth, not just part of it. The hearings had begun after he took an oath swearing to tell the truth, to answer all questions, and to remain silent about the proceedings.[38] The inquisitors' questions listed below show how the discourse between Andrés and his judges was structured. Although these hearings cover much of the same ground that had already been dealt with in Andrés's deposition in Guatemala City, they are more detailed and often contain revealing disjunctures created when the inquisitor picked up on an issue or phrase and asked for clarification or elaboration. The hearing began with the court asking Andrés to state his name, birthplace, age, civil status, occupation, and how long he had been in the secret prison. Then he was to give his genealogy, instructed, no doubt, to state it in the usual sequence: 1) parents, 2) paternal grandparents, 3) maternal grandparents, 4) paternal aunts and uncles, 5) maternal aunts and uncles, 6) brothers and sisters, 7) wife and children. Andrés, like all prisoners, said as much as he wanted to about his family, with no apparent restrictions.

Next came questions to determine whether Andrés could be linked with any previous evidence of heresy. What "caste and lineage" were the relatives that Andrés had declared? Had any of them been "imprisoned, penanced, reconciled, or condemned by the Holy Office of the Inquisition?" Was he a baptized and confirmed Christian? Had he heard the mass, confessed, and taken communion at the times ordered by the Holy Mother Church, and was he in possession of an indulgence (*bula de la santa cruzada*)? Then, with no directive indicated in the transcript, but doubtless as prompted, Andrés made the sign of the cross; recited the Lord's Prayer,

Hail Mary, creed, and commandments; named the sacraments; and "responded well to the rest of Christian doctrine." Following this, did he know how to read [and write], had he studied in any faculty, had he ever left these kingdoms? Then, and most importantly for our purposes, he was to relate his autobiography (*discurso de su vida*). The hearing concluded with the inquisitor asking Andrés if he knew or could presume why he had been put in the secret prison of the tribunal.

At this point the legal rituals called for the admonition of prisoners. So, as if Andrés had withheld incriminating information, the judges warned Andrés to search his memory and unburden his conscience by confessing all, not just part, of the truth of his guilt. Only in this way would he save his soul and receive mercy instead of justice. Andrés's second and third hearings, each ending with an admonition, followed in short order (December 15 and December 17) as inquisitorial procedures required.[39]

On January 19, 1769, the prosecutor (*fiscal*) read the accusation made up of eight articles. Because Andrés admitted to bigamy and the collected testimony confirmed this, he was an "apostate heretic of our Holy Catholic Faith or at least suspected of being one." On hearing the formal charges against him for the first time, Andrés, extemporaneously responded article by article. The adversarial atmosphere allowed for a degree of spontaneity as he rejected motives attributed to him to explain his actions. The notaries gave the prosecutor a copy of his responses and with this the indictment was complete.

The case now moved to the trial as such. Andrés had the right to counsel and on January 28 the court appointed Licenciado don Ignacio Dávila de la Madrid. Dávila listened to the reading of court transcripts of Andrés's depositions, the prosecutor's indictment, Andrés's responses, and whatever additional documentation might be relevant ("everything else necessary"). In the presence of the inquisitors, his counsel echoed that of the judges: he told Andrés to confess the entire truth and retract any false testimony in order to speed the trial and receive mercy instead of justice. The trial began on January 30 with a reading of summaries of testimony (*publicación de testigos*), edited to hide the identity of witnesses, to which Andrés replied.[40]

On February 4, Licenciado Ignacio, after consulting with Andrés, made a formal statement for the defense. It followed the normal pattern to concede guilt but plead for mercy. Licenciado Ignacio stressed that Andrés had repented, made a full confession, and in effect had denounced himself by coming directly to the tribunal after breaking out of jail. He also asked the judges to bear in mind the "hunger and privation" Andrés had already suffered during "more than five years" in a Guatemalan jail, hardship he put into perspective with the comment that "even here in this court some prisoners have been known to die of hunger."

A copy of the defense went to the prosecutor, who declined comment, and the judge declared the trial complete. The next step was to consult an "ordinary" (representative of the bishop)[41] and other legal experts and to decide on a verdict (*voto en definitiva*). On February 18, doctor don Julián Vicente González de Andía, "without an Ordinary present because the most Illustrious Archbishop of Guatemala did not name one," but with the benefit of advice from two audiencia judges, reached a verdict.[42] He ordered that Andrés's sentence be read in tribunal chambers, with doors open.[43] It commuted a term of penal servitude at a *presidio* to the time Andrés had already spent in prison and in travel; ordered that he solemnly renounce in public the light suspicion (*de levi*) that he was a heretic; banished him for ten years from the courts of Madrid and Mexico City, and also from the town of Escuintla, where he committed his crime; required that he make a general confession (and give proof that he had done so by presenting a note from his confessor) and also that he confess sacramentally from Christmas to Twelfth Night of the first year; and ordered that on each Saturday for a year he recite "the rosary of our Lady the Virgin Mary." As for which of Andrés's wives was to be his legitimate one, the tribunal referred the decision to episcopal jurisdiction, where he was ordered back to his first wife. On September 25, 1769, the Inquisitors received certification, in a letter dated September 1 from Guatemala City, that Andrés had complied with the terms of his penance.

The Bigamy File as Drama and Document

Andrés's file shows two important aspects of inquisitorial proceedings.

First, even in a routine case dealing with a minor crime, the inquisitors held to their rules of evidence. In particular they made commissioners and their subdelegates meet judicial standards. Of course their rigor did not help Andrés. It led to such long delays that he himself changed the trial venue by going directly to the tribunal in Mexico City. Second, bigamy documents follow what can be called a "comic fictional mode," in Northrup Frye's terms, because their central theme is "integration."[44] After sinners were tried and punished, they were integrated back into their communities. The court, acting on behalf of God, removed sinner-protagonists from religion, family, and community, and through the drama of trial, the humiliation of punishment, and the efficacy of penance, returned them as purged and reconciled. As heroes of their own stories, bigamists were expected to affirm themselves to a degree by confessing sinful deeds; thus they set the stage to receive mercy and reintegration. Their stage was a very public one. Public readings of sentences, floggings accompanied by the announcement of a public crier, solemn processions through crowded streets, and abjurations and reconciliations acted as a warning, an example, even a diversion to appreciative and enthusiastic audiences. In Andrés's case, this drama unfolded in eighty sub-documents on seventy-six folio pages.

So in the privacy of the court individuals had their say, even though an overall structure of what they talked about was set. Tribunals that wanted to understand motive and circumstance needed to draw out the full details of everyday situations. Bigamy trials especially reflect the banal. First, they deal with one of the most common of all crimes tried by the Inquisition, and a wide range of plebeian types turn up in them. Second, because they concern marriage, testimony always takes domestic life as its setting. The accused speak of friends, family, compadres, bosses, work associates, and neighbors, the *dramatis personae* of their lives. These associates of the accused add details and perspectives that clarify and enrich the accounts by principals. As a result it is hard to disagree with the judgment of Edward Peters that the Inquisition's "meticulous investigatory methods produced the largest and most important body of personal data for any society in early modern Europe, particularly for levels of society that have left very few traces elsewhere."[45] From the drama of the courtroom come ordinary stories set in homes, at work, and in the streets. The worlds of bigamists therefore fuse with those of the lower orders in general.

The shape of the testimony stands as another confirmation of this. It rambles, lingers over odd details, and goes off on tangents. Even though people with little power are speaking to those with a great deal of it, the narratives told to the court have much of the spontaneity and artlessness of conversations anywhere. They point to the circumstances and states of mind that come with chance meetings; they recreate scraps of dialogue; they repeat reactions to a surprising piece of news; they draw backdrops of people and situations that frame the shifting vignettes of daily life. Bigamists, in speaking to judges and facing a prosecutor's arraignment, had every reason to present themselves so as to obtain a merciful verdict. Yet they also placed themselves at the center of their narratives as actors exercising some power in the world. In the dock witnesses asserted themselves more than might be expected.

"Sensitive" matters touching on religious issues might have brought a politics of discourse more directly into play. It would amount to witnesses speaking more guardedly, trying to give the correct answer rather than a spontaneous one, when asked about narrowly religious matters. To give formulaic responses learned in catechism or to disclaim competence to comment on the mysteries of the faith seemed the safest course. The point matters because it can mark in the transcripts a distinction between "everyday"' things that plebeian types knew a lot about, and "theological" concerns that were supposed to be beyond them. Jean-Pierre Dedieu has proposed a test of reliability in testimony which correlates inversely with degree of religious sensitivity.[46] The inquisitors well knew that "distortion," self-justification, and casuistical adjustment of norms to situations included implied or applied religious principles, but witnesses almost never showed an awareness of such fine distinctions as they related their experiences. The work of the court in fact lay largely in pulling out implied religious heterodoxies from the banalities in which they were embedded. But for us the banalities matter more than the constructions put on them by inquisitors. Yet both sides, judge and witness, must be kept in view. Witnesses recounted their experiences, how they situated themselves in their world, and how they made sense of their lives; the court, with its normative thrust, gave a sense of how ideologies and institutions presumed to order behavior and belief.

The dialogues of bigamists with inquisitors, therefore, give us the glimpses of their views and actions that place them as "ordinary" within their society. Yet one might wonder if they were not extreme cases, a restless minority who were more rebellious than their cohorts. I think not, for I have already noted (and as we shall see below), they wanted to settle down and got into trouble by following the rules. As for geographical mobility, there is no precise way to measure it, although Ida Altman, in her study of local societies in sixteenth-century Extremadura, concludes that "leaving home to seek opportunities elsewhere was quite normal" and "marriages often involved relocation."[47] As to the last, the study of bigamists shows that the point may also be inverted: relocation often led to marriage.

Bigamy, after all, was not a behavioral but a legal category. It existed to define deviants who violated a central rule of Christian marriage, that matrimony was monogamous and indissoluble. In particular the post-Tridentine (that is, after the Council of Trent) church narrowed the definition of marriage to a sacramental event presided over by clerics and tried to restrict sexuality to marriage. But men and women were coupling all the time in ways that did not necessarily involve marriage but sometimes led to it: engaging in premarital sexual relations, living for long periods in consensual unions, forming casual liaisons, or engaging in adulteries while "living" with a spouse. Officials deplored illicit coupling (seduction, fornication, adultery, and informal unions of shorter or longer duration) and separated couples or forced them to marry; the population in general, however, tolerated a good deal of it.

Control was an enormous task and a concern to both church and state.[48] Moreover it took the legalistic high ground with, I think, minimal impact on behavior as such. The Inquisition, for instance, consistently confined itself narrowly to the legal definition of bigamy (rather than the substantive issue of illicit coupling), for only about one half of one percent of cases from 1522 to 1700 dealt with the suspicious saying "to fornicate is not a sin," or with simple cases of concubinage.[49] So the "bigamy" category singles out only one kind of coupling because the illicit union had been verbally and sacramentally constituted. Those who contracted such liaisons as private events (the behavior without the ceremony) were legion in Hispanic society to judge by the fact that Spanish women in the Old and New World recorded "twice and even four times" the number of extramarital births as their cohorts in other western European countries.[50] It is reasonable to assume that illegitimate births in colonial Mexico accounted for about one quarter of all baptisms.[51]

But concubinage, often a short-term arrangement, should be distinguished from the long-term and stable arrangement known as *barraganía,* an informal union deeply rooted in Hispanic popular culture and accepted to a degree in Spain's thirteenth-century compilation of laws, the *Siete Partidas.*[52] Illegitimacy rates cannot make such a distinction. Yet a connection between marriage desertions and illegal marriages has been made for eighteenth-century Mexico City with the finding that "nearly one-half of all the illegally constituted marriages in Mexico City were formed by at least one person who had deserted his or her family."[53] Deserters would have been more prudent not to marry, for even though the Inquisition taught people to police consensual unions, the penalties for fornication and adultery were simply to separate the offending couple. Sometimes, however, offending couples were forced to marry and this created the bigamist, just as forcing Jews to convert created the converso. The point needs to be underscored because it emphasizes the coexistence of toleration and prohibition.

Bigamists were men and women who are of interest not mainly because they abandoned spouses, an essentially negative act common enough in early modern times, but because of the risks they took in making a new life. They chose to marry, or when pressured agreed to marry, thus acting according to the basic rules of their society. We should see them, then, not as people bent on disorder but as wanting to fit in and settle down. Yet from new surroundings, new partners, new associations, came new lives. We turn next to the families and youthful beginnings of bigamists to see in more detail who they were and where they came from.

CHAPTER TWO

Family and Upbringing

INQUISITION RECORDS are unexpected sources of information about childhood during the colonial period. As required by trial procedures, bigamists gave information about their families and childhood. It is referred to as "genealogies," brief identifications of parents, siblings, and relatives; and as "autobiographies," the parts that touch on the early years. However spare this material, it nevertheless contains traces of the private world of families and households where children gained the knowledge, skills, values, and attitudes they would take as adults into the larger world. Childhood, the time of this socialization, is defined as the stage of life that ends on leaving home.

Parents raised children as a matter of course, within daily routines. In the beginning children remained close to the household, but as time passed they ventured afield and felt the influence of neighbors, relatives, priests, teachers, and masters. Some parents placed their children in service (to perform unskilled work as shepherds, farm hands, mule drivers, or house servants), thereby delegating their upbringing to employer-guardians. This drastic course, often forced by destitution, meant little or no further contact with their families.[1] "Fragmented families" of plebeians lived in late colonial Mexico City with no male adult present, with "continuous changes and constantly reconstituting [themselves]," living in *vecindades* four or five to a room.[2] The compactness of their social space, the requirement that they "share and coordinate" sanitary, washing, and cooking spaces with as many as sixty to ninety other tenants meant a more collective existence and resulted in more intense and more complex communal ties (and frictions) than obtained within rural or "traditional" stem families.[3] Yet humble households with few resources also kept children in residence long after they might have gone. For them, children became an economic asset, and the longer period of coresidence meant a correspondingly strong parental imprint on their lives.

In this way children became moored to place and way of life; they learned from everyday contact at table, hearth, and bench, and in the streets, shops, and churches of their neighborhoods. The customary knowledge they acquired, too full of "subtleties" to reduce to print, Carlo Ginzburg stresses, came from "the living voice . . . gestures and glances."[4] Whether in person or by proxy, raising children came down to a common objective: to join them to society. This happened in a sequence parallel to the rites of passage as baptism, first communion, confirmation, and marriage marked moments of incorporation, participation, accountability, and autonomy.

We approach childhood not directly but obliquely, because this is all the files allow. Witnesses speak of settings and leave-takings, rather than of processes and influences. Yet something of processes can be inferred by linking settings to the "formed" adults visible in the inquisitorial dock. The look backward to childhood, then, shows leaving home as taking a new direction or keeping an old one. Narrators often place this moment against a backdrop of circumstances and portray themselves as acting and reacting. They also speak of the ties and memory of family that remained ten or twenty years after the departure from childhood. These distant and all-too-brief references sometimes convey the nature of past family dynamics after time, distance, and new surroundings and influences had made their impact. We shall look, then, at settings to deduce formative processes; at leave-takings to test for continuities; and at family ties still remaining at mid-life to see how important they were after childhood had passed.

SETTINGS
The Household as School

From the time boys began to observe their fathers at work, they imitated and helped them by running errands and performing simple tasks. So they learned. In this way Martín Sánchez of Cebreros, a district capital of Roman foundation in the Spanish province and diocese of Ávila, must have become increasingly competent as a blacksmith as he frequented his father's shop.[5] By age fourteen or fifteen, he was working with him as a junior partner and so continued for fifteen years until 1559 when the father died. Martín was then about thirty and, assuming his inheritance of the shop, the expected course would have been to carry on as before.[6] Instead, however, he moved to Seville and later crossed to the Indies. Twenty years later (1581), Martín's lifelong friend Andrés Sánchez, spoke of their boyhood in Cebreros and their half-dozen years working together at the Seville mint. Unlike so many others for whom Seville was only an interlude, a place to secure passage to the Indies, Martín settled where he married, fathered six children, was widowed, and married again.[7] Ultimately, as we know, he went to the Indies, but on impulse rather than with advance planning. Serving as a "soldier" on the fleet, he saw Mexico and "the land seemed good," he testified in 1581, so he returned for his wife and immigrated.

By the time Martín was arrested by the Inquisition, he had been in New Spain for about ten years and was then, according to Andrés, a man of "more than 50 years, thin, light-bearded, olive skinned, and one-eyed." The latter, caused by a work accident in Seville, occurred when an iron filing flew into his eye. Other blacksmiths on Tacuba Street, Andrés added, had also known Martín in Seville. But not before Seville, which suggests a common trajectory for many tradesmen in the Indies: emigration from scattered Spanish towns; association based on work for shorter or longer periods in Seville; passage to the Indies at different times; and renewed contact as work and proximity brought them together again. At every stage of Martín's long journey from Cebreros to Seville to Mexico City, he earned his living with the skills learned from his father. Although we have only a bare outline of Martín's movements,[8] they nevertheless show that his work and social ties remained closely linked to the trade he had learned as a child.

Just as his father's blacksmith shop became Martín's school, so the buying, transporting, and butchering of cattle for towns became Antonio de Acevedo's (born ca. 1550). While Martín had learned the skilled trade of blacksmithing in his childhood, Antonio's childhood prepared him to become a merchant. Meat contracting was his father's business, based in Tordesillas, a town of some importance situated on the banks of the Duero River (in the Spanish province and diocese of Valladolid),[9] and from age fifteen (before that Antonio had attended school) he acted as apprentice and associate "traveling to and from various fairs in León, Valladolid, Medina del Rioseco, and Extremadura to market cattle."[10] By his mid-twenties, Antonio, as a full partner, handled meat contracts for villages on the outskirts of Medina del Campo. His life, so far, projected a pattern for the rest of it: a base of literacy from schooling, apprenticeship, partnership, and eventually ownership of the family business. With good prospects at home, Antonio stayed close, married a local woman, and fathered three children.

But then he fell into debt, and ran off to the Indies about 1575, pushed there by his setback. As did many of his contemporaries, he doubtlessly thought he could find in the Indies the wealth that would allow him to return, pay his debts, and resume, maybe on a grander scale, his life in Tordesillas. To help him he had an obvious contact, his uncle Christóbal de Acevedo, a merchant of Mexico City who made Antonio his factor in Oaxaca. That position, Antonio said in his autobiography, required that he "travel through Oaxaca and the Mixteca" with goods provided both by his uncle and by other merchants. In the city of Oaxaca, Antonio also had a modest store with "stock and cash worth over 3000 pesos" that served both as a retail outlet and a base for sending out itinerant peddlers.

The imprint of Antonio's childhood setting amid his father's mercantile transactions remains visible in the man of thirty-four in the inquisitorial dock speaking of his life as a provincial merchant. A childhood in New Spain also presented opportunities to learn the family trade. With the mulatto Diego de Hojeda (born 1558; a legitimate son with a mixed racial background), the parental imprint imposed itself even more firmly. As members of the silk workers' guild, his father in Puebla and grandfather in Mexico City (Spanish silk-weavers from Medellín, Spain) taught Diego

their trade: "in Puebla to age five" (with his father Francisco) and "in Mexico City with his grandfather [Juan] he finished learning it." Diego's statement, more than we might expect, gives weight to the years before five as a time of training when surely most of it came after joining his grandfather's household. In any case he did finish the training, but instead of working as a silkmaker he took jobs as a muleteer and carter. This, however, must have been to avoid silkmaker cohorts who would have noticed the illicit second marriage he contracted. When side-stepping no longer mattered, at the stage when he was sentenced to five years rowing in the galleys, Diego affirmed the worth of silkmaking and his skill at it. No doubt a ploy to escape the rigors of galley servitude, his plea "to pay his debt in a monastery serving in his trade of silkmaker which he knows very well" presumes the logic and values of his society. Otherwise it would have made no sense as a plausible trade-off.

To the kind of settings we have seen so far, we may add the variable of illegitimate birth.[11] Was it in fact a stigma in colonial society? Possibly yes, if we consider that Felipe Robles Quiñones, a merchant specializing in trade with China, arranged a formation for his son Cosme, born in 1586) with lower social and economic prospects than his own.[12] Despite the father's efforts to assure a good future for his son, the social barrier of illegitimacy proved to be formidable. Cosme lived in a stable household with his unmarried parents to age twelve, learning during this period to read and write from a priest named Mendoza. At age twelve, his father and mother (he uses the plural "parents" in his autobiography) placed him with a master in Mexico City to begin an apprenticeship in silkmaking. Cosme must have had problems with this man, for after two years he ran away to Zacatecas and found farmwork on *estancias*. But after six months, his father found him and returned him to his training. Cosme put in three more years to become a silkmaker but instead of working at the trade, signed up for a tour of duty as a soldier at the fort off Veracruz, San Juan de Ulúa. It proved to be an interlude of only eight months, for a bad heart led to a discharge. He then fell back on his silkmaking training to earn a living.

What was the outcome of Cosme's careful upbringing? By 1604, we see Cosme imbedded in a network of men of his and associated trades in

Puebla, but marginal types of racially mixed castes. He had married, and the low social status of his marriage fits with his low standing. His bride was the mulatto Juana Baptista of Guajoçingo, almost certainly illegitimate, the daughter of a free black woman and an "absent" Spaniard.[13] As for Cosme's network, the mulatto Alonso González de Peralta, a taffeta weaver of Guajoçingo, acted as his padrino, or sponsor, at the wedding, and guests attending it included a silkmaker, a tailor (*jubetero*), "other vecinos," and the *estanciero* Gabriel de Alvarado. After the wedding Cosme and Juana served Alvarado, himself a marginal figure living on land deep in the Indian countryside (a half league from Guajoçingo).[14] The move underscores, once again, Cosme's lowly status. Working as a silkweaver would at least have allowed for a life in the city, where the Hispanic world concentrated. And, in fact, after two and a half years in the countryside, Cosme did return to the city, when he and Juana moved to Puebla and stayed for a year and a half in houses belonging to Juana's mother.

So a disjuncture appears between Cosme's childhood and early adulthood. Although he was illegitimate, his parents were Spaniards, and they nurtured him in a family setting and placed him in training with a master. The father's exertions to find Cosme when he ran away and to reinstate his apprenticeship demonstrates his commitment to his son's future prospects. Yet from this comes an adult Cosme of lowlier than expected standing: he marries a woman of caste, he associates with marginal types in his work, he lives in the houses of his black mother-in-law, he banishes himself to the countryside for long periods, and he works at his trade only sporadically.[15] A year before he went to trial (in 1608), Cosme returned to silkmaking by setting up a "silk store" in Toluca, this after another two-year stint in the countryside (on his uncle's farm near Ixtapa), at which point we lose sight of him. It seems possible, however, that he will continue to use his childhood training, possibly now more consistently than before.

The parental direction that can be inferred from childhood settings oriented, more than it fixed in detail, how children would turn out. Too many unexpected and unforeseen circumstances called for the adjustments, decisions, and associations that led to variation. Again, however, the

Joseph

childhood setting of Joseph Miguel Reyes (born ca. 1730) in a family of storekeepers made a lasting imprint. Joseph, more clearly than Cosme, was marked from early childhood as a marginal figure in Hispanic society. He grew up in the Indian countryside (in Calpulalpa, a subject town of Tezcuco), far from Spanish towns; at twenty he married Tomasa María de la Cruz, a "principal" Indian woman native to the town who spoke at least some Spanish. Before and after his marriage, Joseph lived and worked with his parents and three brothers.[16] He mentions no special training, only that the family ran a general-purpose store and did agricultural work (*labores del campo*), the latter probably a reference to raising crops and stock for their own use. All four brothers (and one sister), then, lived among Indians in an isolated town and, from every indication, would continue to do so after their father died. Joseph, however, broke out of the pattern in 1752 when he got into trouble for gambling.[17] Authorities (most likely Indian authorities) put him in jail, from which he escaped and fled to the mining camp of Real del Monte. After two months, he claimed, he returned to Calpulalpa, but Tomasa refused to live with him, a decision that must have been supported by local authorities. So Joseph left and signed up for a term at a military outpost (presidio). In his new world at the presidio, Joseph reconstituted his old world, marrying a second time and setting up a store, which also served as a gambling center.

In hindsight, storekeeping at the presidio seems an inevitable continuity with childhood. But choice, not fate, determined Joseph's course, as he could have chosen to remain among the marginal Spaniards in direct contact with the Indian countryside. From his childhood, after all, he would have acquired the general knowledge of country folk. In this, he stood with 80 percent or more of the population who, in settings of farm and ranch, learned to assess and deal with the endlessly varied circumstances associated with stock and crop raising.

The stable and seemingly uneventful upbringing of the mulatto Felipe Rodríguez (born 1725) therefore exemplifies that of many others. Felipe spent his first twenty years with his parents, resident workers on haciendas near Mexico City. What did he learn? We have no listing but on leaving home at the age of twenty, he found work as a farmhand and a mule

Felipe

driver, presumably the work he had always done. Along the way he also picked up the rudiments of Christian indoctrination, although without the "understanding that he should have had."[18] This much, brief as it is, suggests a firm continuity and lack of opportunity in the lives of poor men (and women), more in the eighteenth century than before, as generation after generation they worked land owned by others and raised children without means or motive to set out on their own.

They may be contrasted with another type of the eighteenth-century countryside with the means and connections to get ahead. The Spaniard Juan Gómez Franco acquired his own land near Córdoba and grew tobacco. How he came to do this goes back to 1711 when, as an eleven-year-old boy, he set out for New Spain (from Yguera de Vargas, Extremadura) with his father Pedro. Pedro settled in Córdoba, grew tobacco for ten years, and in 1721 returned to Spain with Juan. During his sojourn Juan had grown to manhood and, doubtless with increasing responsibilities, helped Pedro. By then Juan had spent half his life in the Indies; had learned to grow, cure, and market tobacco and to read and write; and had become part of a local network.

Once back in Spain, however, he apparently meant to stay. He married Inés María de Escobar of San Lúcar and whatever work he did in the following seven years surely had little to do with his boyhood formation in New Spain. But the marriage then failed. Inés took a lover who, with her blessing, plotted against Juan. He came to fear for his life and around 1730 returned to the Indies, and to the growing and processing of tobacco in Córdoba. And with considerable success, to judge by his will that put his net worth at 60,000 pesos in 1756. Shortly before making his will, after a twenty-year "bachelorhood", he married a second time (in January 1751). By then he stood out as a provincial notable, a status confirmed in 1752 (shortly before he was arrested by the Inquisition), with a viceregal commission naming him lieutenant in the Córdoba militia.

So Juan made a life in the Indies, and its shape had much to do with the formative years with his father. That it ended badly—he died in the inquisitorial prison on January 17, 1756, after a four-year confinement—should not obscure his successful career.[19] In his will he named his son in

Spain, don Sebastián Gómes de Escobar, his only and universal heir "if he is still alive." Otherwise the estate was to go to pious works. To his second wife, the Spaniard doña Francisca Basilia Rodríguez, a native of Córdoba, he left only a townhouse in Córdoba. Doña Francisca, in fact, had been running the tobacco farm in Juan's absence and in a letter of 1752 sued for compensation for "my industry, credit, attendance, and work from cultivating to harvesting, curing and bundling the tobacco." For all his success, however, Juan's final resolution of his life lay not with what he had created in the New World but with that part of himself he had left behind in the Old.

School

Schools supplemented the schooling that was taking place within households. From the late fifteenth century in Spain, well before the rest of Europe, church synods required that parishes provide schools and masters to teach children reading, writing, singing, and Christian doctrine.[20] So it became a common adjunct of childhood settings and its impact can be tracked to some degree in the inquisitorial files.

In New Spain going to school meant different venues and content for boys and girls. Boys went to a parish school where a *maestro* taught them reading, writing, arithmetic, and Catholic doctrine; girls went to an "*escuela de amigas*," where a poorly trained mistress, in her own home, offered rudimentary instruction in reading, in the memorization of the catechism, and in sewing, weaving, and embroidery.[21] So, with this gendered distinction, children received some skills and quite a lot of religious indoctrination. For girls, the objective was a life of subordinate domesticity; for boys, it could be a first stage in preparing to enter one of the professions, commerce, or a trade. Memorizing lists, formulas, and prayers led to little understanding of doctrine, as Jean-Pierre Dedieu has established, yet the link between religious instruction and reading no doubt accounts for the large number of people who learned to read with no apparent "need" for it.[22]

The mestizo Joseph Muñoz de Sanabria, who grew up in the city and the outlying villages of Querétaro, was such a person. Until 1705, when he was around twenty, Joseph lived with his parents, worked as a shepherd, and learned to read and to write. He apparently retained his skills, for when the Inquisition detained him in 1726, he was carrying a book, *Ramillete de Divinaciones*, and stashed among his possessions were two letters (one from a sister and one from his wife), a promissory note from "one Diego Phelipe vecino of Guanajuato and the tenant of a rancho," plus some "other papers." The book, apparently a collection of divinatory formulas, must have been something he referred to frequently, possibly as a roving oracle to isolated country folk. At this level then, Joseph, the son of a small farmer, a simple shepherd and, later, a mule driver, operated as a functioning literate. The essential point, of course, is that people had to use such knowledge or they would lose it.

What should we make of a muleteer's brief autobiographical sketch that stresses details of schooling to the exclusion of almost everything else in his young life? At the very least, it underscores importance by emphasis. The case in point is the muleteer Pedro Pablo Rodríguez (born 1721) who, in the dock in 1767, said that his father (a muleteer and farm worker but dead since Pedro was two) and mother (also by then dead) had been "taken for and reputed [to be] Spaniards." He himself had been born in Tomatlán (jurisdiction of Purificación, Jalisco) [in 1721] and

> when very little they took him to Guadalajara where he began to learn to read. Afterward he returned to the said pueblo where he finished learning to read and to write with his master Thomás Rodríguez Calderón. And then being of an age so that he could work in the job of muleteer, he went to Mexico City and to various places in the north, always with mules.

Pedro's statement hinges on the transition from boyhood to manhood. The first he characterizes solely by his schooling, the second he signals the onset of his working life driving mules. The divide lies at the point of finishing schooling and becoming old enough to work.

The Domestic Settings of Daughters

Our discussion has concentrated on boys rather than girls for two reasons: first, males form the bulk of our sample, and second, the files, even those with a woman as principal, say more about men than women. Women, of course, had fewer options. The usual step that launched them into "adult" life was marriage, and even that meant merely their transfer from the wardship of father or guardian to that of a husband. Here, for example, are some typically elliptic accounts by women of their childhood. In a deposition given in 1691 the mulatto Lorenza de la Cruz said that she "was born [1661] at the Amanalco sugar mill [Cuernavaca] where she grew up and there [at age sixteen or seventeen] she married the said Gerónimo." Bárbara Martina, a *loba* of Indian and mestizo parentage, gave a comparable statement. Born about 1745, she spent her early years with her parents on *ranchos* (her family moved frequently) in the Pachuca mining district and at sixteen married a shepherd of the district.

The upbringing of a creole Spaniard named Mariana Monroy (born 1649) points to a similar sheltered pattern, but from Mariana's sketchy account of it, given in the dock in 1678, a few elaborations applicable to Spaniards, albeit poor, stand out. Raised by her widowed mother who did piecework as a seamstress, Mariana said that she "grew up in her mother's house [in Guadalajara] because she did not know her father and was occupied serving her mother until she was 14."

From her mother Mariana learned to sew, and from a local woman described as a spinster (Antonia Ortiz, no doubt in an escuela de amigas run out of her home), to read and to write. She had memorized and retained the religious material drilled into girls by these mistresses, for she impressed her examiners with well-spoken recitations of the prayers, credo, and commandments, and of the fundamental points of Christian doctrine. At fourteen Mariana married Manuel Figueroa, a newly arrived peninsular Spaniard chosen by her mother. As we shall see in chapter 4, she was unhappy in this marriage (at least in part because Manuel treated her more as a servant than a wife) and to free herself she stressed that she had entered into it against her will.

The pattern repeats itself monotonously: girls confined mostly to domestic settings, learning wifely skills such as sewing and cooking, rehearsing female virtues of modesty, and subordination, and then marrying. The upbringing of María Ignacia Zapata, a natural child of Spaniards ("my mother Mariana Deita Salazar . . . now dead in Sochicoatlan, had me out of wedlock [in 1765]; my father is unknown") parallels that of Mariana.[23] Probably from her mother María learned to sew and to spin and at twenty-three was calling herself a seamstress and spinner. From her mother as well as a *maestra* of Sochicoatlan she learned to read, she said, but only in the rudimentary way for religious purposes: "to spell out the letters one at a time in order to get through the prayers of the catechism." She did not learn to write. When she was twelve, José Hermenegildo Freyre a *castizo* from nearby Meztitlan, seduced her, took her to Tlacolula (near Tianguistengo), and married her.

It is hard to escape the impression that the meager accounts of their early years given by women in the bigamy records represent in fact, a spare and narrow range of choices and opportunities. Not until these women were away from their families and caught up in the drama of their usually troubled marriages do they speak about their lives with the detail and agency that places them as actors, albeit often beleaguered ones, in their worlds. Before that we get the repeated formulaic accounts indicating close parental supervision (with hints of variation by class, caste, and cultural linkage, although these are rarely spelled out), rudimentary training if any at all, and the passing to a new stage of life at marriage. Within these statements a suggestive detail sometimes emerges. That the mulatto María Ignacia Cervantes (born 1753) "went to school [and] only learned the prayers of the doctrine and to sew, but not to read or write"[24] once again points to a different meaning of school for girls and boys.

Family Settings of Gentry, Professionals, and Merchants

So far we have the childhood settings of modest households. Here we make an incursion into those with the resources and lineages to exercise more power and influence in their worlds. None of them ranked in the high nobility, but all aspired to wealth and position, mostly in provincial towns as professionals, merchants, and gentry. The Benavides family, for example, were people of New Christian background from the Spanish city of Toro, a district capital in the province and diocese of Zamora, who were physicians (father and son), moneychangers (grandfather and son), and notaries (two sons). The youngest son Gerónimo, born in 1532, concerns us here.

Although his father died when he was an infant, Gerónimo said (in the inquisitorial dock in 1579) that he stayed in school until he was twelve, "growing up" in his mother's house because he did not know his father. *precoz* At twelve he left home to elude the consequences of a sexual liaison, entered into after a widow extracted his promise to marry her. Gerónimo thereby cut short an upbringing that surely was meant to resemble that of his older brothers. To get out of the marriage, he got out of town. He went "with a soldier" to Perpignan, then under siege by French forces, but arrived after the siege had been lifted.[25] So, Gerónimo went on to Naples where, for five or six years he shipped out "on a lateen fitted out as a privateer whose *patrón* was a Catalan named Jacome Chipriote, son of a Greek."

Some time in 1549 Gerónimo went to Seville, stayed for the usual eight or nine months that it took to secure passage to the Indies, and in 1550 embarked "as a sailor" on the fleet. In Santo Domingo, Gerónimo attached himself to the entourage of the audiencia judge, Licenciado Alonso de Zorita. When Zorita moved to the Guatemalan audiencia (in the spring of 1553), Gerónimo went with him and no doubt thanks to Zorita received the somewhat lowly position of constable.[26] When Zorita was promoted to the Mexico City audiencia (in 1555), Gerónimo again followed him and again emerged with a constableship, this time in Veracruz. He held the post of royal constable (*alcalde de la carcel de corte*) there for seventeen years and in 1574, by then in possession of the title of "His Majesty's Notary," he purchased the position of notary in Jalapa for 1,500 pesos.[27]

By his early forties, after starting out as if the hero of a picaresque novel, Gerónimo had consolidated his position in the Indies. In 1565 (the year his patron Zorita returned to Spain), he married Marina de Ribera in Mexico City, the sister of the notary Guillermo Román, possibly a man Gerónimo had served as an apprentice. Gerónimo now possessed a position commensurate with his family background and in line with the direction he had been headed as a boy.

Although Gerónimo's formation had gone awry, it had been no fault of his family. Like his brothers, his childhood in a household of professionals points to the family concern to lose no ground in the struggle to be more like nobility than commoners. In this they would have measured themselves against the likes of the Hoz Espinosas, claimants to gentry status in the village of Poza (in the provincia of Palencia), people of means and reputation, Old Christians and hidalgos, who also saw to their son's childhood with evident care. As an only child Agustín de Hoz Espinosa Calderón (born 1546) stood to inherit the six farms that his father Pedro de Hoz possessed. Pedro kept Agustín at home until he was nine or ten (ca. 1556), then sent him to Burgos for schooling. There he learned to read and to write and he began a course of studies in the arts; after two years he went to the court (Madrid)[28] as a page, first in service to the marquesa de Poza, later to don Luis Méndez de Haro.

Schooling in Burgos and three years in Madrid provided sufficient grooming for young Agustín's parents to call him home to marry and take his place among provincial notables. He returned in 1561 "to his parents' house and they married him to a maiden named Cazilda, daughter of Miguel Alonso, a nobleman from Soto de Bureba, three leagues distant from Poza." Agustín lived with Cazilda in his father's house for nine years before she died while giving birth. By then he held the position of alderman (*regidor*), judge of the rural constabulary (*alcalde de la hermandad*), and administrator of poor relief (*majordomo de pobres*). The Agustín of twenty-four is enough beyond his childhood upbringing to underscore how smoothly it meshes with the roles he was destined to inherit rather than to struggle for.

Merchants, like professionals, sought to approximate the status of the nobility. And from the seventeenth century they were having considerable success, using their wealth to secure titles, offices, and respectable marriages.[29] To conserve and increase wealth, therefore, loomed as all important. The Malagueñan merchant Diego del Alamo in Spain provides an example of a father dealing with a son who failed to grasp this essential point. Manuel's dissolute habits (imitative of the nobility?) pointed a dagger at the heart of family aspirations because they threatened the basis of the Alamos' importance. To reform his wayward son, Diego sent him to the Indies. We pick up the story in 1776. Manuel is twenty-nine and has had primary schooling (reading, writing, and arithmetic) and some grammar. But as heir to and participant in the family business, he remains completely out of step with the entrepreneurial values responsible for his family's wealth. As he expressed it later (June 4, 1788) to the inquisitors, his

> nature was to spend on country houses, musicians, on many horses, and other diversions—honest ones but too draining of his parents' estate—because he did not understand that excessive spending is an offense to God . . . The truth is his father scolded him, saying that he had to stop, that he had to realize that in the end he would ruin them.

And so to the Indies he went, but alas no cure awaited him there. If anything its free air incited him to new excesses. On making landfall at Veracruz, Diego sold his "good clothing" and other effects that "had cost 1,800 pesos in Spain" and gambled away the proceeds on card games and cock fights. Although he had assumed the honorific *don* (common as it was by then), he became so destitute that he dropped it, together with his surname, out of shame at being reduced to taking the lowly post of night watchman in Zacatecas. Still under an assumed name, Manuel moved up slightly when he began to travel about curing the sick "with the knowledge . . . of medicine he had learned from medical books." Manuel, therefore, used his schooling to educate himself through books rather than through an apprenticeship but, as he appears in the inquisitorial dock in 1787, showed no sign of having set himself on a course to return home. In fact just the opposite; he had given up hope that his father would call him home.

Parental concern for the continuity and advancement of family standing runs through elite childhoods. For elites, wealth or property acted as a sign or basis of status. To control marriages and inheritance mattered most, but from bigamy files we also find parents tending to values, comportment, bearing, and skills that go with familial traditions and aspirations. While wealth and traditional values were important, so were elite networks and the patronage expected from those with power and influence. In childhood training, younger sons fared as well as older ones, especially among professionals where training and therefore some level of competence, stood, at least in part, as the basis for patronage. In comparison with the lower orders, patronage came to well-established hidalgo families as a birthright. A good example of the professional class is Gerónimo de Benavides (the young *pícaro* who worked his way from runaway, to privateer, to constable, to notary). The intent and pattern of his upbringing was comparable to that of his brothers and fell apart, not because of his father's death, but because of his liaison with the widow.

Leave-Takings

The death of a parent disrupted a child's upbringing because it unbalanced household structures. But as we have already seen with Gerónimo, a household headed by his widowed mother carried on to raise a young child within a pattern earlier set for older siblings. Children in small and homogeneous communities also grew up much as they would have had the death of a parent not occurred. At age four, for example, Manuel de Campuzanos Palacios (born 1695) lost his father who drowned while fishing in the Bay of Biscay when he and his brother capsized in a *chalupa*.[30] So Manuel went through boyhood without his father and one uncle. But there were two other uncles, both of whom owned chalupas. And like the other men of Laredo, the Basque coastal village that was home, Manuel no doubt took his place in the small vessels that fished the treacherous waters that had claimed his father.

At eighteen Manuel left home, taking up "maritime occupations," as he said in his autobiography, and since then he had "always" been engaged in them. In this he referred to service on crown ships: a fleet to the Levant, an escort to the Indies fleet, and, on land for a year in Santander, as quartermaster (*guarda almazén de víveres*). In the 1720s, he made several trips between Cádiz and the Indies as a steward and at least one as a helmsman. Marriage to a local woman, also at eighteen, coincides with leaving home and, at the same time, reinforced Manuel's ties to the Laredo way of life with a father-in-law who, like his father and uncles, "used to farm and, in the winter, would fish." Simply growing up in Laredo inclined Manuel to the sea, and for what it was worth, he learned to read and to write and received instruction in Christian doctrine in the "public" school.

Manuel's career as a seaman brought him to the Indies on several occasions, but in 1730, crossing as helmsman of "The Cock of the Indies" (*El gallo indiano*) with various notables aboard, he decided to stay.[31] He did not explain why, but his conduct on landing suggests that Manuel intended to solicit patronage. Listen to how Manuel, in the autobiographical part of his hearing, recounted his first days in New Spain. Leaving Veracruz for Puebla he

> joined the señor Inquisitor and six or eight other passengers in whose company he arrived at Puebla. The others continued on to Mexico City but he stayed in the inn waiting for the Inquisitor to depart in order to go with him and with don Dionisio Caro who promised to loan him a mule for the trip to Mexico City.

En route Manuel failed to ingratiate himself with the inquisitor, who stopped at Guadalupe (on the outskirts of Mexico City) to wait for colleagues yet to come while Manuel continued on to the capital. He stayed there for about ten months,[32] made contact with merchants, probably men from his *tierra,* based in San Felipe el Real (Chihuahua), and traveled north with them. One of them made Manuel a partner, provided him with goods, and sent him to the mining camp of Santa Rosa de Cosihuiriáchic, eighteen leagues to the southwest. There, Manuel said, he "engaged in commerce" (from 1731 to 1732),[33] but work as a factor at a small mining camp hardly could have matched Manuel's initial hopes for patronage and now had taken him a world away from his childhood setting of coastal Laredo. Yet his ending up in Cosihuiriáchic has a logic to it: in the same degree that Laredo's homogeneous society of limited choices shaped Manuel's boyhood, its outlook on the sea also presented him with an invitation to venture into the wider world. Yet once he had ventured, he gravitated to a tiny part of it where his countrymen had already established themselves.

Just as a community, more than a household, shaped Manuel's childhood, so too another kind of community (in this case a Jesuit sugar mill, with its rhythms of production, work routines, and religious observances) served as the childhood setting for Mateo de la Cruz (born 1627).[34] When Mateo was still a baby, his father, a foreman, left with an administrator who had been replaced; his mother died soon after. No one from Mateo's immediate family—father, mother, brother, sister, and a paternal uncle, all of whom worked and lived at Xalmolonga (Malinalco)—became his guardian. Instead Mateo went to the household of his padrino Francisco Mulato, a humble man with only a racial label for a surname. He grew up on the estate weeding cornfields (*milpas*) with other young boys until he began to help with the mule trains. In this it is hard to imagine that his life was any different than it would have been had his own parents raised him.

At seventeen he married María Ana, also from Xalmolonga, thereby underlining the narrow confines of his existence. Three years later he traveled north to take a higher-paying job as a miner. His account contains apparently idiosyncratic details: not the name of the mining camp, for example, but that he came to owe capitán Juan de Morales 150 pesos; barely a mention of the sickness that forced María to return home, but stress on the detail that he stayed to work off the debt rather than accompany her.[35] Why? Did debt outweigh husbandly duties? Because the debt explains why he had to be separated from María. He would have had no choice but to clear it before leaving the area. And so Mateo continued as a miner until about 1655 when "working as a pickman he fell and injured his chest and tail bone." His injury prompted his return to the less dangerous, less arduous, and less remunerative work of farm laborer. He spent four years "cultivating a small milpa" in the Indian pueblo of Xochipalan, located in a hot and dry area (jurisdiction of Iguala, now in Guerrero state). At thirty-nine, Mateo had come full circle from weeding milpas on the Jesuit estate as a boy, to tending his milpa deep in the countryside as a man lamed by injury.[36]

With Manuel and Mateo, the setting of compact communities shaped their childhood much as it would have had they not been orphaned. By contrast, children passing to the guardianship of a relative might suffer greater disruption. At seven, for example, Baltasar Márquez's (born 1587) parents ("humble, country people" from Jerez, he said) died and he passed to the guardianship of his uncle. But the change must have unsettled the boy, for he ran away to Seville "with some other lads." He gives no details about his life in Seville (perhaps he lived by his wits in the fashion of the young pícaros depicted so vividly by Cervantes), only that he remained there for three or four years.[37] He then went to Arcos de la Frontera and, for ten years, served as a farm hand (apparently to a single employer). From Arcos, Baltasar felt the pull of Seville and from there, in his early twenties, he embarked for the Indies.

Baltasar's childhood, as a time of nurturing and training in a household setting, amounted to little. His account passes quickly over his early years and time in Seville to stress the settled period in Arcos. Yet his running away marks such a clear transition, in fact a rejection of his uncle, that it points by implication to at least an imagined contentment in early boyhood with his parents. Arcos, in a household working as "a servant in things of the country," returned him to that life. At fifty (in 1633), Baltasar called himself (in his autobiographical statement) a farmworker and a shepherd. His summary of work in New Spain merely lists places (for example, Veracruz, Otumba, Querétaro, Texcoco, Chalco) and the names of masters for whom he worked. The inquisitors would have understood Baltasar's shorthand: he was presenting himself as a servant living under the authority of masters rather than as a masterless vagabond. The work itself needed no elaboration, for the specific tasks associated with farm and ranch work were well known. So Baltasar did jobs that required no specialized training, but he moved more frequently than might be expected, possibly because he found no long-term work, possibly because he sought more generous employers.

If Baltasar chose to leave his uncle's household, Juan Antonio Ramírez (born 1716) had no chance to remain in that of his parents, Spaniards from Puebla, who died when he too was seven. Juan had family in the city who might have raised him,[38] but instead his cousin took him to Puerto Alvarado, south of Veracruz on the Gulf coast (now Veracruz state) and placed him in service to a fisherman. So Juan became separated from an uncle and aunt, cousins, and three brothers. Ten years later (in 1733), not they but Juan's master sponsored, and possibly orchestrated, his marriage. In the intervening years Juan learned to read a little. He could manage print in books, he said, but not the cursive script of handwriting. He could not write.[39] He also lived for a time in Veracruz where he "learned the trade of tailor," he said in his autobiography, but instead of working in the trade, he returned to Alvarado to fish. In this his boyhood setting (the household of a fisherman in a coastal fishing village) looms as the strongest imprint on the emerging adult.

Baltasar, who ran away, and Juan, who was taken away, both faced change when their parents died. Other boys ran away from home while one or both parents were alive. Some clearly were running *from* home, but without a clear idea what they were running *to*; others simply took advantage of a chance to go when it came. In either case they had some control over when and with whom they would go. Here is how the mestizo Pedro Mateo (born 1642), as part of his autobiography (given January 24, 1667), spoke of his leave-taking:

> Already pretty big ("*siendo ya grandecillo*") [when his father died], he ran away from his mother's house to the Briçeños's estancia near Pueblo de la Barca (Guadalajara) where his cousins lived. He grew up there until he was a young man ("*hasta ya mancebo grande*").

Thus Pedro divided his growing up into two stages. An early childhood ends with his assumption of a kind of incipient maturity—he is "pretty big," and he takes a master. But not just any master, for his objective is to join his cousins. As mestizos on an estancia, they represent the Hispanic world, and so going there meant taking leave of the Indian world of his mother's household. A second stage ends on reaching young manhood, and from this moment Pedro takes charge of his destiny more directly than before.

Another young runaway, the *lobo* Bernabé Christóbal ran away from home at eight; his going links more to opportunity than to any evident aversion toward home. The mayordomo of a great estate was passing through his hometown of Querétaro in 1704, and he had the chance to go north with him and serve as a shepherd. About twenty-five years later Bernabé refers to his leave-taking in two slightly different ways: the first, he had "run away from his parents [when] little [and] went to the Kingdom of León where he served Mireles, mayordomo of the Count of Peñalva"; and that "Eugenio Mireles took him to Nuevo León, raised him, and [in 1715] arranged his marriage with Lorenza María, free mulatto, native and *vecina* of the sheep ranch."[40]

Bernabé, in effect, chose Mireles as his guardian, for young boys (and in theory grown men) could run not to "freedom" but to service and the supervision of a master. Later pairing him with another of his servants was easy enough, but the mayordomo apparently interested himself little in Bernabé in other ways, neglecting, for example to have him instructed in Christian doctrine or to hare him confirmed. Only at age twenty-seven was he confirmed, long after his term of service with Mireles. Work as a shepherd continued to be Bernabé's occupation as an adult, not only in León (where Peñalva had his herds) but elsewhere. Bernabé's boyhood break with his family was decisive and permanent; his choice of an employer-guardian shaped his adult life.[41]

Unlike Bernabé who, once he had taken leave of his parents, spent the rest of his childhood with a single master, Juan Lorenzo de Castillo (born 1680), a lobo "tending more to mulatto than mestizo," changed masters frequently after leaving home at age eight. He went with a second master after only a year and, although he gives no details of his service until age twelve, by then he worked as a muleteer for a third master. To judge by how frequently he changed masters (he had had four by age fifteen and seven by twenty-eight, having served terms of service of one, two, or three years in places ranging from Querétaro to Sempoala, from Parral to Mexico City), Juan exercised considerable control over his life.

Juan's mobility fits with working as a muleteer, his father's occupation as well. So even though Juan spent only his first eight years in his parents' household, the time mattered nonetheless. Juan must have watched his father's comings and goings, helping as best he could, with chores of feeding, watering, tethering, and with the packing or unpacking of them.

His leaving for Querétaro removed him permanently from parental supervision, but Juan's wide-ranging travels as an adult and, most recently, those from his home base in Mexico City, allowed him to maintain some contact with his family—at the time of his arrest his widowed aunt, still in Orizaba; his mother, also widowed, in Puebla with his unmarried sister; his brother, "married to a morisca named Manuela," in Mexico City.

Muleteers served as a ready means for boys to run away because they continually passed through towns and villages, always needed helpers, and were going places that might seem more interesting than home. Boys in coastal towns who had access to the comings and goings of ships, as did Juan de Lizarzaburo, had at hand a comparable way to leave home. Juan grew up in Rentería on the Bay of Biscay in the 1640s. At fourteen, although no longer a mere boy, he said that he "ran away" from his parents' house on a ship going to Andalusía. From that beginning Juan worked on the coastal trade between Cádiz, Seville, Córdoba, Andújar, Badajoz, and eventually to the Indies. If his early years had made him familiar with work carried out by his family (his father was a shopkeeper and his uncle a blacksmith), the presence of ships in the harbor offset family example.

In the Indies Juan stayed in the maritime track that his leave-taking set him upon. He served as a soldier in coastal fortifications, first in Puerto Rico (three years) and in Santo Domingo (twelve years). Then sickness changed his course. He had contracted syphilis somewhere along the way and now traveled to Mexico City to receive the mercury ointment treatment. "After a long wait," he said, the hospital admitted and treated him, but from then on he remained ashore, working as a peddler out of Mexico City and San Juan Zitácuaro (now in Michoacán state). Juan made Zitácuaro his home for ten or twelve years, running six mules to points "throughout the diocese of Michoacán" and to Zacatecas, Querétaro, San Luis Potosí, and Sombrerete. But his illness gradually wore him down. In 1690, when he appeared in the inquisitorial dock, he was no longer working and, as we shall see in chapter 4, was living apart from his wife in Copandaro, an Indian town ten miles or so from Zitácuaro. The trajectory of Juan's life—from the self-assured and almost-grown boy leaving home to the spent fifty-year old complaining that his "natural forces were failing"

(July 10, 1690)—shows us a man overtaken by age and disease after a hard life at sea and in the Indies.

Boys who grew up amid the bustle of Triana, Seville's barrio of seamen and transients, must have felt a correspondingly strong pull of the wider world. As the focus of ships and shipping to the Indies, it gave boys the chance to leave home at any time. Juan de Barrera (born 1648) had no seafarers in his family, but took the chance to go at about age ten. Before that he says little (in his autobiography of 1689) about his family and childhood. His father and eponym was a tailor from Burgos who, with his brother, had migrated to Seville, married a local woman, and lived a settled life practicing his trade. The tailor's family had grown rapidly (Juan was one of seven children), and Juan had been sent to a neighborhood master to learn to read and to write. To leave, he

> arranged to go as cabin boy with Salvador Sánchez, a pilot who was making a voyage to the island of Santo Domingo and since then his work has been, sometimes as a cabin boy, sometimes as a sailor, to sail on various ships from Spain to these Indies, to Porto Belo, Cartagena, Havana, Vera Cruz, and from them back to Cádiz or San Lúcar.

In 1670 Juan made his last Atlantic crossing. He stayed in New Spain for a while, married the Spaniard Ana María Milanés (in 1672), and for five years (his testimony says nothing about his work during this time) lived with her in Tehuacán. Then about 1677 he returned to the sea: a voyage across the Pacific on the Manila galleon, service in the Caribbean in the armada of Barlovento, and work on ships plying the Pacific coast to California. Approaching age forty, Juan showed no sign of departing from the pattern established by that first voyage to leave home.

From our examples, then, boys ran away from home at seven, at eight (two), at about ten or twelve, and at fourteen.[42] They took leave decisively and permanently, but rarely said why. Silence as to motive suggests that such leave-takings fall within the range of unexceptional behavior for plebeian, if not elite, Spaniards. However "personal" their individual reasons, cultural assumptions presumed how and when boys entered society: at seven or eight years, for example, to begin an apprenticeship and by eight, ten, or twelve to serve as cabin boys, helpers with mule trains, shepherds, and servants. The contribution that young boys could make to family enterprises when they existed (stores, farms, ranches, freight haulage, shops) had to be balanced against the costs of keeping them and also against their personal inclinations. After all, ambition, boredom, anger, fear, or resentment directed against family or local authorities also pushed boys from home. But even personal perceptions and impressions were embedded in the culture but with limitless variation possible. A third variable, opportunity, depended on place and circumstance, providing boys with occasions frequent or scarce for approaching potential masters, mostly muleteers and ship captains, but also sometimes clerics and estate administrators.

FAMILY TIES
The Scattering of Families

The mobility of Spaniards' scattered families, sometimes sending fragments in several directions, sometimes simply bifurcating them as when an uncle in the Indies became the destination of a nephew in Spain. But whether leaving first or following a relative, the network of relations and compatriots left behind was unlikely to be a part of one's life again.

Boys who detached themselves from their families and tierras at an early age inevitably lost track of their collateral relatives. Let us look at one more of those boy argonauts in the enterprise of the Indies, the Portuguese Manuel Romano, son of a pilot, with six or seven uncles involved with ships and shipping on both sides of his family. In the inquisitorial dock in 1579, Manuel summarized his early years: "Born in Tavila [in 1559], he grew up in his parents' house until age nine and then went to sea. He made five voyages to New Spain and Santo Domingo as a page and cabin boy."

Still only twenty, Manuel had already been in the Indies for four or five years, and had worked herding cattle on estancias near Veracruz and in the north. By then he could only identify his family in the vaguest way—"six or seven . . . men of the sea that he didn't know." In this he can be compared with Juan de Barrera (born 1648) of Triana, who, as we saw, ran away from home at about age ten. Juan left behind four brothers and two sisters, all young and unmarried, and twenty-five years later knew nothing more about them.

We have already seen that some of those who went to the Indies reestablished themselves with relatives who had gone before. Antonio de Acevedo (born ca. 1550), who crossed to New Spain about 1575, met up with two of his uncles, one of whom was a merchant of Mexico City who placed Antonio as his factor in Oaxaca and the Mixteca. The rest of Antonio's family remained behind in Tordesillas, in Tordehermos (a neighboring village where his mother's family was based), and in the regional center, Valladolid. They were mostly merchants (but included a priest, a farmer, and a physician) and wives or widows of merchants. But to judge by his wife's letter of 1583, the family had become increasingly unimportant to Antonio in the eight years he had been in New Spain. The letter, one of many that she wrote, is full of news and poignantly describes her loneliness and hardships, but Antonio rarely answered. Nevertheless his letters, hit-and-miss as they were, at least provided "some relief from my suffering," she said, "for without them I would have taken you for dead."

Families within the Indies

If moving to a new world across the Atlantic weakened family ties, so did moving within the Indies. The second was played out at a regional scale, albeit a vast one in comparison to Spain. But the point does not depend solely on distances. Inquisition files show that the frequent movement of people frustrated efforts to gather evidence as, for example, when Juan Ignacio Bustamante had no way to confirm Bárbara Martina's parentage because he could not locate her baptismal record. He knew that she had been born about 1745 at Rancho de Santa María, deep in the Indian countryside and, it seems, very close to the small village San Mateo Yxtlahuaca, outside the pueblo of Tolcayuca (now in Hidalgo state), which was visited irregularly by clerics from Tezontepec.[43] He also knew that her parents moved frequently. When the rancho changed owners Bárbara's parents and the other renters departed (she was then a small child) perhaps because the new owner canceled their leases. What had been a community was permanently dispersed. Investigating twenty years after the event (in 1768), Bustamante could not find a single person still on the rancho who had witnessed Bárbara's baptism. "They have all vanished together with the priest and any registers they might have kept. Bárbara Martina's earliest upbringing [he added] was a wandering about with her parents."

Mestizos gravitated more often to the Hispanic than the Indian side of their families, although these could not always be neatly differentiated. Perhaps in areas where acculturation was well advanced, it was mainly a matter of degree. Bárbara, for example, remained only in contact with her mother's family whom she termed "mestizos"; she had no contact with her father's, whom she termed "Indians." Pedro Mateo (born 1642) also lost contact with his Indian relatives. Although he called his mother an Indian (from Xalostotitlán, now in the Altos de Jalisco), she failed to make a permanent imprint on him, even though in his early years he had no contact with Hispanic relatives. Pedro could say a little about his grandfather, "reputedly" an Indian, and his "step-grandfather", his mother's uncle who raised her as an orphan. On the Hispanic side he had only Magdalena, an aunt married to a mulatto, whose sons worked as muleteers, an occupation that often connected Hispanic and Indian worlds, but more within terms set by the former. As we saw above, Pedro ran away from his mother's household when still young and joined mestizo cousins from his father's family on an estancia. Pedro Miguel, *alcalde* of the native population of Xalostotitlan, confirmed Pedro's failure to integrate himself in the life of the Indian town: "he has not been present in this pueblo," he said through an interpreter, "but is always away from here."[44]

Networks of relatives stayed in touch selectively as work, mutual assistance, and proximity, not blood ties in themselves, promoted close ties. Thus a family asset (a store, some land, or a team of mules) could become the focus of a family network. The mules of Nicolás del Valle of Tehuixtla (now in Morelos state) supported his family during his lifetime; after it they served as a reason to stay together. Our glimpse of the family comes after Nicolás died. Juan, the eldest son lived with his wife, younger brother and sister, and widowed mother (probably in her house) and had taken charge of his father's freight business. Two sisters were married to men in a nearby pueblo; one owned mules of his own, the other worked as his helper. Two of Juan's uncles (one from each side) also fed into the network. The first lived at rancho Tepetlapa, a subject village of Teputztlan on the road to Acapulco, the other in the town of Tistla, about two thirds of the way to Acapulco from Cuernavaca. All in all, the several units of the family complemented each other in the hauling of goods between the capital and the port.

The high mortality rates of earlier times culled children from families. Those who lived past childhood would have seen an equal number who had not.[45] Christóbal de Ovando (born 1735) had ten brothers and sisters, but in his early forties only three remained. María Ignacia Cervantes (born 1735), the youngest of seven children, was the only one to survive childhood. Antonio de los Santos Chavarría (born in the 1670s) survived his wife and all seven of his children. Of the latter, only Joseph Francisco (born 1706) lived beyond childhood and he died at age 30 in Hospital de Amor de Dios of Mexico City. Christóbal de Castroverde (born 1576) could name six brothers and sisters who died as children but not "the rest." María Jesús de la Encarnación (born 1750) lost two sisters: one was named María, the other she could not remember. We need not pile up more examples. These underline that those who survived still 'lived' with those who had not. The tallies of dead siblings, some with names forgotten, means not indifference but resignation. Fate, with no evident criteria, had taken many to an early grave while leaving the rest to await a later one.

As the years passed, survivors must have known that family long ago left behind no longer existed except as a faded image of a distant time and place. Juan Rodríguez, after forty years in the Indies, dusted off his memories of family in a village in the mountains of Oviedo. He mentions two brothers and two sisters, one of whom married before he left home. He would have known that they, together with nephews he had never known, might very well be in their graves. Few from his village would have recognized him had he returned.

Conclusion

As enclosed and partly autonomous places, households nurtured children; as social and productive units, they connected them to lineage, community, and culture. The families that made up households mattered, but not all in the same way. Children who remained at home for a longer time, for example, received a correspondingly stronger parental imprint. They came from poor households, (but not the very poorest), where they could be an asset, and from comfortable ones, where the cost of supporting them was easily borne. Whether contact ended at five, ten, or twenty, and whether by running away, moving on, or taking a mate, children left home as socialized and in possession of some knowledge. Boys without specialized training foraged widely for work (or patronage), those with it gravitated to workshops and construction sites to practice their trades.

As they entered a wider world, young people kept track of their kin, at least to a degree. If relatives showed no particular benevolence or generosity, family connections still probably stood as the most resilient and enduring bonds. When active and current they served as a network of reciprocal give and take; when absent, as time, distance, and the original qualities that made them supportive or confining eroded them, they nevertheless lived on as a part of personal identity. In either case they oriented and shaped adults. By the time bigamists appear in the dock (mostly at midlife after many of their relatives had died, and in Mexico City, usually far from the towns and villages where they began their lives), links to family had loosened.

The death of parents occasioned transitions: to guardians, to a master, and sometimes to a picaresque life of temporary jobs and constant movement. But even without death, boys made such transitions by running away. They went, as we have seen, with a master, patron, or employer, and learned a trade, served as cabin boys, helped with mule teams, herded livestock, or worked on farms. If these moves provided a vehicle for running away, they also reestablished boys in familylike settings, headed by patriarchal figures who assumed their guardianship, set them to simple, routine tasks. Still, boys who left home exercised more independence than we might have expected, as they chose masters, jobs, and destinations. Many of them, especially those from Spain who went to the Indies, lost touch with home.

Even the most doting of parents, in whatever form they existed, could not have controlled all the elements involved in raising children. Locale, economy, family, and character carried too many variables and surprises to allow for any easy predictability. If the autobiographical statements rarely linger over them, they nevertheless give an indication of the ways that children deviated from directions presumed by parents, guardians, masters, and teachers. If raising children was meant to control how they would turn out as adults, early formations proved only partly able to withstand the unexpected and unforeseen.

Girls, like professionals and the gentry, had a more protected and more closely supervised childhood. It centered on hearth and home and so offered far fewer chances for enrichment (wealth and calidad made for some variation) than that based on more contact with a wider world enjoyed by their brothers. Marriage ended their childhood but not their legal minority or, as we shall see in chapter 4, their determination to escape marriages that became intolerable. They moved to the custody of a husband, but their lives, as Silvia Arrom has shown for the women of Mexico City, were not confined only to the "domestic sphere" and neither were they "defined exclusively as wives and mothers."[46] In the next chapter we focus on marriage, to see how and sometimes why women and men married and thus became fully incorporated into society as adults.

CHAPTER THREE

Marriage

IF MARRIAGE MARKED the transition to adult standing, it did so for a man
more fully than for a woman. A woman shifted from the custody of her
parents to that of her husband, thus in law and custom her condition hardly
changed. Both, in Nancy F. Cott's words, approximated "an indenture
between master and servant" little different from other "dependency
relations . . . [of] traditional society."[1] If Spanish women retained ownership
of their dowries (when they had them), their husbands nevertheless
controlled this property and also retained legal guardianship over children.[2]
Canon law held a more egalitarian view of marriage (at least in prescribing
reciprocal duties between husband and wife) but, as Silvia Arrom has
noted, its norms remained theoretical: rarely observed by laymen and
seldom enforced by clerics.[3] So wives, as part of a new social unit, lived
as subordinates to husbands, bearing and raising children in a domestic
setting. Husbands, on the other hand, inherited the patriarchal mantle
which gave them uncontested "jurisdiction" over wives. And even if newly
married men often continued to live for a time in their fathers' households,
the conjugal relationship sooner or later became the basis for authority
over a separate household composed of wife and children and also,
sometimes, of servants, relatives, younger siblings, boarders, orphans,
and possibly a widowed mother.

Theologians from the time of Gratian in the twelfth century to the Council
of Trent had worked to join the contractual and sacramental elements of
marriage under church jurisdiction.[4] Primarily this meant setting up the
supervisory processes to insure that marriages took place publicly, fully

in view of the church and the community. The aftermath—feasting, celebration, and consummation—could take place much as it always had. Mutual consent, the pledge of a man and woman to marry in the future (betrothal) or in the present (marriage), remained the essential core of marriage. The rest could be dispensed with or, as with the blessing, be pronounced later. Courtship, whether conducted by the father in an arranged marriage or by the couple directly, always included consultation with, and usually the approval of, the family.

So the church, the couple, and the family were concerned with marriage. The church defined it as a sacrament, but one to be enacted by the couple itself, for it claimed not to "perform" marriages but to set rules on when, how, and who might marry.[5] Tridentine canons nevertheless restated in more detail than before that the church must "administer" marriages. They grouped barriers or impediments, for example, into those of greater and lesser seriousness. The first, dispensed with only by the pope or a bishop, set minimum ages (twelve for girls, fourteen for boys), forbade force, and disqualified candidates closely related by blood or affinal ties (to prevent incestuous unions), who had a spouse still living (because marriage was a permanent union), or who suffered physical problems (of a type that would prevent them from procreating children).

The less serious impediments, dispensed with by parish priests and vicars, involved procedural irregularities—for example, failure to publicize the marriage in the proper way. In parishes candidates underwent a screening process, the *diligencia matrimonial,* to discover possible barriers, a process opened to the community by announcing the forthcoming marriage from the pulpit on three successive Sundays or feast days. If no impediment arose, the priest issued a license, presided over the public exchange of marriage vows, either during or after the celebration of the mass (the nuptial mass as it appears frequently in the documents), preceded by words of instruction and followed by the priestly benediction, the exchange of a ring, and, after the Pater Noster, embraces and the kiss of peace.[6] Afterwards the priest recorded the union in a parish register, for the permanent record of the community.

By insisting that persons marrying must do so of their own volition, the Council of Trent would prevent forced marriages. But more importantly the measure established the church as arbiter in cases of parent-child conflict. Clerics may have sided with parents in oppositions (most probably never went to a formal hearing), at least as often as with children.[7] But that mattered less than asserting the primacy of clerics over the process of marriage once and for all. The idea was not new (the requirement that marriages be publicly announced and solemnized dated to the Fourth Lateran Council 1215), nor did it happen overnight. But after Trent new penalties for non-compliance were stated. Clandestinity, for example, marriages contracted without a priest present, became an invalidating impediment, whereas before it had been considered valid if troublesome.[8]

Assertion of exclusive jurisdiction over marriage rubbed against the regal pretensions of secular states. France, for example, never promulgated the Tridentine decrees. Instead it passed a law requiring parental consent for marriage, thereby undermining Trent's central concern: to assert the primacy of the doctrine of consent and the church's jurisdiction over it.[9] Spain, in theory equally jealous of regal prerogatives, reserved the right to review and prevent publication of papal bulls and briefs when they ran counter to social convention and law.[10] So Tridentine decrees entered the Spanish empire only on Philip II's "own terms and at the pace that he himself chose to dictate."[11] But he saw nothing subversive in them and so, unlike France, Spain acted as partner rather than adversary of the church by incorporating them into civil law.[12]

Tridentine marriage regulations form the backdrop for the marriages in the bigamy files, but as we shall see, they do not override individual invention and customary practices. In their autobiographies, bigamists relate how they came to marry in two general ways. In the first they portray themselves as submitting (occasionally after considerable resistance) to the agency of brokers, most often parents, masters, or clerics, who promoted the marriage. In the second, they "marry" sacramentally or consensually on their own. This, in cases of elopement or "abduction," sometimes meant defying the woman's parents or, when property and status were not at issue, proceeding without reference to parents who remained unconcerned one way or the other.[13] We shall also see how bigamists, involved in sexual liaisons (brief or extended, begun with no intent to marry) turned these relationships into marriages. They began with men and women seducing one another, running away, and cohabiting. But clerics, officials, and sometimes even ordinary people kept an eye on suspicious "friendships" to see if they needed to be "solemnized" with a priestly blessing, and policing of this kind pressured some bigamists into marrying.

Brokers

The mating of two people, before and after the church increased its supervision of marriage, was ordinary, instinctive, and expected. It followed conventions deeply imbedded in law and custom having to do with procreating children, transferring property, socializing children, gaining advantage through family alliances, and following customs informed by a patriarchal ethos. Although insisting on the centrality of the doctrine of consent in marriage, Trent did not alter the ways that parents, masters, and clerics arranged the marriages of the young. Bigamy records might make it seem that such people often arranged inappropriate marriages because, by definition, bigamists abandoned their first spouses and remarried. As we shall see in chapter 4, however, the failure of first marriages came about for a great many other reasons than how the matches were contracted. For now we shall be concerned not to evaluate the interventions of brokers, but simply to see how they, the couple, and other interested parties played their parts to effect marriages.

Parents

In 1559 Francisco Díaz was the groom in a marriage arranged for him by his father, a chairmaker of Cartaya (Huelva). He was about ten years old at the time, well below the canonical age of fourteen for boys, and, as we might expect, faced an older and larger bride with fear and bewilderment. As a man of thirty-five relating his life story in the inquisitorial dock, Francisco said that he remembered "very well" that morning twenty-five years before in the town of Lepe, near the coast on the Gulf of Cádiz about midway between Huelva and Ayamonte (in the diocese of Seville). "They brought him . . . to the main church to marry a young woman . . .

and the priest gave the nuptial blessing. And once blessed he fled out of fear of the woman who was as big as a Philistine and this one, a boy, was afraid of her." The bride, Juana García, the daughter of a gravedigger, "had been brought up" by Juan de Córdoba and Juana García. Juana, as the eponym of her mistress-guardian, most likely had gone to Córdoba's house as a serving girl at an early age.

After the wedding Francisco and Juana returned to her master's house for a wedding meal and "for two weeks lived a married life."[14] Yet Francisco "truly" did not remember, he testified, "whether he knew her carnally because he was so dazed." In any case an older brother, Pedro, came to the rescue by arranging his passage to the Indies.[15] Thus Francisco escaped the marriage decided for him. Years later, however, he remained perplexed that his own father had been "the one who arranged it."

Francisco's marriage had little in the way of property, honor, or status at stake. One commoner married another in a socially if not personally suitable match. Given the latter, it seems that Francisco's age, taste, and sensibility counted for little and that the goal of securing a family alliance, a purpose of plebeian as well as elite marriages, dominated the decision.

Parental objectives appear more straightforward in families of some, if relatively little, status. Although María de la Cruz, a widowed seamstress, could not endow her daughter Mariana Monroy (born 1649), she nevertheless could represent her as of a respectable creole lineage, long rooted in Guadalajara. This plus the fact that Mariana was a beauty of medium height, full figure, white skin, rosy cheeks, small nose, dark eyes, and black hair gave María some reason to hope for an advantageous match. When Mariana reached age fourteen, María pressed her to marry a newcomer, Manuel Figueroa, about twenty, who "sometimes said he was from Seville [Mariana testified fifteen years later], and sometimes from Ayamonte." And so she did, "to please her mother . . . but not willingly because she did not want to get married." In the context of a bigamy trial, Mariana's argument stressing her lack of consent implies that a valid marriage had not taken place.[16] At the time, however, it seems more likely that she readily had deferred to her mother.

Could she have prevented the marriage by resisting? Probably not, for parents and guardians presumed the right to arrange marriages and when faced with filial resistance countered with threats and abuse. The Spaniard Rita Lobato (born 1726) possessed little honor as an illegitimate child fathered by "a certain priest" and also, apparently, no dowry.[17] Yet because she lived in an Indian town (Santa Ana el Grande, now Honduras) she, through her Spanish mother, doña Isabel Lobato, laid claim to superior status and, for what it was worth, also flaunted the honorific *doña.* She got away with inflating her worth because honor was relative in frontier zones where Hispanics were surrounded by large Indian or slave populations.[18] In such places, eligible marriage partners must have been rare, and so Ignacio Buscarones's arrival in 1737 would have been closely noted. He was about twenty, a Spaniard native to Orizaba, roving the countryside in search of a patron or employment; and he found work with don Felipe Ruiz de Contreras, doña Isabel's son-in-law. It was his master don Felipe, Ignacio testified in 1744, who "persuaded him and arranged his marriage to [Rita]." But Rita said no, and as a result, "doña Isabel punished and abused her so much that twice she ran away and took refuge in the house of the three Medina sisters in the pueblo."

In fact doña Isabel failed to break Rita's opposition and so instead of risking a public marriage at the church, she persuaded a priest to come to her house where, with only her and one other witness present, he pronounced the nuptial blessing.[19] Her caution proved wise, for following the ceremony young Rita redoubled her opposition by insisting that she was not married and had never wanted to marry. Temporarily, at least, a truce could be declared, as doña Isabel, on the grounds that Rita was too young to consummate the marriage (she was eleven and canon law stipulated twelve as the minimum age for girls), said that Ignacio should wait until the following Easter. By then, however, she was saying that she "hated" (*aborrecía*) Ignacio and "in public said that he would not be joined with her daughter." Ignacio tried to resolve the dispute by asking the priest to intervene, but by now doña Isabel was using Rita's opposition as grounds for saying that a valid marriage had not taken place. As a result Ignacio left town thinking that he had not really married Rita.

The case, then, illustrates how doña Isabel, to marry her daughter and then to "annul" the marriage, honored church procedures in the breach more than the observance. First she used a priest as a cover of legality to override Rita's resistance; then she argued that consent had been violated, to deny that a marriage had taken place. The file gives no reason for her about-face, only a picture of it, as she at first intimidated Rita and manipulated the priest, and then as she sided with her and disregarded him.

More commonly parental use of church authority came in suits on behalf of a daughter, claiming that a suitor had promised to marry her (thereby establishing a binding betrothal), had taken her virginity, and then had abandoned her.[20] Pedro Muñoz Palomir, a Spaniard from Villa Conil (province and diocese of Cádiz), was not guilty of this entire sequence, but he did delay a marriage arranged by his uncle to Juana López de Heredia long enough that Juana sued for breach of promise. An ecclesiastical judge placed Pedro in jail while he heard the complaint, and in 1707 ordered the marriage to take place without delay. The judgment found that the oral agreement made by Pedro's uncle was binding even though, as don Pedro, marquis of Herrera, a witness, observed, Pedro had objected with "violence and repugnance." As a result, Herrera recalled, Pedro "left Juana's house on the very night of the ceremony on the pretense that he was going to change clothes and never came back."

The young man ran away to the Indies, perhaps his only option given that family and local authority stood firmly against him. It may seem surprising that in 1707, with the principle that marriage be a *consensual* contract so well established in canon law, the judge forced it in this way.[21] But a woman's honor (or more precisely her family's honor) was at stake, and the judgment looked to repair that by the overriding consideration that the promise to marry constituted a binding contract. Requiring that it be fulfilled solved everything and nothing: Juana's honor had been vindicated, but she experienced not even one day of married life. Until her death some thirty years later, people of her village would know her as "Juana the badly married."

Pedro went through the motions and then freed himself with the traditional "self-divorce."[22] Resistance at an earlier stage conflicted with the deference that young people owed their elders. But in most cases, attitudes of parents and children coincided more than they clashed, because children freely "chose" prospective spouses according to values instilled from childhood. This in fact constituted one of the central rules of the marriage market, that in racial and class terms like married like.[23] Yet there were disagreements, and children sometimes had to decide whether to defy parental authority by resisting a marriage or submit to it by acquiescing in an undesirable one.

One way to finesse the issue was to marry without parental consent. Such a course, of little concern to laborers and peasants without land, mattered a great deal to people with property and with a concern to maintain family status.[24] Catalina de Vega, a young Spanish woman who married clandestinely, thus provoked parental outrage. In Mexico City one night in 1563 Catalina agreed to marry her young suitor, Pedro de Ribero, as he courted her through the iron grill of a window in the house of don Bernardino Pacheco de Bocanegra, one of the richest and most powerful men of Mexico City.[25] Catalina was thirteen, a native of Seville and in Mexico City only since 1561, having come to the Indies with her father, the widower Tomé de Vega. Tomé had purchased the position of notary in Coyoacán, a Nahua town on the outskirts of Mexico City,[26] and placed Catalina in don Bernardino's household where she served his wife, doña Isabel de Luján, a woman of considerable substance in her own right.[27]

Even in the household of such important personages, Catalina did not repress unruly habits. At least, Marina Díaz, who had known her all her life, implied this in testimony she gave in 1573: "She was a fickle young woman; would take advice from no one because she had too much pride; and she boasted that she took advantage of the said Bocanegra's absence to get married." Marina's characterization fits what would have been said about a girl who had so boldly disregarded her masters' authority. The betrothal, words of "future consent", not only made a binding contract, but began "the process of marriage" that became complete with sexual relations. Pedro found this out by consulting Father Jorge de Mendoza, chaplain of the *colegio de niñas,* and, as a result, he tried to begin a married life with Catalina. She, in the meantime, had faced a furious doña Isabel who scolded her, placed her in protective custody in the colegio de niñas, and started a legal inquiry. Tomé de Vega threatened to attack Pedro.

Catalina acted independently of her master and therefore fits Marina's description of her as insubordinate. This I think explains doña Isabel's anger: a thrall in her husband's household had acted with no regard to her and her husband's authority over her; she had thereby insulted and dishonored them. Tomé de Vega's outrage has a different explanation. His project to match Catalina with a man of honor and substance, perhaps in a marriage arranged by her masters, had been thwarted. If doña Isabel set upon Catalina as the target of her wrath, Tomé set upon Pedro as the target of his, on the convention that honorable women seduced or abducted were not party to what had befallen them but instead were innocent victims.[28] With Catalina inaccessible in the colegio and the imminent threat to his safety, Pedro decided to flee. Later father Jorge testified (July 27, 1573) that Pedro told him "he had to leave this city because . . . the said Tomé de Vega was after him to punish and do him harm."

It took about a year for ecclesiastical authorities to confirm the marriage and release Catalina from custody. But to no avail, for Pedro had disappeared. In fact he had gone to Peru, but no one knew that until later. As Father Jorge remembered it:

> About two years after the said Pedro de Ribero left Mexico City [1565], he received a letter from him sent from the city of Lima . . . together with others for the said young lady, for Tomé de Vega, for Bocanegra, and for the mother [superior] of the colegio where Catalina de Vega had been put in custody. [Pedro] said that he was well and had returned to Lima from an expedition of conquest [*entrada*] that he had gone on with a general and other soldiers. From the entrada he got two or three pueblos [in encomienda] and was waiting to find out how much they would be worth. [Pedro] begged him [i.e., Father Jorge] to deliver the said letters and to make the said Tomé de Vega hand over his daughter because she was his wife. He said he would come for her and would

bring a lot of gold and silver and would take her and that he
[Father Jorge] should advise him of the resolution of this.

If mediation should fail, Pedro added, would Father Jorge begin a lawsuit
in Pedro's name? So if Pedro had not followed standard procedures, he
nevertheless had taken his vow seriously. And now that he had raised
himself to the status of encomendero, he seemed confident that Tomé and
others directly involved (and failing that, the intervention of an ecclesiastical
court) would see him in a different light.

But Father Jorge could not find Catalina or her father (so he claimed),
and the mother superior had in the meantime died. As for don Bernardino, by then he may have been disgraced and banished following his
implication in the conspiracy that formed around Martín Cortés from about
1563, which was cut short by his arrest and that of others on July 16,
1566, and the subsequent beheading of the Avila brothers three months
later (October 3).[29] In truth Father Jorge seemed indifferent. He lost Pedro's
letters and sent no reply. His lethargy illustrates a principle: those in need
of a broker in colonial society should choose compadres and relatives rather
than strangers. As much as anything, Father Jorge's lassitude left this
marriage, and consequently the lives of Pedro and Catalina, unsettled for
more than thirty years. Only in 1596, when Catalina petitioned to take up
the long-lost marriage, did a resolution appear. Addressing it to the Holy
Office, she said that

> the said Pedro Ribero has just come to this city in order to
> live with me as his legitimate wife and I need to receive the
> nuptial blessings. I therefore petition your Lordship to . . .
> give me a report of what happened so that I can receive the
> said blessings and live a married life with the said Pedro
> Ribero my husband.

At forty-six, then, Catalina is properly subdued and cautiously
awaiting the completion of her marriage, the nuptial blessing, before
beginning a long-delayed married life with Pedro. But for her guardians
and her father, she would never have been separated from him. But for

the Inquisition, she would have forgotten him and lived out her years married to Alonso Sosa. As it was she lived with Alonso ten years before the Inquisition prosecuted her for bigamy, thus disallowing the relationship.[30] The judgment consigned her to a "marriage" that was only an abstraction, one never consummated or experienced, and with a man whom she would not meet again for another sixteen years.

Catalina's marriage to Pedro in 1563 came just before the Council of Trent tightened its prohibitions against clandestinity. In any case, Tridentine reforms would not have disallowed this marriage, only required that it be formalized publicly in a nuptial mass or at least a nuptial blessing. After about a year, as we have seen, the church sided with Catalina against "parental" objections, but this came too late for Pedro who had already fled. Catalina, apparently in good faith, married again, but this was technically an adulterous relationship and any children she might have had in her prime child-bearing years would have been *adulterinos*, a particularly odious category of illegitimacy. So Catalina paid the price for her initiative because others presumed that it had not been hers to take. Her marriage disrupted her father's aspirations for her, and also, quite possibly, his chances for staying on good terms with don Bernardino. Instead of a wealthy and powerful compadre, Tomé de Vega had only disaffected former employers, irritated at his daughter's affront to their honor. Although Father Jorge insisted at the outset that Catalina and Pedro had indeed married, his inability to counter the anger and opposition of a father and an employer, especially one so powerful, reflects the personalized politics of life in the largest of Spanish colonial cities.

We should see Father Jorge, then, as adjusting church teachings to fit the realities of power and influence. As did everyone else in Hispanic society, priests tied themselves to patronage and family networks, cultivating some and not bothering with others. And in certain circumstances families needed to court priests as well.[31] The Mesquita family failed to appreciate this in 1558 when they tried to marry a daughter, Francisca de Alvarez, to a local encomendero, Francisco de Aguila. But Martín de Mesquita, the head of the family and local notable (he held a city magistracy, alcaldía ordinario), arranged the marriage with no reference to the church. At the time, Francisca, a creole Spaniard, was twenty, and Francisco, a peninsular Spaniard claiming to be an hidalgo, sixty. Mesquita proposed the marriage in September, 1557, his motive, surely, to secure for his family Francisco's encomienda. Although it yielded only 400 pesos a year in tribute, the prestige of joining the encomendero class and the gaining of access to workers from Indian towns was a prize to covet.

All went according to plan and in June 1558, the couple "joined hands as husband and wife," Francisca testified, and "married with the words of present consent at the door of her father's house." Catalina, a black slave of the household, and Martín de la Mesquita, Francisca's brother, witnessed the exchange. Three months later, toward the end of September, Francisco and Francisca repeated their exchange, but in a more festive occasion: "last Saturday night," according to Francisca, "clandestinely, with the words of present consent." Both occasions, then, were clandestine, because the wedding had not been announced, no priest presided, and no nuptial blessing was given. And the couple, as well as the entire Mesquita household (father, mother, brothers, sisters, two brothers-in-law, and servants), were implicated. Francisca testified later that "Francisco had her virginity," probably in the period following the original exchange in June.

Anticipating Tridentine rulings, a vicar annulled this marriage on the grounds that it was "not a true marriage because it was not preceded by the reading of the banns and not [conducted] in the sight of the church (*in facie ecclesiae*) as is the rule and custom of the Holy Mother Church." So much for the assumption of the Mesquita family that they could contract a marriage strictly as a private, family event. Yet in spite of these objections, clandestine marriages, once they slipped through, were supposed to be binding (especially when a woman of honor had lost her virginity), when checked for impediments and confirmed with a nuptial mass or blessing.

So why, in this case, did church authorities insist on the narrowest definition of valid marriage? The answer has to do with politics. The church, at least as represented by the prior of the Dominican convent, had already foisted a marriage, by proxy, on an unwilling Francisco to one María Valdés Sotomayor. Thus he was already "married," but curiously the church did not annul the marriage to Francisca for that reason but, as we have seen, because a priest failed to preside over it.[32] Although the fault easily could be repaired, as it often was, with a priestly blessing at a nuptial mass, the vicar insisted that the affront be expiated with a fine: 30 pesos for both Francisca and Francisco, 15 for each of the Mesquita children, and an unspecified sum, possibly 30 pesos, for Mesquita himself. Two years later (March 2, 1560), Mesquita, appealing for a reduction of the penalty, said that the fine "would destroy me and my children because I have many of them and am very poor."[33] His distress and his inability to pay (the fine was commuted to labor on a church) underscore how useful the encomienda tribute would have been. The judgment, then, gave occasion for the church to assert its control over marriage, but in general and procedural terms rather than as an instance of bigamy.

Bigamy records have allowed for some glimpses of parents arranging their children's marriages from the midsixteenth to the early eighteenth century, but from the standpoint of children. This yields a sometime exercise of parental authority as arbitrary, ill-considered, and resented. Some of this comes after the fact, but much of it does not. It shows us children in conflict but not in the dock, as they perceived marriage arrangements as having little to do with their own contentment. Overall, however, parents exerted their authority, a matter of honor even in plebeian households, sought tactical advantage (on however humble a scale) through family alliances, and made matches that approximated their own social and economic standing. The last, in modest households, came mainly through the negative test of trying to avoid a drop in status or prestige.

Masters

Masters considered all members of their households to be under their authority, and their presumption to arrange and patronize marriages differed little from that of parents. At best attachments to masters, as with all forms of clientage, involved affection and trust, and this formed the broader context of whatever economic benefits the relationship yielded. Ana Díaz, a Spaniard, had been born in Fez (Muslims had taken her parents captive) around 1519. By 1570 she was well established in Zacatecas, counting among her possessions "some houses" and a black slave named Juan Sape. In her community she was known as a healer of both "poor and rich." Although she did not indicate how and when she arrived in New Spain, she must have come at least twenty years before and then established herself in the household of Alonso Carreño of the mines of Zultepec (in the southwest part of what is now the state of Mexico), most likely as a servant, but also as mistress mother of children fathered by him. But this led to no undue presumption on her part, for she continued to call him "lord and master," and in 1554, at his order, in his house, and under his supervision, she married Pedro Rodríguez. After the marriage she looked to Carreño as patron just as she had before it, serving in his household but now with Pedro. Then, after about a year and a half, Pedro requested leave to move with Ana to Zacatecas and Alonso granted it. There, rumors that Pedro had a wife in Portugal bedeviled the marriage until Pedro departed, ostensibly to go to Portugal to get the affidavits to disprove them.[34]

In Zacatecas Ana waited more than a year with no word from Pedro and then, by letter, explained her trouble to Carreño. In reply he once again made a major decision for her. "Alonso wrote back not to wait for Pedro," she testified in 1572, "that he too had heard that Pedro was married in Portugal, and that if [Ana] should find a suitable young man she should marry him and that he would patronize and help him." Again, then, Carreño endowed Ana and her marriage prospects with the promise of patronage.

As servant, as mistress, and then as "daughter" to pass on to another man in matrimony, Carreño treated Ana as more than a mere employee. Their tie can stand for the familylike protocols that became part of all employer-employee relations. A typical expression of this bond came in the arranging of marriages. Normally masters would match servants within their own households, and what better way to do this than view a newly arrived worker as a suitable partner for a daughter or relative? In his mid-thirties Francisco de Riberos (born 1576 in Conde, Portugal) was employed by Antonio de Carmona of Seville to act as master of a small boat that ran along the Guadalquivir river between Seville and San Lúcar. Before this he had knocked about for years in the Atlantic shipping lanes, engaged mainly in the slave trade between West Africa and the West Indies.

Riberos testified that he stayed with Carmona for at least a year and a half, probably a longer-than-normal stint for him, "because he always gave good pay." After a time, he added, "[Carmona] became fond of him and tried to marry him to Mariana de los Reyes, saying that she was his relative."

The negotiation began correctly enough with Carmona asking Riberos if he were married. Riberos answered yes, to María Francisca in Conde, although it had been eight or nine years since he had news of her, and acquaintances from his tierra had said she was dead. Carmona took this as a qualified "yes" and wanted to proceed. Francisco, however, wanted to check to see if María Francisca was alive. Carmona apparently agreed, but three months later still had not found anyone to travel to Conde. Evidently in a hurry, and without consulting Riberos, he then arranged for three witnesses (one his own wife) to attest in a marriage investigation that Riberos was single. The statements, of course, were perjured to speed things up, for had the witnesses declared Riberos a widower, the marriage could not have proceeded without positive confirmation of María Francisca's death. These shortcuts, Carmona knew, placed Riberos at risk. After giving his own deposition, he returned to his unsuspecting shipmaster and consigned him to his fate. Francisco, in his autobiographical statement seventeen years later (January 1620), recalled the moment. "There was nothing to do now [Carmona said] but entrust [the matter] to God . . . [for] he could now marry the person arranged for him. [Carmona] also offered to help him however he could and so this [witness] determined to marry Mariana de los Reyes, vecina and native of Triana." Francisco's account conveys that the process began tentatively, picked up momentum, and then reached a point of no return.

We need not doubt that Carmona's fondness for Riberos was genuine to wonder why he could not find a more suitable candidate for the marriage. The circumstances, in fact, suggest a family emergency, the need to find a husband quickly for Mariana, possibly because she had been seduced by an unacceptable or now absent suitor or even raped. In the three months intervening between Carmona's initial approach to Riberos and his extraordinary performance before the ecclesiastical judge, the family was searching for a man to marry Mariana. He of course would be of the plebeian ranks (all Mariana's family were carpenters and mariners) but respectable, known in the community, and already connected to the household. Riberos, except for his possibly still-living wife in Conde, fit perfectly. And if the worst happened and Riberos were arrested for bigamy, not Mariana and the Carmona family, but he alone would bear the infamy, loss of honor, and punishment. Family came before friendship, paternalism was a means not an end.

In the same way that plebeian masters married their relatives to employees they also married their daughters. Bartolomé de Renaga, a muleteer based in San Juan del Río (now in Querétaro state), for example, found Domingo Rodríguez, a mestizo from Puebla, in his early twenties, to be "industrious and accommodating," and so proposed that he marry Luisa Ramírez, Renaga's mulatto step-daughter.

How masters "courted" these young plebeian men can be seen in more detail in the case of Pedro Mateo (born 1642), a mestizo native to Xalostotitlan (now in Jalisco state) but who grew up on cattle ranches south of his hometown. At eighteen he gravitated back to Xalostotitlan and found work with an Indian named Pedro Hernández who asked him to marry his daughter, Francisca. At first Pedro declined, saying that he was poor, just a boy (*muchacho*), and without money for the marriage investigation and other expenses. Hernández countered that he would arrange everything, pay the costs, and establish Pedro in his household. So Pedro agreed. And Hernández did his part, but in a way to let Pedro bear the costs after all. After choosing padrinos he supplied Pedro with a new name, Mateo González, and, aliases for his parents in order to present Pedro as Indian. This meant a reduced fee but more importantly set up a deal to commute the fee: the priest agreed to enter "Mateo González" in the marriage register as an Indian in exchange for Hernández's pledge "to some day harvest his maize crop." The obligation, of course, would be passed along to Pedro.

Thus Hernández worked within marriage procedures as set by the church, but adjusted them with the help of a cooperative priest to further family ends. An incident that occurred a year or so later makes this even clearer. Pedro decided to leave the Hernández household and go back to an estancia where he had formerly worked. As he prepared to take Francisca with him, he recalled in his autobiographical statement that Hernández had said "no, that he would beat him before allowing him to take her . . . He said 'go', that he would support Francisca just as he always had while he was raising her and after she married." Hernández, in his own mind, had not "given up" Francisca when she married. He had merely added her consort to his household. Married or not, this plebeian pater familias expected to maintain her and had no intention of releasing her from his service.

Masters on a household scale such as Hernández and Renaga each chose a son-in-law after assessing the young man's strength, industry, and malleability. The last consideration was perhaps linked to youthfulness that presumably could be molded into loyalty to the new household and family. This was crucial, for in addition to recovering the costs of marriages, masters wanted to keep their daughter-servants as part of a productive unit. The process should not be seen as cynically motivated, as if acting out a petty tyranny to mistreat underlings (although in-law ties were often abusive), but as stemming from the ethos of clientage that embedded labor within personalistic bonds. Hernández's impatience with Pedro came because the young mestizo failed to make the transition from outsider to family.

If masters arranged marriages directly, they also facilitated them indirectly. They might, for example, advance money to cover costs. This was not necessarily routine, because it included an element of risk. When a priest of Santa Clara ordered José de Mora (born 1718), a Spaniard native to La Piedad (Valladolid) to quit his "illicit friendship" with María de Josepha de los Reyes (they had lived together for eight years), José agreed to marry her. He asked Joseph León and his wife, Indians of Santa Clara, to act as sponsors, but he recalled, they "declined because they were poor Indians and not able to confer the honors and the candles but [José] answered that they should do it anyway because his master had offered to charge everything to his account."

In fact advancing money in this way could also be a way to hire a worker. So it became in 1735 for Nicolás Antonio de Arauz, a mestizo from Calpulalpa (now in Mexico state), in the impromptu offer of one Pedro Aguador (Peter Waterman) to cover the costs of his marriage. Nicolás had been pasturing some hogs for a gatekeeper (of Mexico City?) who lived just beyond the village of Guadalupe. After delivering the hogs, he was heading north when, as he testified, he "met an Indian named Dominga" who lived with her mother and three brothers, selling food to travelers next to the pueblo of Santa Clara, beyond Guadalupe, on the royal highway (*camino real*). Nicolás took up with Dominga, and Pedro eventually offered to pay the costs so the two could marry.

Pedro bound Nicolás to him through debt, ritual kinship, and by settling him in his household. Was the loan a device to indenture Nicolás at less than market wages? Probably not, for a large floating population in Mexico City could always be found to perform unskilled labor. Moreover, Pedro's cash advance on wages was money at risk (minimized in his mind, perhaps, by the newly established *compadrazgo* bond) that might not be repaid if Nicolás chose to skip town. And, in fact, Nicolás did skip after four months, although it is not clear if by then he had cleared the debt. Probably he had not, and Dominga, working as a house servant, would have completed the obligation.

From the examples of Nicolás and José, one might infer that masters readily provided credit to employees in the form of advances on wages. Here the relationship was mainly employer-employee, but that slid naturally into patron-client and compadre-compadre, even though neither master played the directing role in bringing about a marriage. It is important to notice the process, for it points to ways that masters bonded with workers at many interlocking levels: as patrons, creditors, benefactors, compadres, landlords, advisers, and friends. More importantly it transformed mere employees into clients and compadres, thereby cementing deeper loyalty. If this was a linkage that from the employer's standpoint might have been merely instrumental, it was not consciously so. Paternalism inhered in mastership, the exercise of authority over others. Even humble figures aspired to the role. Witness Pedro Aguadero, a man with only his occupation for a surname, acting as patron in the same way, if not to the same degree, as personages with far greater resources.

Love Matches

A marriage arranged by parents or clerics for social and economic ends, as we have seen, could seem arbitrary and inappropriate to the contracting parties. Another model of marriage, what Beatrice Gottlieb calls the "love match," obtained when the contracting parties found each other, became "sweethearts," and eventually made it known to parents and community that they intended to marry.[35] If parents objected, usually because they perceived their son or daughter to be marrying a partner of lower status, lovers might seek clerical intervention, sometimes by eloping first, or they might find themselves thwarted.[36] Usually, however such cases consisted of routine supervisions of initiatives by young people or of the contracts settled on by their parents, in the case of arranged marriages.

First an instance of a thwarted marriage. About 1556 sixteen-year-old Gómez de León, a native of Seville, fell in love with the daughter of a merchant who resided in the neighborhood of the Duke of Medina Sidonia. Pedro de Trujillo, Gómez's confidant at the time (by 1570 Trujillo was a notary in Mexico City) testified (in 1571) that "seventeen or eighteen years ago,"

> Gómez de León was having a love affair with a girl of about fifteen . . . [Pedro] does not remember the girl's name except that because she was small and talkative they called her *La Merlina*. And to meet her, the said Gómez told [Pedro], sometimes they would open the door and he would spend the night. And the merchant moved from Seville . . . and took with him his whole household including his two daughters.

As if playing the role of the tricky servant, a stock character of the comedies of that era, a trusted black servant, probably a slave, facilitated Gómez's entries.[37] Probably at the outset, to legitimize the sexual relations, Gómez and Merlina became betrothed. In the house but with Merlina's father unaware, the servant and a sister witnessed Gómez and Merlina exchanging the vow to marry with hands clasped. Thus they had married and consummated their marriage, but out of view of the church. Thus it was "clandestine." These circumstances regularly constituted the elements for breach-of-promise suits, when the groom, most typically, failed to transform an engagement into a marriage or to solemnize a clandestine marriage with the nuptial blessing of a priest.

In this case, however, Merlina's father moved his household to Badajoz (Spain) before any of this became public knowledge. Pedro recalled Gómez coming to him

> one morning when the said merchant was departing . . . and when they were alone told him with bitter tears that the merchant was taking his whole household, his daughters, and his sweetheart. And he knew that *La Merlina* was his wife and that they had married . . . in the presence of Merlina's sister and a black who used to open the door.

Pedro told his friend to speak to the ecclesiastical judge, for he too believed that Gómez had married. This explains why five years later (1558) he denounced Gómez to the Inquisition after he married Francisca de Torres. The reasons for the merchant's departure do not appear in Gómez's file, but some of them can be inferred. The timing, haste, and completeness of it suggests that it links to his discovery of the betrothal and deflowering of his daughter. If he investigated Gómez, he would have found the young suitor wanting in several ways. Though the son of a woman of distinguished family, he was fathered by a priest and therefore an illegitimate child of the most despised kind. In addition around Seville Gómez was notorious as a gambler. I suspect that the merchant judged his calidad as well below his daughter's. Rather than assenting to this "marriage" by letting it become public knowledge, he spirited the girl away, presumably to a place where a more appropriate suitor could be found.

If young people married clandestinely to bypass the authority of parents, that very circumstance, in this case, made the marriage vulnerable to parental annulment. In taking his daughter away, Merlina's father skipped over church authority to secure his own house. To avoid such an outcome, couples needed to publicize their union as a fait accompli and have it sanctioned by the church. Pedro, as we saw, understood the mechanism well in advising his friend to appeal to an ecclesiastical court.

For some reason (possibly he feared retribution, possibly he felt restrained because of his lack of honor as an *espurio*) Gómez failed to do this.

Not all young men acted so tentatively, and not all young women so docilely. In 1613 the Spaniard Agustín Vázquez found his youngest daughter, Catalina (born 1591), a mulatto like Agustín's wife, stubbornly committed to her beau, no matter what he said to oppose the match.[38] He was Juan Vázquez (no relation), a muleteer who had worked with or for Agustín; but that connection in this case worked against Juan. Catalina's attempt to gain her father's permission for the match, neighbors testified, came to heated arguments, periodic shouting, beatings, and a final blowup, when Agustín threw Catalina out of his house and threw rocks at her. In the face of such resolute opposition, Juan sued to remove Catalina from parental jurisdiction, thereby blocking Agustín from further interference. But that may have been unnecessary, for Agustín in the meantime disowned Catalina. In the end, Juan and Catalina went through all the approved procedures and, in spite of rumors that Juan was already married, exchanged vows in Tepozotlán, in the presence of a priest and friends.

Agustín tried to subdue Catalina with the usual parental instruments of control: disapproval, intimidation, threats, violence, and finally disinheritance, whatever that would have amounted to in his plebeian circumstances. When his daughter dishonored him by refusing to submit to his authority, he withdrew. Here the will of two young people determined to marry defeated a father's opposition. This must have occurred frequently with greater or lesser histrionics. Lesser, for example, in the case of Sebastiana, an Indian of Malinalco.[39] In 1644 her daughter, the mestiza María Ana, wanted to marry Mateo de la Cruz, a *mulato-lobo* from the nearby Jesuit estate, Xalmolongas, but she opposed the match and so did María Ana's brother and sister (her father, not married to Sebastiana and absent, played no part in the incident). The opposition, then, consisted of voicing disapproval but nothing more. When María Ana persisted, they refused to participate or witness the marriage, so she asked an acquaintance in the village, the mestiza Ursula de Lara, to attend her in the ceremony. Ursula testified (in August 1666) that the wedding day began when

> María, a mestiza whose surname she doesn't remember, came to her house one morning about eight o'clock and told her that her mother would not let her marry Mateo de la Cruz . . . and begged her to go to the convent with her so she would not have to go alone and so [Ursula] did and witnessed the marriage as godmother.

Only at the last minute, therefore, did María Ana speak to Ursula who, to judge by her ignorance of María's surname, had only a casual friendship with her. This is corroborated by the fact that she apparently learned for the first time of María's problem on the wedding day. María Ana's isolation came as a surprise to the priest, who wondered why the bridal party consisted of only two people.

In the cases of María Ana and Catalina we find no stated reasons for parental opposition. It seems, however, that common concerns focused on social and procedural matters. The first involved seeing that the calidad of a suitor matched that of his intended; the second that impediments defined by the church would not mar the match. Petrona de la Candelaria, a mestiza of Mexico City, valued the assurance that her suitor, the lobo Juan Lorenzo del Castillo, was unmarried more than her own virginity, which she had already surrendered to him. In 1706, having had an "illicit friendship" with Juan ("more mulatto than mestizo," she said) for about a year, he asked Petrona to marry him. Petrona was then about seventeen and living with her mother; Juan was about twenty-six. "She resisted," she testified three years later, "saying to him that as long as he does not bring a paper, or a person who knows him, she doesn't want to marry him." She referred, of course, to acceptable proof that he was free to marry. As it turned out, Juan, in spite of being already married, produced affidavits that satisfied Petrona as well as her mother. Petrona's handling of Juan's suit shows us, then, how Petrona followed social norms selectively, adopting relaxed standards of "illicit" sexual activity but holding firmly to marriage procedures defined by the church.

If Petrona accepted sexual relations outside of marriage, the Spaniard Juana Montaño held, more conventionally, that sex came only after marriage or betrothal, not before it. In this she exemplifies the assumed link between an unmarried woman's honor and her virginity. The Spaniard Marcos de la Cruz (born ca. 1625 in Pátzquaro) accepted her standard, as we can see by the account of his infatuation with Juana, which began in 1657. At the time he was already married and so had good reason to think twice before getting involved. But he did not or could not. In the dock in 1671, the inquisitors asked him to explain why, given his correct understanding of the permanence of matrimony, he would commit bigamy. He answered that he had been "dragged down by human weakness because he wanted her so much and, since she was a virgin, there was no other way to gain access to her because Juana said he could have her only if they married. Thus carried away and defeated by passion he committed the error." Marcos had lost all judgment in the throes of his "uncontrollable sexual passion," a basis for marriage that parents increasingly attacked as irrational, unstable, and in the words of one father, "the effect of a lascivious juvenile appetite."[40] In fact he was twenty-seven, hardly a juvenile, and already married. Yet he was out of control, and Juana used his condition as a basis for talking about marriage.

Eloping was a simple and effective way to counter parental opposition. It consisted of running away, exchanging vows, engaging in sexual intercourse, and returning to report a fait accompli to a priest or ecclesiastical judge. If parents persisted in their opposition, they would usually be isolated by ecclesiastical and legal procedures (mainly the removal of the young woman from parental jurisdiction, as we saw in one case above), which would legitimize what had been effected by stealth. Legitimation through a nuptial mass was, of course, the decisive step.

All of this was common knowledge possessed by plebeians such as Pedro Mateo, a mestizo who had always worked on cattle ranches. At age twenty-five (in 1666), he said that he could not recite the creed because "he forgot it." Nor did he know anything else about Christian doctrine for, as "a poor miserable one (*pobre miserable*) he has not had anybody to teach him."[41] Yet lacking as he was in doctrinal knowledge, Pedro nevertheless knew how to spirit the mestiza Nicolasa de Chávez from her parents' household when they rejected his suit.

After the elopement Nicolasa's parents found them and brought their daughter home. But it was too late. Pedro could now enlist the church on his side and did so by going to Father Tomás de Alcocer, a parish priest who, a year later, testified that "the said Pedro appeared before him saying he and Nicolasa had exchanged marriage vows." Father Tomás therefore took Nicolasa from her parents, deposited her in the house of a respectable citizen, and prepared to bless the marriage. By then the rumor was circulating that Pedro was married elsewhere, but Father Tomás ignored it, probably because he heard it from Nicolasa's mother and discounted it.

In fact it was true, and later the inquisitors asked him why he had contracted a bigamous marriage. He answered that he had been "blind and compelled by the arrogance of Nicolasa de Chávez's mother who said that he was a poor Indian." Thus the reason for opposing Pedro fits with a standard interpretation of parental opposition suggested by J. A. Pitt-Rivers, C. Lisón-Tolosana, and Verena Martínez-Alier: the perception that the suitor fell below his intended in social standing.[42]

The case of Pedro takes us further into the process, however, because it documents the suitor's reaction. Taking the judgment as an insult, he resolved to have Nicolasa whatever the cost. So here parental opposition had an outcome contrary to its intent. It shifted Pedro from the suitor of Nicolasa to that of defender of his honor. But why was the comment so insulting when it may very well have been true? Pedro himself admitted to some confusion when he testified that he did not "know if he is Indian, mulatto, or mestizo, because he did not know his father or even who he was and he only knew that his mother was Indian." Thus he may have been illegitimate as well, or at least perceived as such. But the insult had less to do with biological specifics than with Pedro's calidad. Labeling Pedro an Indian presumed him a servile type unworthy of Nicolasa. Here again Nicolasa's mother spoke the truth, but it was a question of degree. All indications projected Pedro to a low place in society, but not, in Pedro's view, so low as a "poor Indian." Plebeians constantly haggled over calidad, it seems, in the social marketplace. At the lower end of the hierarchy one could claim a higher or lower place within a range (admittedly a fairly limited one), and so heated disagreements arose in the disparities between self-designations and the attributions of others.[43]

Rustics as well as men of higher status used elopement to repair the dishonor implied by the opposition of a girl's parents. The response fit an expectation for males in Hispanic society that they dominate and conquer women.[44] It included "taking" women from the household of their fathers for the purpose of marriage or seduction, an extraction that could be carried out by trickery as well as by stealth. In 1727 the mestizo muleteer Manuel de Lizona combined the two when Sebastián Ruiz Medrano of the mining camp of Guadalcázar (now in San Luis Potosí state) refused to allow Josepha Medrano, an Indian foundling he had raised, permission to marry him. Why? Not for social reasons, but almost certainly because he wanted to keep Josepha as a servant in his household. Manuel countered with a clever scheme. After a season driving mules, he had earned enough to buy pieces of silk, wool, Brittany cloth, and ribbon from his boss's store, which he brought to Ruiz's house. He presented the goods and asked Sebastián to "give them to the señoras."[45] "Now let's be on good terms," he added, for "I've found a cave that seems to be used by robbers where there's a lot of goods and we must go there, for it's not far away, on the side of the peaks that lie between San Luis Potosí and Guadalcázar."

With an embellishment or two (say, for example, the untimely return of the robbers) the account approaches something from the *Thousand and One Nights*. Even so it must have been a local classic, to judge by don Manuel's well-rehearsed retelling with the actors' words given as direct speech and with the scene carefully drawn. The rest of his testimony dwells on how well the scheme worked, that indeed Manuel the trickster used Sebastián's greed to achieve his ends. The older man suddenly warmed to his daughter's suitor and agreed to ransack the cave with him. He hitched a team to a cart and, with Manuel giving directions, the two men headed into the rough country. Once there, Manuel pretended to be confused, told Sebastián to wait with the cart while he scouted ahead, and moved quickly out of sight. He then circled back to Guadalcázar where Josepha awaited him and then "abducted" (*hurtó*) her. They traveled eastward to Valle del Maíz, married, and afterward returned to Guadalcázar. Later, Josepha's biological father, who gave Josepha to Ruiz to be raised, referred to Manuel's "capture" of his daughter as undertaken with her consent. Ruiz, as was usual in elopement cases, accepted the accomplished fact. Besides he had some consolation in the gifts that Manuel had brought in the first place.[46]

ILLICIT FRIENDSHIPS
Seduction

Because the church confined sexual relations to marriage, it goes without saying that a hasty promise to marry, whether sincere or not, would accompany some liaisons. We noted in chapter 2, for example, that Antonia Sánchez, widow and hatmaker of Toro, exacted such a promise from twelve-year-old Gerónimo de Benavides (born 1532) before she accepted the boy's proposition to engage in sexual relations. Gerónimo spent three nights with Antonia "knowing her carnally," but this, and the fact that he had betrothed himself to do so, horrified his older brother Pedro. Still in Toro thirty-five years later (1577), Pedro remembered that "he did not want his brother Gerónimo de Benavides to marry the hatter, saying to him 'look at what you've done, that it would lead you straight to the devil' . . . and he persuaded his brother to go to New Spain because that woman would be lost and that was [his] conscience."

Antonia's attempt to use sexual relations with an inexperienced boy to marry him can be compared to the raping of a young girl that included no plan for marriage. Ana Pérez (born ca. 1514) was raised in Zamora in the household of an aunt and uncle. She testified (in 1539) that

> in Zamora she knew a Christóbal García carnally. He had her virginity [when] she was in her aunt's house and after he had it, the husband of the said her aunt, brother of the said Christóbal García who had it first, also had sexual intercourse with her [on two occasions]. She was a young girl (*muy muchacha*) and one day she was alone in the house and in bed and he [Christóbal] entered her room and had carnal access with her.

Even as transmitted to the third person by the notary, the account seems to reflect a child's trauma, for the statement goes over the same ground, with slight variations, three times. Ana, it seems, had never been able to go beyond the event itself, which had stripped her of her honor as a woman, perhaps before she had been aware of possessing any honor. Her account focuses on Christóbal, the agent of the deed (who he was and when and how he took her virginity); the scene, weighted with normality (a day at home and she alone in bed); and the act itself, the familiar figure of her uncle entering her room and, somewhat euphemistically, "having her virginity." The account is emotionally distant, but the details point to strong feelings nevertheless. And is it not remarkable that after this initial violation, sexual relations continued with both of the adult men of the household? For the rest of the story, Ana stresses the agency of her aunt, who effects a conventional justice: "afterward when her aunt found out how [Christóbal] had corrupted her she made him marry her."

Rape and marriage are followed by six or seven years of married life with Christóbal and the birth of six children. At this point, perhaps in 1530 or 1531, Ana revealed, apparently for the first time, the details of her sexual initiation to a priest in the confessional. But why only then? Perhaps through contact with catechal teachings, she became aware that marriage to an uncle was an invalidating impediment. The priest, in any case, told Ana that her marriage to Christóbal was invalid, and so she left him and the children and went to the Indies to begin a new life. In New Spain she cohabited with Beltrán de Peralta until "believing that she would serve God by removing herself from sin she married him." After a year, however, Peralta took up with an Indian woman of Veracruz, saying, Ana remembered, "he was married in Spain to a Francisca Morena who lives in the city of Baeza [diocese of Córdoba] and with her had a daughter." But that did not stop him from contracting a third marriage, to the Indian woman. Ana in the meantime also married a third time, after stating her situation to local priests and receiving a dispensation.

Some of Ana's marital complications (those stemming from her involvement with Beltrán de Peralta for example) may be traced to the state of flux existing in the Indies during the first half of the sixteenth century. However, we must not let that obscure Ana's initial predicament and its resolution: the loss of her honor was repaired by marrying her to the man who had taken it. Ana's aunt enforced the "solution" with her considerable authority in her household. Ana, in fact, places the aunt at the very center of her narrative: it was her house, her husband, her finding out, her making Christóbal marry.[47]

At some level sexual relations implied betrothal and marriage. That was the case when doña Clara Ochoa and Francisco del Valle, a Spaniard of Mexico City, came together under the watchful eye of doña Clara's family. Both parties claimed high social status, and the result was a highly charged drama over doña Clara's honor. It began in August, 1654. Francisco, just finishing a term as governor of Tuxtla (now in Veracruz state), was traveling to Coyoacan to rejoin his wife, an invalid, who had remained behind during his term of service. We learn of it from his autobiographical statement given in the dock of the Inquisition in June, 1656.

At Puebla he found "lodging" at the home of doña Clara Ochoa, located on the road to Cholula (now in Puebla state). But instead of a brief stopover, don Francisco settled in for a more leisurely stay as he and doña Clara dallied in an "illicit friendship." After a couple of months, doña Clara's relatives decided that their liaison must be legitimated by marriage. To this end, they circulated a report that don Francisco's wife had died, sent messengers to tell him, arranged for city officials to offer condolences, and then urged him to marry doña Clara. The new widower understandably tried to delay the process. He wanted the alleged death confirmed, but the family portrayed this as stalling. To increase the pressure they applied economic leverage: he would agree to the marriage or else repay immediately an outstanding debt of 2,300 pesos. Refusal would have meant the seizure of Francisco's property and person until he could pay.

Trapped, don Francisco consented while secretly plotting to evade the marriage. He continued to request correct procedures, for example that the banns be published in Mexico City, which would have been in order since he was a vecino there. Doña Clara's relatives declared this "unnecessary" and, as they orchestrated a rapid run up to the marriage, made don Francisco a virtual prisoner in doña Clara's house. In this predicament, don Francisco decided on a desperate plan to escape. After nightfall at the entry of the house he arranged a meeting with his sister's blind servant, the mestizo Christóbal, and directed him "to bring him a horse from [her] estancia" so he could escape to Mexico City in a pre-dawn gallop.[48]

But doña Clara herself overheard the conversation and told her brother and cousins. In the meanwhile an unsuspecting don Francisco returned to his room and retired early. But alas there would be little rest, for at 10 P.M. an angry crowd, led by doña Clara's brother Juan Ramos, burst into his chamber. With drawn dagger and a pistol in his belt, Ramos angrily confronted the startled Francisco: "So you wanted to abandon doña Clara and make her a laughingstock." Then, as if the protagonist of a melodrama, he turned to the others in the room and recounted Francisco's plan to run away. Facing his adversary once again, with threats and oaths he shouted that Francisco would marry that very night or "he would have to kill him." In fact he had already sent for a magistrate (alcalde ordinario), who arrived at 11 P.M. together with even more family partisans. The magistrate, according to don Francisco, was

> more irritated than all the others. He said to him 'you don't have an out, you are going to have to marry now,' and he ordered that he be seized and taken to the jail for the debt he owed to the king, to the said Matheo de Ledesma, and to other persons, that he would have to die in jail if the relatives of the said doña Clara did not kill him first.

Don Francisco was defeated, and his final antagonist was a peer and colleague. His dalliance had turned into a nightmare. His attempt to delay the denouement, even to adhere to normal processes, had been thwarted. His plan to flee had backfired. But even so, Francisco tried one more time to escape with a direct appeal to a fellow magistrate once they were alone:

> On the way to the public jail he pleaded with the said alcalde to take pity on him, that he was a nobleman who had held offices and administered justice and that he should [therefore] take him to his house and enclose him in a room until the

truth as to whether his wife, doña María de Acarce, is dead can be investigated. And even in case she was dead it was not his convenience to marry the said doña Clara for many reasons. [For one] she was so poor that there was no advantage whatsoever in marrying her. [For another] he could not permit the large blot and affront to his lineage [that marriage to her would bring, for] afterward how would he be able to face the Viceroy or his friends?

Francisco supposed that class and professional bonds might overcome his counterpart's ties to his community. But they did not. Did he suppose that the performance at the house had been merely theatrics? Possibly yes, given the tone of Francisco's appeal with its candid and unflattering assessment of doña Clara's worth relative to his own.

With no escape, the marriage took place and afterwards don Francisco immediately left Puebla never to have further contact with doña Clara. From the standpoint of her family, his departure was no longer a problem, for they had vindicated her honor. The entrapment of Francisco was of his own making, at least in part, for he seemed to have used the promise of marriage (whenever his first wife should die?) as the backdrop to forming the liaison with doña Clara. Even more striking is the political point that a man so well connected in the viceregal court could be so powerless in a provincial city. An important family of Puebla had enough local influence to isolate an outsider completely and, most importantly for our purposes, church officials were completely integrated into this local network.

Any woman who engaged in sexual relations, whether for the first time or habitually, could claim that the promise to marry had accompanied a liaison. This implied connection obtained strongly enough that it even affected the mulatto innkeeper Leonor Vázquez of Mexico City, a "woman of the world" who in truth had no such concerns.[49] She dispensed her sexual favors freely and apparently enjoyed herself with many men. Testifying in 1565, when she was in her late twenties, she remembered an occasion when a twenty-year old mulatto had "stopped to sleep two or three nights" in her house in Mexico City. The man, Christóbal de Ayala, testified that he had "carnal access with her as if she were his mistress, but Christóbal never promised to marry her nor did she him, for she had already promised to marry the mestizo Francisco Mendezín before knowing Christóbal."

For Leonor, then, it amounted to a straightforward liaison without complications. Others at the inn, lodgers or customers in for a drink of pulque, must have thought the same as it became "public" and the occasion for ribald comments.[50] One lodger, Francisco Velázquez, who was a permanent resident of Mexico City and probably a regular at Leonor's, remembered that one jocular exchange ended with Leonor saying to Christóbal: "Yes, I would like to marry you." He noticed how the remark had silenced Christóbal and how Leonor, a bawdy type apparently enjoying Christóbal's uneasiness, repeated the comment. At this point, he testified, "an Indian woman urged Christóbal to marry Leonor," that is, to respond to her comment in kind. And so he did. A liaison, a flirtation, a facetious remark had suddenly become serious as Christóbal took Leonor to the vicar to apply for a marriage license. But here Leonor had the sense to stop, to get away from Christóbal, and to run to "a mestizo [her fiancé Francisco]." Later, running into Leonor in the plaza, Christóbal gave her several hard slaps and dragged her to the archbishopric's jail. Doctor Anguis, vicar of the archbishopric, questioned each of them and upheld Leonor's prior betrothal to Francisco. He also ordered Leonor whipped "because she had not told the truth to Christóbal in representing herself as free to contract marriage."

The little drama of Leonor and Christóbal illustrates the complex interplay of sexual mores and matrimony. Neither of them presumed a necessary connection between sexual intercourse and marriage. But once that connection was made, albeit, at least for Leonor, in a joking way, the banter was easily misinterpreted. Discussion of marriage, especially when a man and woman "agreed" to marry, was more serious than sexual liaisons as such, for it constituted a betrothal. The crucial moment that transformed this exchange came with the innocent intervention by the Indian woman. She did not get the "joke" but instead pressed Christóbal to take Leonor's comment in its literal, not just its ironic sense.

So, the picture is one of people socializing, joking, and intervening in each other's lives (possibly in Nahuatl or a mixture of Spanish and Nahuatl, to judge by the presence of the Indian woman and the taking of testimony from Leonor through an interpreter),[51] with advice and urgings of various sorts. Moreover, the group of mostly mulattos took the Indian woman's suggestion as seriously as anyone else's. Through the entire episode Leonor must have known that she could not follow through with her charade, but social posturing fueled by drink quickly achieved considerable momentum from which Leonor would have found it difficult to extricate herself. That she eventually did shows that she too respected matrimony, or at least feared the penalties that came from violating norms that defined it. However irreverent and brazen her joking, she knew that betrothal firmly set her on the way to marriage. Christóbal knew this too. Witness his initial hesitation, his decision to go directly to the vicar, his angry confrontation with Leonor in the plaza, and his suit for breach of promise.

In the above examples falling under the category "seduction," sexual relations were linked to marriage in that they were seen to presume either betrothal or marriage. Given this association the promise to marry clearly played a part in persuading women concerned to protect their reputation to engage in sexual relations. Admitting as much in 1722, the Spaniard Miguel de Herrera testified that "he solicited some women, promising to marry them but as a pretext to satisfy his lust, not with the intention to keep the promise . . . Sometimes this became public and people thought he married [these women] but he did not."

Miguel's words, "pretext to satisfy his lust" have the tone of the formulaic speech prompted by confessionals as a kind of ritual contrition. Many, in fact, must have repeated such phrases to authorities to distinguish between "feigned" and "serious" promises.[52] But it might be difficult for those who heard such promises to make the distinction. This may have been the reason, Miguel speculated ingenuously, why "some" women claimed that he had married them. In fact breach-of-promise suits over an alleged promise to marry, according to Lavrin, make up the most frequently heard kind of complaint in ecclesiastical courts, thus indicating the widespread use of this model of seduction.[53] The outcome of the complaints against Miguel have been lost, probably because he ran away quickly and avoided apprehension and prosecution. He must have been a common type, however, in using to his advantage the conventional tie between marriage and sexuality.

Abduction and Concubinage

Seduction, abduction, concubinage, and marriage can be seen as a continuum. Couples passed through some or all of these stages, which in one way or another went from courtship to stable pairings. Marriage always stood at one pole, however, as the proper resolution for any of the others. Earlier we saw one kind of abduction that in fact was nothing more than an elopement in the face of parental opposition. Even more commonly, abduction occurred as a part of illicit friendships, the coming together of men and women with no particular intent to marry, at least not right away.[54] Yet these can be seen as informal marriages, for they become cohabitations rather than one-night stands.

As with elopements, they began with a man "abducting" or "stealing" a woman. The language accurately mirrors a structural rather than phenomenological reality in that women (except possibly for widows) lived as minors under male jurisdiction. In theory they acted largely through the agency of men, but this was a male view of things. "As far as men were concerned," in Edward Shorter's words, "she [a woman] did not make things happen; they happened to her."[55] To take a woman from that jurisdiction irregularly (without permission, consultation, or leave of the church) indeed amounted to robbery. In truth, however, this language and these assumptions do not pick up the agency of women who did "make things happen" by consenting to, encouraging, and sometimes engineering their leave-takings.

Parents heading plebeian households with minimal property and status, placed no great importance, in Ramón Gutiérrez's words, on "whether or whom their children married."[56] These types accepted the abduction of a daughter as a routine event of no particular concern. In 1582 or so the Spaniard Miguel Muñoz, a native of Triana living in Celaya, found one day that his daughter Isabel had been abducted. She was then about fourteen and as he described her, "a mestiza . . . his bastard daughter." In Celaya (Miguel had lived in Mexico City when Isabel was born), Isabel had little claim to status in Hispanic society. Indeed it may have pleased Miguel that Isabel and her beau spared him the bother of a formal wedding, which would have entailed some expenses. In a nonchalant way, he testified (in 1588) that she had been abducted six years before, when

> a *vaquero* [serving] Gaspar Salvago—he doesn't know his name except that he is a mestizo and he lived on the estancia Los Llanos, three leagues from here—took her from [Miguel's] house in this town . . . He heard that [the mestizo] took her to Guadalajara and then to Zacatecas . . . where three years ago she married Francisco Ortiz, native of Cádiz, who serves as a soldier in the presidios of that kingdom and his daughter lives with her mother-in-law in the new inn next to the Tlalpuxagua mining camp [now in Michoacán state] and he doesn't know if she married before with someone else.

Yet Miguel had a pretty good idea of Isabel's movements. He knew, for example, that she was not living with her husband but, probably servant-like, with his mother, running the inn. As for the abduction itself, two aspects of the statement give the impression that he considered it a commonplace. For one, he never bothered to pin down the identity of the abductor. Instead he defined him socially through his master, his work, and his "quality" (calidad) which place the young man, in our terms, as a propertyless wage earner of mixed race—roughly speaking, Isabel's social equal. In addition to Miguel's casual view of the abductor, let us also note his apparent indifference as to whether it had resulted in marriage or not.

Isabel's abduction led to marriage but in a round about way.[57] Officials arrested her abductor, not for taking her but for another unspecified crime, and sentenced him to the galleys; they sent her to serve in the household of an audiencia judge in Guadalajara. After three years another man, the one Miguel heard she had married, ran off with her, and in Zacatecas they tried to pass as married. Officials spotted them as living together illicitly, arrested them, and arranged their marriage.

The two abductions of Isabel both initiated marriagelike cohabitations. Officials "annulled" the first because of crime and ratified the second by

to Francisco

to Miguel

formalizing it. The initiative, planning, and commitment implied by running away, then, amounted to a kind of folk marriage. When officials moved to transform these informal unions into proper marriages there was little reason to resist, except possibly to avoid the costs or, in the cases of the already married, to avoid bigamy. After formal marriage, life went on as it had before, except that couples were now bound by a formal and sacramental tie instead of an informal one. The latter had the advantage that it could be ended at any time without further complications. Many such unions must have ended neatly and quickly for one or another reason.

Such an ending proved fortunate for Bernabé Cristóbal, termed a lobo to signify his racial mix of mulatto and Indian, because he was already married when he began a period of cohabitation with a woman. He worked as a shepherd and therefore spent long periods away from his wife, Lorenza María, a mulatto whom he married in 1708. During one such absence, in the sheepshearing hut on the heights of Ibarra (now in the state of Aguascalientes), he met María, an orphan and like him a loba. She had been raised by an Indian named Antonio who tended the hut and, with María's help, cultivated a plot of land. Contact in this isolated place led to Bernabé and María running off together. They settled in the Huaxteca, the area of the Gulf coastal plain under the jurisdiction of Pánuco, where, as before, Bernabé worked as a shepherd. After a time, however, María's brother, acting as a kind of guardian of his sister, tracked her down and took her away. So it ended with no damages and no recriminations, as if nothing much had been at stake.

Nevertheless men and women who spontaneously came together in various ways sometimes set into motion a policing reaction. The routine and the mechanism of policing consensual couples can be seen from a vignette that must have recurred countless times in New Spain. It consisted of a priest visiting isolated settlements and haciendas and marrying couples living in concubinage. Our example concerns Manuel Romano of Tavira (Portugal), who in 1577, at age eighteen, was working as a vaquero on the estancia of Pedro Núñez, six leagues from Veracruz. There he lived in concubinage with "Juana India" and in his autobiographical statement testified that about a year and a half ago a priest . . . who used to visit estancias in the district came to visit and told him to clasp hands with the said India and the said priest then took their hands in the presence of Pedro Núñez and other vaqueros who were two black slaves and a free mulatto. He doesn't know what the priest said or how the rest of it went except that he took their hands and afterward he slept with her just as he had before.

The marriage made no sense, for as Hispanic society assessed it, they were badly mismatched. He was an immigrant, albeit a humble one, from the peninsula; she was a native, possessing only the generic "India" for a surname, speaking only Nahuatl. Their union had been a sleeping arrangement and nothing more. Why then did the priest marry them? Officially, of course, to regularize an "illicit" friendship. But more fundamentally, I think, to help a master keep and control his servants. This compromised no Christian principles, for within the natural order, as a seventeenth-century confessional manual makes clear, masters held authority over servants no less than fathers did over children: "not only the body, but more importantly the soul, is under his guardianship."[58] There is little doubt that Núñez, who paid the priest and was on friendly terms with him, easily arranged the marriages of his cohabiting servants. An overworked cleric on circuit, trying to keep up with the demands of a far-flung rural parish, no doubt welcomed and counted on such cooperation.

As might have been expected, Manuel left Juana after a couple of months. He traveled north and near San Miguel married the free mulatto Juana de Herrera. In doing this he corrected to a degree the social and cultural mismatch of the marriage with Juana India, for Juana the mulatto had a surname, a family, and a place in the Hispanic world. In his bigamy trial, Manuel said that he "did not take that which happened with the said Indian to be a marriage." He stated three reasons: it had not been preceded by a matrimonial investigation and the reading of the banns; it had not taken place in a church; and it had been "arranged" (this last from Juana herself) "to keep him on the estancia."

Manuel, at least for his trial, distinguished between what he considered mere concubinage (not taking seriously the priestly intervention on the estancia) and proper marriages.[59] So did others, and with good reason. The mulatto Francisca de Paula, testifying nine years after she married Manuel de la Trinidad Rodríguez explained that "as a weak woman she had a friendship with her husband before and didn't want to marry him because she well knew his bad character but her mother and sister forced her."

The state of mind she refers to takes her back to 1739 when she was nineteen. In accepting the "friendship" and, at the same time, rejecting the suit for marriage she made a crucial distinction, for marriage tied a woman permanently to a man of questionable character; cohabitation did not. But Francisca's mother, Damiana, also played a role in the drama. She called the friendship a *mala vida* or "bad life" connoting her moral disapproval but also the concern that Manuel was subjecting her daughter to an unsettled existence. "He has never wanted to subject himself to live a settled life," Damiana said in 1748, "but kept moving, today here, tomorrow elsewhere, jumping from one pueblo to another." By then the eighty-year-old woman must have realized that her original moral concern had been misplaced. As a result of the marriage, Francisca suffered "many hardships," she said, and Manuel "gave her bad treatment." All of this Francisca had anticipated in her original preference for concubinage rather than marriage.

Conclusion

Marriage is complex. It takes place as a private transaction and a public one; it springs from passion and from planning; it is based on consent yet subject to pressure, cajolery, and intimidation; it enabled licit sexual relations and occasioned, through the promise to marry, illicit ones. Bigamy records give some indications of how and why pairings took place because they include the testimony of the young people who were setting up new households. Naturally they received advice and the attention of parents and relatives, of masters who considered themselves guardians or patrons, and of the post-Tridentine church, which claimed exclusive jurisdiction over the sacrament. They resisted or cooperated with interventions in one way or another depending on their temperaments, personal inclinations, and ideas about how life should be lived.

Inés Hernández, alias Florentina del Río, a Spaniard born at the very end of the fifteenth century, certainly had her own ideas. She faced the prospect of living alone (her husband had long ago disappeared) or remarrying. In 1525 she chose to marry, thereby risking bigamy. The justification she gave to the inquisitors, consisted of an axiom of popular culture: "Better to live [as a bigamist] in one sin than as a single woman in many." In fact the saying paraphrases a passage from the *Siete Partidas* that excused informal unions (called *barraganía*) among men:

> Holy Church forbids that any Christian man have *barraganas*, for to live with them is mortal sin. But the wise men of old who made the laws permitted that some men might have them without civil penalty, for they held that it was *a lesser evil to live with one woman than many*, and that the paternity of the children would be more certain."[60]

Inés's version conflates bigamy with barraganía, inverts gender, and disregards the underlying intent to control for paternity by restricting women to a single sexual partner. She shows, therefore, how legal principles, at the level of popular culture, could be stretched to suit individual purposes.

By keeping an eye on the views and behaviors, on the actions and reactions, of the contracting parties we can view processes of marriage formation in real-life contexts. So we have named individuals and told their stories. If their approaches to marriage and life fall within a "system of predispositions" arising from upbringing and place in society, they nevertheless were personal, varied, and subject to contingency.[61] So much so that they defy easy formulation as a system. What does come through is their humanity, as they complained about and resisted the brokerage of others or submitted to it; as they ran away to marry or to cohabit; as they fell under the purview of policing mechanisms and submitted to marriages to correct their illicit cohabitations.

However casually marriages were contracted, the parties understood its importance as a context for their lives and for forming a family, the essential unit within which they would exercise some leverage on the larger society. Symbolically the contracting of marriages mattered as well for, as Beatrice Gottlieb has stressed, bigamists went "through the complete series of proper procedures" to effect "normal" marriages."[62] By this they defined themselves as respectable citizens, conforming to social expectations. Nevertheless we have seen how young people viewed outside interventions as distasteful, disappointing, and threatening. Outsiders, for example, all too often brokered marriages for reasons of their own and, as a result, sponsored inappropriate matches. Marriage, a supremely organizing moment at the threshold of adult life, could become a fundamentally disorganizing one as cupidity, passivity, and legalistic interventions based on church doctrine rode roughshod over the sensibilities of the contracting parties.[63]

Yet people learned. Passivity before marriage brokers correlates roughly with youthfulness and inexperience, self-assertion (as can be seen in the way people approached second marriages or, sometimes, preferred to cohabit rather than marry) with experience. The exertion of more control, sometimes only in its negative form, by exercising greater caution, may have come from the higher risks attending illicit second marriages. Nevertheless, men and women contracted second marriages in much the same way that they did first ones. Even informal unions, the coupling of men and women without the step of a formal marriage ceremony, replicate the courting process normally issuing in marriages.

So men and women coupled, before, during, and after they married, and sometimes they married twice. When the latter happened the inquisitors wanted to know why. Bigamists and their spouses tried to explain, and to do so spoke of their marriages, separations, and reasons for marrying a second time. These explanations will be our window on domestic life, the subject of the next chapter.

CHAPTER FOUR

Married Life

MARRIAGE AFTER TRENT increasingly came under church control in its design to channel all religious life to the parish.[1] As Tridentine reformers reaffirmed traditional doctrinal positions, they also set out to improve religious practice. And by the end of the seventeenth century (probably earlier in Spain and the Indies), they had succeeded.[2] Married life, however, falling as it did beyond the requirements of attendance at mass and the partaking of the sacraments, barely felt the intrusive winds of Trent. Once marriages had been contracted, domestic patriarchies presided over families, as they always had. Pastoral exhortations urging husbands to respect wives and moderate harsh treatment merely reinforced that authority, for the "good government" of the family, that most basic of society's cells, depended on the male heads of them as the essential agents of social control.[3]

Parish priests and ecclesiastical judges concerned themselves with family matters, perhaps most particularly with drunkenness and adultery, but had no thought of interfering with the structure of the family. Interventions, when they occurred, acted to "avoid disorder," as François Giraud has noted with regard to cases of sexual violence, and thereby to restore an "equilibrium."[4] But if the church intruded little into the domestic arena, what mechanisms did regulate married life? Probably the traditional ones of popular culture: pasquinades, mock trials, and ritual humiliations. But once again to traditional ends: to defend patriarchal authority, to protect the local pool of marriageable women, and to insist on the inviolability of sex roles.[5] So the deeply rooted norms of popular culture possessed considerable inertia, thus contrasting, in John Bossy's phrase, with the "silent revolution" of Trent that moved from the top down.[6] For our purposes the point matters, because it underscores the church's limited engagement with domestic life. Once couples were properly married, clerics had little to say about the quality of life within marriage (the occasional exhortation to act less harshly perhaps accompanied by reference to the iconography of the peaceful domesticity of Mary and Joseph) that would place it in opposition to traditional norms. These, for example, viewed a husband's adulteries as acceptable, but a wife's as worthy of death; looked at a husband's beating of his wife (and children) as the exercise of discipline but a wife's beating of her husband as infamous. Although the church had theoretical positions to encourage moderation, these, as we have noted, reinforced the traditional patriarchal order. Deviation from this key norm would be frowned on by the church and disapproved of by the populace. Otherwise, clerics, parents, masters and neighbors showed little inclination to intervene in quasi-autonomous household units headed by men.

One might think that the marriages of bigamists, at least first ones, were by definition less successful than those of nonbigamists. But the issue is not so clear-cut. As we shall see, bigamists lived in harmony with partners they eventually separated from as well as in discord. They were adulterous and sometimes ran off with another partner, but who can say whether in greater numbers than the population in general? Separations came often enough because work, debt, and flight from the law occasioned absences and the loss of contact; second marriages followed after a new life had been established. Bigamists contracted them because they thought their first spouse had died, because officials forced them, because they became carried away by passion, or because they thought they could get away with it. In any of these circumstances, bigamists lived out their domestic dramas with the same concerns that anybody else had: getting along, making a living, running a household, raising children, and maintaining links to bosses, patrons, neighbors, and authorities.

Shaky Foundations

As we anticipated in the previous chapter, forcing an inappropriate partner on a reluctant or passive young person may have been a "marriage" in law but hardly in fact. We saw, for example, the already-married Pedro de Valenzuela arrested, put in chains and, with property impounded, held until he married Francisca, a young "woman of the world" he had picked up in a small town of Nueva Granada (now the country of Colombia). Another case was the boy Pedro Muñoz Palomir, forced against his will by an ecclesiastical judge in Spain to fulfill a marriage contract arranged by his uncle. In another instance, Francisca del Solar's parents surprised Juan Antonio Chacón Gayón alone with her in her house and, threatening to kill him, demanded an explanation. "This one responded," the transcript records, "'I am with my wife'." The answer saved his life, but committed him to an unwanted marriage. In these cases and others, the objective was to force marriages in order to satisfy family honor. Once that had been done, the men were allowed to escape. Pedro de Valenzuela resumed his journey and sent Francisca back to her mother; Pedro Muñoz fled, eventually to the Indies, without consummating his marriage; Juan Antonio stayed with his wife about two years, without enthusiasm it seems, and then abandoned her.

The cases above point to a society taking marriage as a formal nuptial too seriously. It became an end rather than a means, a legalism to satisfy family honor or protect against scandal. It sacrificed content to form because it lost sight of the long term: family life and a stable environment for raising children. It infringed on the doctrine of consent and created bigamy as a by-product of forcing couples living in illicit friendships to marry. In time this "solution" was likely to be discovered and then punished as a crime against the sacrament of matrimony, a more serious offense than various forms of fornication.

At a first level, weak foundations for married life resulted from the parties simply disliking one another. In Zacatecas in 1572 Petronila Ruiz (born 1555 in Havana) objected so strongly to the marriage her master arranged that he overcame her resistance only by locking her up, chaining her, and threatening her.[7] Eventually she "consented" to marry Francisco de Aguilar, but this was mostly a legalism. She hated Francisco no less as his wife than as his prospective wife and within two weeks, this almost cost her her life. Francisco tried to kill her and "he would have," Petronila testified six years later (August 22, 1578), "but for the resistance I had in my legs and the other people who stopped him." But these bystanders could not protect her when Francisco had her alone at home as Petronila explains.

> He abused me in many other ways, branding me on my face and on other parts of my body, beating me, selling my clothes, and not providing me with food because he is an incorrigible man and a criminal so that the said marriage is null because it was forced . . . because in conformity with the law of God, marriages must be in accord with the will of both persons without the intervention of third parties.

Francisco's violence, sadism even, was not entirely arbitrary. Branding, for example, associated with marking slaves as chattel, suggests that Francisco was determined to "own" Petronila. But he could not break down her resistance. In fact just the opposite, for mistreatment strengthened her resolve to escape. Yet however abusive the marriage, Petronila, when dealing with officials, spoke in legal terms, stressing that lack of consent, not bad treatment as such, invalidated the marriage. In this she adjusted her language for officials who she knew would count violated procedures for more than violated wives.

From Petronila's experience we may infer something of the dynamic between masters and the servants whose marriages they had arranged. What in theory constituted the primary relationship, marriage, depended almost entirely on the secondary one, the master-servant tie. Perhaps marriages of slaves constitute the extreme. Pascual de los Reyes broke his primary tie to his master when, about 1737, he ran away, changed his name, and passed as an Indian. As a matter of course he sacrificed his "secondary" tie to his wife and fellow slave, María Olaya.

But free servants, as we have seen, also acted in a similar way. The shepherd Bernabé Cristóbal changed masters in his peripatetic occupation; he also left behind Lorenza María, the woman his former master had married him to. Pedro Mateo, recruited by his father-in-law to attach him to his household as a worker, ended his marriage by changing his job. Did this represent a casual attitude toward marriage? Not necessarily, but it does indicate that marriages instigated by and for masters lived or died because of their continued utility to the master. In a third case Manuel Romano saw his marriage to the Indian Juana, with whom he had been living in concubinage, as his master's way to keep him on his estancia. Two months afterward, he discarded Juana when he moved on to find another job. Even though he contracted it in the presence of a priest, the marriage hardly made an impression.

These cases represent an instrumental, if not casual, view of marriage and depended on the agency of the master. As the tie to him loosened, so too did the marriage tie, a casualty of the *real* marriage between servant and master. In at least two of the three, marriage procedures themselves were seen as flawed, at least in hindsight. This became the focus of the mulatto Beatriz Ramírez, who insisted that she had gone through an incomplete ceremonial sequence. In 1560 she and Diego, an Indian vaquero living on an estancia near Apaseo, publicly declared their intention to marry. The banns were read and the priest told them to go to San Miguel el Grande for the marriage, but they never did. Instead, they lived together as if they were properly married until Beatriz tired of Diego's abusive treatment. "Because the said Indian gave her a bad life (mala vida)," she testified to the inquisitors in 1574, "and beat her whenever he saw her, she left." Yet she also admitted that she knew that the exchange of promises had bound her to marry. Her argument that an "incomplete" marriage was not a marriage merely justified her "self divorce" and marriage to another man.

This argument, similar in a way to Petronila's above, shows how people dissatisfied with married life knowledgeably cited improper procedures to justify "divorce." The process amounted to a kind of folk casuistry, which made the Tridentine requirement that marriages receive a priest's blessing (*velaciones*) an escape clause. Depending on one's objectives, one might avoid the blessing to keep the marriage incomplete, or press for a blessing to make it conclusive. Teresa Núñez, for example, testified (in

1670) that "many times she urged Marcos to arrange the nuptial mass because he was delaying it." Another reluctant groom, Manuel Angel Domínguez, calmly acquiesced in a bigamous second marriage but fled at the prospect of going through the upcoming nuptial mass planned by his wife's brother.

Marriages coming out of abductions, like those that lacked a nuptial blessing, might be viewed as having an uncertain status. The issue hinged on whether the woman cooperated or resisted. In any case, as we have seen, women were legally minors and therefore not responsible for their acts. Thus running off with a man was termed a "theft" or an abduction. Compliance implied elopement, resistance rape, although the distinction became blurred, and rape was rarely prosecuted.[8]

In fact communities seemed to spend more energy tracking down illicit but consenting couples than running down rapists. To avoid such policing, some couples stayed on the move. Antonio de la Cruz, serving as a vaquero near Tlaquiltenango (now in Morelos state) in 1706, married the mayordomo's daughter, María de la Encarnación. But after six months, Joseph del Vario, a sometime worker on local haciendas and a muleteer, ran off with María (she went willingly, it seems), took her to Amecameca (now part of the Federal District) and lived with her for two years. In the meantime Antonio was "feeling lonely," he said, and took up with the mestiza Rosa Munice. Before the inquisitors twenty years later he recalled that "they moved through all of these towns and provinces covering the territory between the Pacific coast and the Mixteca with the story that she was his wife." The illicit nature of their cohabitation remained undetected, but after two years, Rosa, tired of life on the move, termed it a mala vida, and Antonio returned her to her home village Tistla (now in Guerrero state). And so ended this cohabitation, without rancor or complications.

As for his wife, María, Antonio said that she had "run away" with Joseph. Joseph, for his part, said that "he abducted María de la Encarnación [while] peddling clothing." Antonio's version makes María the agent of her leave-taking; Joseph's makes himself the agent. What actually happened points, in fact, to a parallel trajectory for María and Antonio, after María dissolved the marriage by running away. Each re-formed into a consensual union that lasted two years. Although Antonio eventually married again (hence the reason we know about him), María remained unmarried. When she testified to the Inquisition in 1732, twenty-six years after running off with Joseph, she was still living in free union, now with one Joseph Garfías, an overseer of orchards in Atrisco (now in Puebla state).

Husbands, of course, did not take it lightly when their wives ran off with other men. Probably without exception, they found such leave-takings humiliating, an affront to their honor, and an excuse for vengeance. Sometimes they pursued with intent to kill both their wives and their abductors. The issue was sensitive enough that even abandoned women who returned to their families and lived "honorably" might fear the vengeance of husbands. Eleven years after Teresa Núñez and her three daughters returned to her family's house in Guadalajara, she testified (in 1670), her husband Marcos appeared at odd hours at night to spy on her. Perhaps he hoped to catch her consorting with another man, thereby giving him an excuse to kill her. Such a motive is easily imagined, for Marcos had married a second time and killing Teresa might have seemed a way to avoid prosecution for bigamy.

Joseph Muñoz de Sanabria announced just such a plan to his second wife, María Rosa, explaining that killing his first wife Josepha would "save" their illicit marriage.[9] This was in 1726, after five or six years of married life, and shortly after María discovered that Joseph was already married. From the Silao jail Joseph asked María to help him break out of jail. In her denunciation of him (July 6, 1725) she testified that

> in jail he repeated that he would kill his first wife and within
> six months would go and live with [María] in the North
> where she was to await him. She said that more likely he
> would receive his first wife and serve God by living with
> her. The said Sanabria made so many entreaties that she
> agreed [to meet him] but only to quiet him so she could go
> to the Commissioner [of the Inquisition] to report the matter.

On first reading, it might seem that María Rosa rejected the plan only because she doubted that Joseph would go through with it. She must have wondered, however, why she should believe that he would compound one crime (bigamy) by committing an even more serious one (murder). Even more telling, the comment shows María Rosa imagining a likely alternative: why not simply resume married life with his legitimate wife?

In any case María Rosa was afraid, for she moved quickly to escape Joseph. Yet men may have spoken about killing a wife more commonly than we might have thought. Imagine, for example, Thomasa de Orduña's feelings on hearing her husband Sebastián recount his killing of his first wife. She had just told him that a neighbor said he had had another wife and, as she testified later (December, 1671), "he said it was true, he had been married, but because he found his wife with a man he had killed her and with that she did not deal with the matter further." If this seems a placid acceptance of Sebastián's self-possessed explanation, what else could she have done? Society would have agreed that infidelity justified vengeance. More directly, of course, the exchange reminded her that sexual misbehavior as a married woman brought the harshest possible sanction.

So far we have seen little of day-to-day married life, only some instances of it beginning badly. The unhappy runaways from such marriages often denied that a marriage had taken place. They said that they had not consented or that procedures had been incorrect or incomplete. Lack of consent, experienced as a personal violation, links most often to separating; incompleteness of procedures, a technicality constructed later, to justifying second marriages. Both form part of the popular discourse on Christian marriage, as did even the tactic to seduce women after promising to marry them. Miguel de Herrera, as we saw, carefully differentiated between betrothal, the promise to marry (words of future consent), and marriage (words of present consent). The distinction, a fine one not so visible to his partners, shows him carefully skirting church regulations. It was also invoked by the older brother of twelve-year old Gerónimo de Benavides, who promised to marry a widowed hatmaker in order to sleep with her. Before this engagement could become a marriage, he arranged Gerónimo's flight. The innkeeper Leonor Vázquez got into trouble not because she engaged in sexual relations with Christóbal de Ayala, but because she joked with him about marriage. She answered for her irreverence with a whipping. But that was better than the penalty for bigamy; typically for a woman of her station, lashes, abjuration of her error, and three to five years confinement.

Abandoned in the Old World

If men and women found ways to escape impossible marriages and to flee unwanted engagements, they also walked away from marriages considered, at least by others, appropriate and workable. Women left behind by men at least felt abandoned; they wanted their husbands back, their marriages restored, their children supported. Why then did men leave? Not in the main because they were "pushed" by an unhappy domestic life but because they were "pulled" by the larger world. Departure should be seen, therefore, as a process more than an event. It began as men went to war, took jobs, served masters, or tried out a liaison (all absences presumed temporary), and culminated as husbands moved farther and farther away from their old lives, until finally they shifted to new ones.

The way that three men (Nicolás, Francisco, and Luis) spoke of their leave-takings from married life illustrates the pattern. In 1524 Nicolás Chamorro married Juana de Moñón in Medina de Rioseco (province of Valladolid). Married life lasted "some days," Nicolás said, and [later] Juana gave birth to a daughter. "Afterward," Nicolás testified in 1537, "he went to Valencia and Andalusia to look for a living and was in those parts for three years without returning to his house. Then he passed to these parts [the Indies]. Just as he was about to embark he received word that Juana had died and then he left without inquiring further or knowing [more]."

The second, Francisco García (born 1523), spent his youth in Broças and Campomayor [El Campo][10] as a swineherd, shepherd, and muleteer, and married (in 1551) Violante Ruiz Pizarro, part of the numerous Pizarro clan of Trujillo. After three or four years of married life he took his four mules and headed for Seville. After he had been gone for some time Violante searched for him but resented traveling "from place to place, like the gypsies, looking for him."[11] In fact her searching had not been random. Accompanied by her uncle, the weaver Pedro Alonso, she had gone straight to Seville on hearing that Francisco was there. From Pedro's testimony (June 1572) we learn that they found Francisco "living with a mulatto woman. And he returned [home], but Violante stayed three or four months and then came back—three months pregnant—saying that she could not suffer being there any longer because of the mala vida she had with him because of his love for the mulatto with whom he was in concubinage." Francisco's testimony (July 1579) differs from Pedro's, in that he has Violante returning to El Campo after a few *years*, not a few months, and himself going to the Indies nine years after that. This makes her the deserter more than the deserted. In Puebla, where Francisco worked for a year as an innkeeper, his paisano Sayago from El Campo (dead by 1579) told him, so he claimed, that Violante had died.

The third, Luis Rodríguez (born 1556) of Moguer (province of Huelva) had been married to María de Cabrera for only three months (in 1575) when he went to Seville to practice his trade of pastry chef (*pastelero*). Finding work and settling on Sierpes street, Luis moved in with Juana de los Reyes, the daughter of another pastelero. A couple of years later he heard that María had died and he married Juana. Six or eight years after that, in 1585, he sailed as a cook on a ship going to the Indies. Although he had been paid only 10 ducats of the 80 he was to receive for the trip (the remainder to be paid on arrival back in Seville), Luis nevertheless jumped ship in Veracruz and remained permanently in Mexico.

All three of these abandonments began in an apparently innocent way. The search for work took each of the men to Seville, where two of the three established consensual unions. As time passed each became settled in a new life and received "news" that his wife was dead. Killing the old life (signified metonymically by the wife's death) validates the new one and correlates with going to the Indies (coming just before departure in two cases and just after arrival in the third), a further stage in the creation of a new life.

As men worked their way towards a new life in a new world, women remained behind in their old worlds. So much so, in fact, that in 1525 Seville seemed to the Venetian ambassador to be "in the hands of women."[12] Women expected their husbands to return and became desperate and angry as temporary sojourns turned into permanent disappearances. Witness, for example, the plaintive letter that Isabel Pérez wrote in 1583 to her husband, Antonio de Acevedo, after an eight-year absence.[13] "Every day I miss you, for it seems such a long time and I am so melancholy and wounded by your absence." She related news of the children ("Luis is with my brother Juan Pérez who is teaching him doctrine, virtue, and to read"; "Antonio . . . goes to school and applies himself well"; "Ana is well, and God be served, a good girl and a very gracious young woman"), the cousins, an aunt and uncle ("They kiss your hand many times"), her mother ("better but very tired"), and his father ("He is well and is the butcher of this town"). Although Isabel asks Antonio to send money, she adds: "I would rather see you, for without you I feel so used up and lost . . . that sometimes I feel dead." So Isabel reminds Antonio that his old world is still intact, that it still consists of everything that should matter to him—wife, children, family—and awaits his return to resume his place in it.

In fact Isabel *constructed* Antonio's world as intact, by stressing that nothing essential had changed. She could do this because she had some contact with him through letters. There came a point, however, when women lost contact, stopped making such constructions, gave up hope, and tried to make a new start. Beatriz González, of Málaga, saw her husband Juan embark for the Levant in 1521. She testified that for ten years "she raised her daughters with much labor and fatigue, without compromising the honor of her person or her life."[14] During this time neighbors and relatives (including in-laws) would "say to me every day that the said Juan González was dead or that he had died in Italy." Eventually she agreed, gave up on her old life, and embarked for the Indies. She justified this course to the inquisitors in the strongest terms: "By right all those who are absent in distant and remote places should be presumed dead so that their wives can remarry without penalty."

Women took longer to give up their old lives because they remained in them, whereas their husbands periodically absented themselves anyway. Beatriz, most immediately, had two daughters to raise. Yet temporary absences after a time seemed permanent, and so women agonized in the eighteenth century no less than the sixteenth. First efforts lay in reestablishing married life to its full integrity as we can see, for example, in the letter of Mariana de Itá (of Cádiz) to her husband in 1746.

> Agustín, I would like to know what motive you have to not
> remember a daughter and a wife whom God has given you.
> I would like to know if it is ill health that causes you not to
> bother yourself at all. I charge you with enjoying yourself
> and forgetting us. Remember you have but one soul and
> you will lose it for not tending to your obligations . . . and I
> pray to God that you will return as every day I do *novenas*
> asking God to bring you back. I think I shall become blind
> so many tears have I shed.

But years went by, life continued, and abandoned wives had to carry on.[15] They might be absorbed in the household of a father, brother, or brother-in-law, look to live off the charity of a relative of their husband when they had none of their own, or support themselves and their families through their own labor, often by becoming domestic servants. A common concern, to return to Isabel Pérez's letter to her husband Antonio, was "to shape these children in discipline and virtue." Another was the social limbo women found themselves in, a "suspension in the air," as one termed it, as neither wife nor widow.[16] The urge to transform oneself from deserted wife to widow must have tempted many, for it solved a lot of problems. But a missing husband had to be certified as dead, for no statute of limitations existed. How could women establish whether their husbands were alive or dead?

For one thing they made inquiries. Antón González, pilot of an escort ship in the Indies fleet, remembered how Isabel Gerónimo approached him in 1579.

> Five years ago he was passing through Ayamonte on the way
> to Cádiz. He spoke with a woman there and she, knowing
> that he had just returned from the Indies, asked him if he
> knew any men named Cañada in New Spain. He answered
> yes, that he knew a So-and-so Cañada. 'Know this, then,'
> she said. 'He is my husband. And this girl that you see'—

showing him a young woman by her side—'is his daughter and mine. He has been gone now for twenty-two years'.

With that Isabel entrusted González with letters for her husband. Catalina Rodríguez made similar inquiries when she approached Father Juan de Pinilla and other travelers from the Indies in search of news of her husband, Christóbal Quintero. Father Juan testified (in 1542) that

> two years ago he was at his *posada* [inn] in Seville and a woman whose name he does not know came up and asked after Christóbal Quintero, a black staying in Veracruz. He told her that he left him married in Veracruz to a woman of Castile, that he had shown him a *probanza* [proof] showing that his first wife died. And the woman said 'how could he marry, the evil man as he is my husband and I am alive'.

A year later, Catalina spoke to Martín Hernández (a vecino of Seville who probably sailed regularly on the Indies fleet) and sent him back with a strong message for her husband. Here, from his deposition given in Veracruz, is how Martín remembered the incident:

> It was [Saint Mary] Magdalena's day in July [22] 1539 and he spoke with the said woman and saw her alive. She asked if her husband was alive and he said yes. She then said to tell him that he'd better come to these parts, that he'd better send her money to support her, that if he did not she would go there and take him away from the wife that he now has.

On returning Hernández duly relayed the message and received the response "she can go to the devil." Hernández, as far as we know, did not upbraid Christóbal for lax morality. But González, the pilot from Ayamonte, eventually ran down Isabel's husband, Pedro Cañada, who was then about to remarry. When Pedro claimed that Isabel was dead, González testified that he had then shouted "you dog, enemy of God, you're lying. I just spoke with her and I left her alive."

So strangers sometimes took the part of women who enlisted them to help locate their husbands and pressure them to send money, to return home, or to abandon illicit marriages or the plans to contract them. Their efforts were not necessarily to much effect, at least in these cases, for Pedro went ahead with his marriage in spite of González's reprimand, and Christóbal rejected out of hand Catalina's claim to him.

Was the next step for a woman to go to the Indies? Possibly, if she was in good health, could afford passage, and had family to go with. The last mattered in two ways: it gave women protection for the journey and allies for confronting their errant husbands. After all, an absence of ten or more years amounted to divorce. By the time a missing husband had been found, he no doubt had formed strong ties to a new place, new associates, a new spouse, and new progeny. Now newly rooted, the reappearance of one's old life in the form of a wife's message, or worse her arrival, sparked dismay, hostility, and disbelief. We already saw Christóbal's reaction to his wife's threat to take him from his new wife: "she can go to the devil" might very well epitomize most old-world intrusions into the new worlds of bigamists.

Yet wives persisted by refusing to accept their husbands' "divorces." Juana de Herrera, in the fourth of five unanswered letters to her husband Francisco Rangel, asked him to return to Mexico City from the north, insisting that she had an absolute claim on him. "Many people here know that you want to [re]marry. Watch what you do, for you are a Christian and my husband and you know very well that before God, when you left you didn't even say farewell and I didn't know a thing about it."

Note that she concerns herself less with the marriage Francisco might contract (perhaps because she knew it would not have legal standing) than the one he has failed to maintain. This ordering repeats itself in her coupling of a warning not to marry with the apparently trivial complaint about the hastiness of his departure. Yet the latter mattered, for it denoted the callousness of Francisco's abandonment. Her condition rankled all the more because, as she put it in a letter to him, she had "found out that it goes well with you and that you have money. For the love of God you ought to give some to your daughters who have nothing." In all of this Juana speaks as a woman presuming her marriage to be intact (as indeed it was in the eyes of church and state). That confidence pervades her formulaic but affectionate sign off, "God keep you happy until he lets me see you which is my desire, your wife who esteems and loves you."

Abandoned wives presented married life as companionship, economic partnership, and project to care for and nurture children. Women wanted this not in the abstract but concretely with the man they married; men wanted it too, but generically, by reconstituting domestic life in other places with other women. The pattern can be seen in the case of Francisco del Puerto who found himself "temporarily" in the Philippines. But time went by, and he became ever more permanently cut off from the happy marriage, two daughters, and network of family and friends that earlier had blessed his life in Málaga. When Francisco told his story to the inquisitors in 1721, he was fifty-four, and by then had been apart from his wife and family for more than twenty years. In Málaga, he testified, "many people envied" his happy domestic life, but then a cargo ship in which he had an interest was lost and he therefore fell into debt. "Seeing that he had become a slave, he said to his mother and wife that he would like to go to the Indies to see if he could get on his feet again."

And so he went, with his mother's blessing and his wife's permission. What happened next is not clear, except that Francisco, so far away, got the idea that his wife and mother had died. They did not hear from him for nine years and did not even know where he was. His mother, doña Juana de Arriola, in a letter dated October 3, 1705, one of many she wrote to try to reestablish contact, gives an idea of the family's distress with Francisco's interminable absence.

> I am completely broken in health because of your absence, or, to say it better, because you have forgotten your obligations. I can see a daughter [in-law] living with many burdens who is carrying them with great virtue. My heart is even sadder when I see the two daughters that you left who are naked, not able to hear the mass for lack of clothing, and with their mother in the same plight. Would that our Lord open your eyes and give you to understand your hardness of heart, for

when honorable men, because of the accidents of life absent themselves, they are not thereby freed from meeting their obligations to their wives and children.

Doña Juana's rebuke of her son can stand for the voices of other women (wives, mothers, sisters) left by their husbands in Spain. These range in tone from shrill and angry to fatalistic and resigned. They repeatedly express distress that the head of the household had removed himself from his economic and paternalistic roles as provider and leader. They show us that from the sixteenth century a divide had opened up in the valuation of domestic life. On one side men, pulled by the wider world, valued marriage and family life relatively; on the other women, focused mainly on their households, valued it absolutely. When a man such as Francisco del Puerto finally got around to thinking about it, he spoke movingly of his former life and happiness in Málaga. But he, like other men who established themselves in the Indies, had reconstituted his life in a new place with a new woman. We turn now to follow men whose work and the call of wider worlds pulled them from their marriages.

Work and the Larger World

So far we have seen that bigamists went to the Indies as a matter of course to escape debt or a spouse as well as to seek their fortune. The excitement of the early Spanish expansion into new lands exerted a strong pull on men and Diego de Villareal can stand for the type. He had arrived in Mexico about 1522, in time to play a secondary role in the conquest, and sustained a wound which required the amputation of one leg below the knee.[17] After marrying María de Aguirre in 1529, Diego settled in the town of Santa María de la Victoria [Tabasco], and fathered four children. But in 1544 he went to Peru, lived for a time in Potosí, and as a reward for his role in "pacifying and populating" Tucumán, received an encomienda in the district of Santiago del Estero (probably in 1552).[18] After his departure María knew nothing of Diego's adventures and subsequent life in Santiago where, according to the testimony of an acquaintance in Peru, he moved about on horseback or on a chair carried by his Indians.[19] In fact he had begun a new "married life," informally of course, with Francisca de Vega, the "servant" who lived with him for nine years and to whom he left a "quantity of gold pesos" in his will. Back in Victoria, María, after six years, gave up on Diego and remarried.

Francisco, modestly successful in New Spain, abandoned his wife when given the chance to go to Peru. So did Jacobe Luxeri, who left his wife, Inés, in Guatemala City in the early 1540s. Jacobe, however, occasionally saw his wife: after twenty years for three or four days while en route to Mexico City where he stayed for three or four years; and en route to Peru once again, once again merely for a few days. He then disappeared from Inés's sight for another fifteen years. A brief file has nothing in it to indicate what Inés thought about this "married life." Jacobe's son Christóbal, however, testified in 1580 that he had gone to Peru around 1556. At the time he was eighteen and intended to collect his inheritance (reports had arrived that Jacobe had died) but found his father alive. Father and son reunited at the mining camp of Almaguer near Popayán and stayed for two years "reacquainting themselves as father and son." Inés waited and finally, in 1579, remarried on hearing (unfortunately falsely once again) that Jacobe had died.

The early period of conquest and settlement pulled forcefully at Jacobe and Diego. But the larger world had pulled men from their homes before the Indies opened up and would do so afterward. For the women left behind, expecting news or the return of their husbands, disappearances amounted to the same thing, whether in the heroic mode to go to Peru or to another region in search of work. Moreover temporary absences had a way of becoming permanent ones, sometimes in spite of the intention and attempts to reestablish contact. Hernando de Rosas, for example, after living for six years with his wife Ana de Salazar in Mexico City, signed on (in 1605) for a tour of duty in the Philippines. "I am the most wretched of men," he wrote Ana in 1615, "for in ten years I have seen only one letter from you even though I have written every year." If he had failed to meet his obligations as a husband, he added, it had not been "for lack of love, desire, or resources, which, thanks be to God," were considerable. These he listed as 1,000 pesos cash, a house worth 600 pesos, two slaves, and successful businesses. But they, and he, remained in Manila, hostage to dangerous sea lanes across the Pacific.

> If I have failed to come to see you it is not my fault but yours. I have written letters, one with auditor Diego de Chandía . . . and twice embarked with my goods [for New Spain] but they unloaded them, for year after year there is nothing but war and more war. So you can well believe that the fault lies in trying to govern the many enemies of these islands. And so señora, my very own, once again I beg you to come to my rescue by letting me see your letter . . .

Work and Mobile Types

If the circumstances of living in an expanding and far-flung empire pulled men away from home, so too did their search for work. Most emphatically here we are concerned with mobile types such as seamen, muleteers, or shepherds, whose work took them from home as a matter of course. We have, for example, a precise chronology of Diego González Carmona's career and can infer how it affected his marriage with Elvira Sánchez.[20] Both came from the mountain town of Araçena (jurisdiction of Huelva) and married in 1578. They lived together for two years and then, in 1580, Diego joined Spanish forces invading Portugal. On returning Diego testified (in his autobiographical statement of 1614) that he was based in Seville for eight years.

> The first four [years] the said Elvira Sánchez, his wife, came to see him from Araçena and she was with him two months until the galleons of don Francisco Colonna that came to Cartagena were ready and he embarked on them and spent one year and a half on that armada. He returned to Spain and was there another three years and four months in the port of Santa María and in all this time did not see the said Elvira his wife nor hear whether she was dead or alive.

At this point, Diego had drifted well away from his married life with

Elvira and finished it off by embarking for the Indies "on the fleet of Pedro de Escobar Melgarejo about fourteen or sixteen years ago [in 1600]."[21] "It will be [he added] about seven years ago [1607] that he married a second time in Mexico City understanding that his first wife was dead."

Other mobile types imposed similar pressures on their marriages. Although muleteers moved shorter distances than seamen, they could nevertheless be lost from view as far as their wives and communities were concerned. Here is how a routine leave-taking could turn into a permanent one. One day in 1731 when Juan Antonio Mascareñas of Sinaloa, a muleteer married for thirteen years to Francisca de Armenta, father of four children, left on a job headed for Mexico City. In southern Sinaloa he became sick at the mining camp of Nuestra Señora del Rosario and his boss left him behind. On recovering he was hired by don Juan de Mosquera based in Acaponeta (now in the northwest part of Nayarit state), fifty miles or so to the southeast of Rosario, to run some mules to Guadalajara; after that he went to Mexico City, to Veracruz, and, hired by "a *gachupín*," to Parral. Then he signed on as a soldier in the presidio of Cerro Gordo.

Juan's movements from job to job have a random quality, as if he were a leaf blown by the wind. And indeed the contingent nature of work pulled men from place to place and, little by little sometimes, further from their old lives. The circumstantial ordinariness of this drift is epitomized by a 1752 leave-taking of another muleteer, the mestizo Pedro Pablo Rodríguez. He and María Marcelina de Baes had been married for four years when, in the words of the prosecutor's summary of testimony against Pedro,

> he told her to make him some tortillas, that he was going to the pueblo of Mascota [now in Jalisco state] with letters sent by the alcalde mayor don Christóbal de Mendoza y Alvarado. So he left with this pretext the Friday after . . . the feast . . . of the Immaculate Conception of our Lady the Virgin Mary [December 8] and with word that he would return the following Tuesday, but he did not until August 1767.

Pedro therefore disappeared for nearly twenty years. His failure to return must have baffled María, for she described (in 1768) her married life with him as a happy one, "living together in all peace, love, union, and serenity and her husband made their living. . . . and together they urged on some mules that he had with which they maintained themselves comfortably."

What had Pedro been doing in all these years? He as well as the prosecutor seemed hard pressed to give a coherent picture, but here is the prosecutor's summary: "He went to various pueblos and places and *even* practiced the office of shoemaker in . . . the mining camp of Cosalá (Culiacán, Nueva Galicia) where he tried to marry."[22] Pedro also mentioned stays in the area of Tepic (now in Nayarit state), Zacatecas, and Santa Bárbara (now in Chihuahua state) working sometimes as a groom or shoemaker but always returning to muleteering. The end came on a routine trip, Pedro said, when

> Domingo Morán sent him with his [Moran's] mules to San Sebastián [now in southern Sinaloa state] to pick up a load of maize. But he did not find any and Morán had him return to Pánuco [now in Zacatecas state] and then go to Acaponeta to try to get some. He ran into his brother there and, because he told him that his wife María Marcelina was still alive in Tomatlán [now in west Jalisco state], he went to Hacienda San Lorenzo. From there he made two trips to the mining camp of San Francisco,[23] one with fruit, the other with meat. Then he went directly to Ameca [now in Jalisco state] and was put in jail.

Eventually Pedro married a third time (he had married María Marcelina as a widower), after living in an illicit friendship with Juana María Bobadilla for a year. The decision, Juana said, was "prompted by violence because of the denunciation the judge of the district made that he would banish him unless he married." In spite of the "violence," the marriage can be seen as a kind of ratification of Pedro's life at that moment, drifted into little by little, until it had reached a point far removed from the old life with María.

The answer to a still troublesome question, why Pedro left a "happy" marriage with María in the first place, remains unanswered. Fortunately, the inquisitors also wanted to know, and in response to their query Pedro said that "he did not find [María] sufficiently faithful and rather than suffer the loss of his honor by his wife, he left and thereby did not have to strike her as a jealous husband." Missing are the specifics. Had María become too bold or a little insubordinate at the festival of Concepción? We cannot know. Perhaps Pedro had forgotten or simply spoke formulaically of honor in a way that would make sense to his male judges. Assuming some basis to the statement, however, we have Pedro recalling what he remembered as a real dilemma, either to "strike" María or to abandon her. In this way a plebeian defended his honor and quit an otherwise happy marriage. If he had too much pride to return to María on his own, the net closing in on him as a bigamist provided the extra push. And the reunion was a happy one. María said that "he greeted and embraced her . . . with expressions of love and of happiness."

Shepherds and Vaqueros

Shepherds and vaqueros, also mobile types, had to be away from their wives regularly and sometimes for long periods. When the Inquisition investigated the marriage of José Francisco Ortiz (born 1743), a shepherd at Hacienda del Pozo in the district of San Luis Potosí (the hacienda ran sheep and goats in an arid country that required much land to sustain the animals),[24] they received a deposition by Miguel de los Santos López, mayordomo of the hacienda, who testified (in 1780) that he had known José "on the rancho called Charco de la Piedra, accessory of the said hacienda of Pozo, since he was about twelve." Miguel had seen "the gathering of people for the wedding and celebration" when José and María married in 1773 and knew that "the hacienda paid the marriage fees." But he did not enter the house at the time of the festivities.

Salvador Carrizal, about seventy and "without a trade before arriving at an advanced age," but then an "ager of stock to be slaughtered," remembered the event only at second hand because he had to be with the animals. Others too busy to stop work, Juan Salvador Pérez for example, said much the same thing. As "assistant to the foreman of the goat hacienda, property of the Hacienda del Pozo, he was with the livestock as required by his occupation." Nevertheless Juan knew José and his wife María Josefa for about two years, and his testimony gives a clear picture of the married life of shepherds.

> María Josepha did not actually live on the goat hacienda but at Pozo [where] the rancheros normally keep their wives. They [the goatherds] always run around—they're like couriers [*correos*] doing different jobs in distant places—and it is more comfortable for the wives to stay on the hacienda although that does not mean that they do not have a married life as much as they can.

This pattern of marriage allowed for liaisons, concubinage, and bigamy or polygamy. The mulatto shepherd Alonso de Alvarado, for example, had three wives. Moreover, the prosecutor of the Inquisition charged, "he usually had an Indian woman as his companion," while herding sheep near San Miguel el Grande. Not until 1691, twenty-five years after his first marriage, did his loose way of life catch up with him. Marriage irregularities easily went unnoticed as men who moved long distances with flocks, lived away from towns and even small settlements, and left their wives behind. One of Alonso's wives, Agustina, remembered her "needless" jealousy of Alonso's Indian consort, whom she had begun to beat: "She stopped when a man told her '*señora*, don't beat her, because Alonso de Alvarado told me that you are not his wife'." Only a licit wife need bother to beat her husband's mistress.

Mala Vida and Discord

If work pulled men from their marriages, the mala vida (abuse, overwork, lack of support, beatings) pushed women from theirs.[25] Women engaged the problem in a discourse informed by norms of Christian marriage, for as common as the mala vida was, it was so designated as the inversion of some sort of ideal "good life." We already saw, for example, that friends and neighbors viewed Francisco del Puerto's marriage in Málaga in such terms. The tanner Joseph de Luque remembered (in 1707) Francisco and his wife María as "a husband and wife with more affection than other married couples; they did not quarrel or inflict the mala vida on one another but always were very lovingly married." Debt rather than discord pushed this couple apart, but with most marriages "external" forces such as debt cannot be disentangled from "internal" ones such as discord. The first often provided the pretext and the second the motivation for separating. Here, nevertheless, we shall highlight directly expressed dissatisfaction with marriages.

Joseph makes clear that the mala vida could be inflicted by either partner on the other. In fact, however, men imposed it on women far more often than women on men, as they directed or neglected the affairs of their households. This occurred because law and custom supported male dominance and assumed male superiority. "In wisdom, skill, virtue and humanity," Juan Ginés de Sepúlveda wrote, men surpass women just as Spaniards exceed Indians and adults children.[26] The role of husband and father, however, included reciprocal duties and the benevolence associated with ideals of paternalism. Mariana Monroy, a creole Spaniard of Guadalajara who married in 1663, recognized the discrepancy between ideals and reality when she bridled at her servant-like condition as wife of the peninsular Spaniard Manuel de Figueroa. She testified (in an autobiographical statement of 1678) that he made her rise at one o'clock in the morning to do household chores and "if she did not do things to his liking he abused and beat her many times." Three years of this culminated in Manuel beating Mariana for failing to serve him "as quickly as he wanted," and she fled to the house of Manuel de Escalante, prosecutor of the *audiencia* of Mexico City.

Mariana's escape was a logical step, for she "hated [Manuel] and always lived in discord with him because he made her work so much." Moreover she prefaced this statement by claiming "she married against her will." The last counted as an argument to invalidate the marriage. Mariana intended, it seems, to have it put before a court to argue for annulment on grounds that the doctrine of consent had been violated. But after waiting all day for Escalante to appear, Mariana gave up (perhaps in the realization that the justice system, no less than onlookers and neighbors, hesitated to intervene in a man's domestic affairs) and instead took refuge in the convent of Santa Catalina. She remained in her sanctuary about six weeks (from Shrovetide until Holy Week). Only then, because she believed (wrongly as it turned out) that the Viceroy was going to punish Manuel by sending him to the Philippines, did she take leave of her sanctuary.[27]

That Mariana believed this shows how she thought her society worked. She thought it natural that the highest official of the kingdom, proxy of the king himself, would concern himself with her mala vida and, solely on the basis of a friend's complaint, exile her husband. The weak, the abused, and the victimized looked to benevolent protectors to act on their behalf.

On several occasions in her trial Mariana returned to the themes of consent and mistreatment. The first, without detail, acts merely to frame the bitter list that itemizes Manuel's tyranny, beatings, and merciless slave driving. To Manuel, Mariana's loathing was also a protest and evidence of her lack of subservience, a challenge to his male authority that must have intensified his harshness. Summing up their relationship at the end of the trial, Mariana characterized it as one of "continuous war, disagreement, and disunion."

Manuel's defective character, Mariana concluded, accounted for the trouble, and in an inspired leap she associates this with heresy. "He has a perverted nature, so bad and so disturbed that she decided that the said marriage was null and void and invalid. In her view it was as if he were a heretic and she considered [the marriage] no longer binding." The progression outlined by Mariana is prefaced by lack of consent but moves from bad treatment to defective character to "as if a heretic," the first and last clear grounds for annulment.

Not many instances of the mala vida can be documented in so much detail. If all wives coming into their husband's households entered as outsiders and subordinates, they nevertheless expected some limitation to their subservience. This came at the hands of husbands who imposed a servantlike condition, a kind of "indenture" as we just saw, and at the hands of mothers-in-law.[28] The mulatto Lucía Guadalupe testified (in 1744) that she put up with five years of such harsh conditions (from 1726) "until she had to run away to this village [Córdoba, now in Veracruz state] because of the bad treatment [*mal trato*] from her mother-in-law, Juana de Pisa, and her husband, the mulatto Antonio de Pisa."

Lucía ran away "accompanied by the Indio ladino Antonio Ramos," according to her neighbor Leocadia Gertrudis. She made her way from Izúcar (now in Puebla state) to Córdoba and became a servant in the house of don Rafael de Olivera. But thirteen years later, she declared that she "desired to rejoin her husband whenever possible." What an odd turnabout (was it tailored just for the inquisitors?) after so much effort to remain out of Antonio's hands. He, at least for a time, had searched high and low for Lucía. A glimpse of him looking comes from the deposition (in 1744) of the Spaniard Juan de Pastrana, who ran into Antonio in the village of Xalostoc (now in Morelos state). "He was crying while telling the story of Lucía's flight and asking help to search for her." On the one hand, then, Antonio mistreated his wife; on the other, he was capable of weeping when she ran away. Likely his grief had more to do with loss of face than change of heart. More importantly, Lucía "solved" her own problem, a point that can be underscored from Leocadia's account of Lucía running away "accompanied," not abducted, by Antonio.

Some fifty years later María Guadalupe Delgadillo Hernández, a Spaniard, also traced her mala vida to a mother-in-law.[29] She ran away twice, first in 1773 after a year of married life, and again nine months after having been returned to her mestizo husband.[30] What went wrong? María testified (in her autobiographical statement of 1780) that she ran away to escape the "punishments and bad treatment" of José and his mother. But before that she had also "explained to José that she would leave him if he did not treat her better." She had also asked the parish priest to intervene. And later, from Mexico City, she wrote letters. None of this did any good. If anything, her complaints made things worse and strengthened the resolve of mother and son to tame her. In this José's mother took the initiative: she restricted María to the house, barred José from giving María even a small coin (*un medio*), and forbade him to sleep with her. Such was the content of the mala vida for María. Young as she was (fourteen at marriage), she stood up for herself by telling José in a letter that he had violated "the obligations of matrimony." In effect, therefore, he had abandoned her, not vice versa, as was true literally.

The mala vida for women, then, meant mistreatment, abuse, and overwork. A male version of the mala vida also appears in bigamy testimony, but for men it meant "discord," a less specific term that included insubordination, disaffection, conflict, which often caused anxiety over manliness. María's husband José, for example, undoubtedly viewed her refusal to acquiesce in her servile condition in this way. With an unruly wife he would be subject to taunts, gossip, and even organized ridicule calling into question his manhood. Men could euphemize conflicts over subordination as "various discords," as did don Joseph Serrano y Mora in characterizing his marriage (1760) of only four months to doña Francisca Ricarda Molina of Málaga. After a dispute Francisca resorted to her mother's house[31] and when don Joseph went to get her servants ejected him from the house. The incident wounded his pride. Referring to it fourteen years later he testified that he had been "shamed by this insult to his honor" and so went to Carcabuey, to Cádiz, and then to the Indies. Doña Francisca said that she did not know where, but she must have known why, don Joseph had gone.[32]

Whatever the "various discords" had been, don Joseph abandoned doña Francisca because he had failed to maintain authority over his wife and therefore lost face. In this he underscores a difference from the mala vida as experienced by women. Unhappily married men did not suffer "discordance" for so long. The mestizo Nicolás Antonio de Arauz managed just four months with the Indian Dominga María whom, as we saw in chapter 3, he took to Mexico City and married (in 1735) with the patronage of Pedro the waterman. In the dock six years later he summarily recounted a brief and troubled married life "with her in the house of his padrino, whom he helped carry water to the houses, . . . and because he could not stand his wife with whom he had no peace, he left her and went to the rancho of Nicolás Díaz with his uncle, Pedro de Arauz, an Indian tributary."

Díaz had raised Nicolás Antonio, and so his arrival amounted to a homecoming even though the older man by then had died. His widow, the mulatto Rosa, and two sons took Nicolás in tow and "at different times" asked if he had married when he was gone. Nicolás always answered no.

So, they counseled him to marry their house servant, the Indian María Rosa, a girl of sixteen or eighteen of "unknown parents" from Guachinango (now in Jalisco state). Nicolás agreed, he said, "thinking that in the epidemic [1736] his first wife would have died." His denial that he was married (was he ashamed of having married Dominga?) and his silent wager that his first wife had succumbed (however plausible given the high mortality rates) shows us a man who had put a brief but unsuccessful old life behind him.

Husbands termed defiance or even complaints as a cause of "discord" as did the muleteer Juan de Santana Izquierdo who in 1783 used the term to characterize his unhappy married life with the mulatto Josepha Castellanos in Piguamo, a village in the mountainous zone of Michoacán (now in Jalisco state).[33] "After six years, having had various disagreements, he went to the pueblo of Tamazula [in the same region, about forty miles to the north] where he has been married now for four years with the Indian Juliana Valerio, vecina of the said pueblo, daughter of Margarita la Ortega and an unknown father." Juan's statement highlights a simple sequence: discord, departure, remarriage. If bigamists created new lives for themselves, this one began with the "push" of an unhappy old life rather than the "pull" of the larger world as we saw above.

Adultery, New Partners, New Lives

Adultery strained marriages but did not of itself break them. Society, after all, accepted a double standard and men sought adulterous liaisons at the same time that they insisted on their wives' fidelity and their daughters' chastity. Thus the Spaniard Miguel de Acosta's good-humored admission (in 1777) of his adulteries: "one and another peccadillo [*fragilidad*] with some other woman" during a six-year marriage to Ignacia de Castro without "treating her [Ignacia] badly and without ceasing to have conjugal relations with her."[34] Ignacia saw it differently and testified that "Miguel treated her very badly perhaps because he was illicitly involved with Teresa de Anaya, unmarried, resident of this town [Molango, jurisdiction of Meztitlan, now Hidalgo state]." We have, then, contrasting visions of adultery: the first, harmless and inconsequential; the second, painful and destructive.

However discordant the double standard for wives, they probably acquiesced in it, worked to regain their husbands' affection, and tried to keep temporary liaisons from becoming permanent.[35] The latter would mean serious trouble: abandonment, withdrawal of support, and, more likely than not, children to raise alone. Yet how could women prevent such drift when mobile occupations offering occasions to establish and renew illicit friendships routinely took husbands away for shorter or longer periods? Here is a typical instance, when in 1714 Josepha de la Nava saw her husband Miguel de Herrera off. "He said he was going with someone who was going to pay him a peso a day," she testified in 1722, "and would be back in four months." In fact, he roamed about, seduced a number of women, and eventually married one of them. Josepha, in the meantime, remained in Mexico City and in eight years saw Miguel only three times.[36] It seems doubtful that in the beginning Miguel intended to abandon Josepha, but finally one of his liaisons in Michoacán pushed him into that step. By the time he stopped by to pick up a hat he had left behind with Josepha (two visits in May suggest that he may have been monitoring the condition of the now ill Josepha and hoping for her demise, thus to remove the evidence of his crime), his new life was well established.

Wives feared adultery because it portended abandonment. If the mulatto María Robles seemed to accept that her husband, the mulatto Felipe Rodríguez, would have sexual relations with other women from time to time, she drew the line when a liaison threatened to break up their marriage. As she summarized twenty-five years of married life that had begun in 1738, she noted that Felipe's work as a muleteer frequently took him away from their home in Zumpango (now in the north of Mexico state). After several years of married life and seeing the birth of three children, Felipe left and stayed away for four years. When María tracked him down, he was living with a woman named Gertrudis. To get him to come home, she threatened to report him to don Antonio Correa (a man who acted as a patron to her?), formerly "captain" of the audiencia chamber. Felipe returned, this time for five or six years and the birth of three more children. His next long period of truancy began in an ordinary way, when Felipe departed with a mule team owned by Joseph Morales. After about a year María again found him, this time in Mexico City, and brought him home. And once again, María recounted in testimony she gave in 1775, she conceived a child but miscarried. The calendar of Felipe's homecomings in María's account, therefore, correlate with the birth of her children. It is as if she is emphasizing that Felipe, not somebody else, had fathered them, and also that she had a married life with him.

María also noted a third long absence "seven or eight years ago [ca. 1767], and for no reason at all, for there was no quarrel, anger, or anything else." Indeed not, for from Felipe's testimony we learn that he had then realized that he was tired of María and simply left. It might be inferred that married life for Felipe and María had been tenuous for some time. But for María's initiatives to bring him home two or three times, Felipe seemed well on the way to drifting out of the marriage. However frequent his trips, together with occasional longer periods away, the marriage still confined Felipe too closely and there came a point when Felipe determined to separate permanently. But note how María and Felipe disagree on why this happened with María unable to imagine a motive even though she had lived with Felipe's erratic pattern of absences for nearly twenty years.

María and Josepha expected their husbands to be away for varying intervals. Josepha, for example, spoke of Miguel's projected four-months absence to work for a peso a day as if it were routine. Nor did María worry when Felipe was away for similar periods. María also tolerated the adulteries that seemed to go with Felipe's absences, as long as they did not imply a cessation of their marriage. The liaison with Gertrudis, for example, had such overtones, and she found a way to stop it. A distinction can be made, therefore, between liaisons of short and long duration. Both of course were sins and officially prohibited; both consumed time and resources to which wife and family had prior claim. Yet a short-lived, passing adultery did not threaten a marriage until it became a regular liaison and the basis for another life.

At such a point, with her husband "permanently" living with another woman, a wife might give up hope. At least the mulatto Juana Martínez did after a five-year marriage to Andrés Ramírez, also mulatto. Their marriage began at an hacienda near Querétaro "on Tuesday, the day before Ash

Wednesday in the year after the *matlazáhuatl* [epidemic] of 1738," Juana testified (in 1750) when they "married and received the nuptial blessing." In fact it was a group wedding, probably to regularize a number of informal unions, as Juana's aunt and "many others" from the hacienda also married. Afterwards they feasted in the quarters of Juana and Andrés with "all the servants of the hacienda." The newlyweds remained at the hacienda for ten months, then went to Guadalajara (six weeks), Mexico City (four months), back to the hacienda (ten months), and then to Ocoyoacac (now in Mexico state) where for three years they both served a priest. Then Juana left Andrés, she said, "because living in concubinage with Agustina Quesada, he subjected her to the mala vida."

Juana's charting of her married life with Andrés seems a fairly routine prologue to the central point: she left him. The wording here matters. She might have reversed it, to convey that Andrés left her. That she did not underscores the assumption that taking a mistress did not in itself mean abandonment of a wife. Notwithstanding Agustina, Andrés had not left Juana, but Agustina's presence in the marriage meant the mala vida for the rightful wife.

Eventually Juana attacked Agustina with a club and tried to kill her two children. The judges, in fact, ordered her not to speak to or attack her rival. Yet the children were an inviting target, for Andrés had fathered them (the eldest was then six, thus indicating that the liaison had been going on at least since he married Juana). But why strike at this moment, and why target the other woman instead of Andrés himself? The timing links to Juana's realization that she indeed had been supplanted. That she attacked Agustina instead of Andrés points, once again, to the disparity in power between husbands and wives. Instead of lashing out at Andrés directly, Juana chose the safer course of attacking the rival who had displaced her.

If losing a husband to a mistress was a process, at the early stage wives might see the danger signals in the loss of affection and support. Francisca de Torres, for example, a woman of sixteenth-century Seville, had to cope with her wayward husband Gómez de León (she married him in 1558), who openly associated with prostitutes, had mistresses for shorter or longer periods, and gambled away his substance. His friend and compadre[37]

Christóbal Ruiz bluntly said (testifying in 1572) that in the early 1560s Gómez had been "a whoremonger who gave the mala vida to his daughter." He recalled Francisca, addressing him as "señor compadre," asking why he had consented to the said Gómez her husband associating with other women?" Note that her sense of the moral economy of compadrazgo relations required at times a reprimand. For in this case Francisca's distress obviously traced to Gómez's adulteries which, in Christóbal's wording, meant that Gómez was giving the mala vida to his daughter, not his wife, and suggests non-support. By this time, in fact, Gómez had confided to Christóbal that he regretted marrying Francisca saying that he had been too young and had gone through with it to get the funds (probably from her dowry) to qualify as a notary.[38]

Men who drifted into consensual unions away from their tierras could pass as unmarried, but because they were unknown ("vagabonds," "travelers," and "strangers" in the language of the Third Provincial Council of Mexico, 1585), they were expected, more than locals, to demonstrate their freedom to marry.[39] But in practice the prescribed vigilance did not seem to screen out already-married strangers so readily. In fact just the opposite, in many cases, for newcomers whose personal histories were unknown and who were living in concubinage were assumed to be unmarried to the degree that officials and families threatened and urged them to marry. In this way the distancing of space and time set the stage for a "trial" life to become a "permanent" one, as it did in the case of Nicolás Cervantes, alias Nicolás Hermenegildo Hidalgo. After marrying María Martínez (in 1754), he lived with her for three years. But in the next three years or so, he spent, in the wording of the sentence (handed down in 1782), only "two or three days [with her] . . . every four or five months" before he "absented himself completely." That Nicolás married two more times reveals less for our purposes than the fact that his third wife, Antonia Josepha, had previously been one of his mistresses while he lived a married life with María. Nicolás testified (in his autobiographical statement of 1782) that "he moved to the city of Salvatierra [now in southeast Guanajuato] and . . . married a third time with the said Antonia Josepha who, years ago . . . he used to know in that city when he made his trips to the North." For Nicolás, an occasional but periodic liaison over a long term prepared the ground for his third marriage and a new life.

Differing versions of Joseph Manuel de Molina's sudden abandonment of his wife, María Rosalia, illustrate perceptions of adultery that are poles apart. The first comes from the mulatto Pedro de Zúñiga, who at sixty could say that he was native to and a vecino of the hacienda of San Agustín in Nueva Galicia (now in Zacatecas state) and had watched Joseph grow up, marry [in 1743], and live on the hacienda with his wife, the mulatto María. He testified (in 1770) that

> they lived a married life for a number of years until the administrator don Miguel de Olea, expelled some peons and he went to the mining camp of Bolaños [now in Jalisco state]. But perverted by a woman, he ran away with her but after three or four months the witness knew that he was very contentedly living again with his wife and a young lad named Simón Lobatero, known as Patales, told him this.

Pedro's story combines two explanations. First, a "structural" one involves a kind of reorganization of hacienda labor brought about by a new boss. Peons are expelled and one of them moves on to a mining camp. Second, a "personal" one makes a conjuncture with the first but a subordinate one: temporary insanity "caused" by a woman. So Joseph is blameless because he was powerless. Somehow, though, he managed to come to his senses (Pedro seems to approve) and return to his wife. In this telling the episode is a minor one, a small aberration in an otherwise stable marriage.

In a second version, María Rosalia's, the episode looms larger, because she states the relevant chronology more precisely. "He made a married life with her—she had seven children, five are alive—until the beginning of the 1760s. Then he separated from her, having abducted María Casimira, and for eight years the witness had no news of him and then he returned and resumed married life until they arrested him."

In María's telling Pedro's "number of years" of married life becomes more than seventeen, his "three or four month" absence becomes eight years. María Rosalia had no idea what had happened, but she, Pedro, and Joseph agree on the centrality of Joseph's infatuation with the other woman. In a familiar plot Joseph himself testified in 1770 that the story consisted of abduction, illicit friendship, the birth of children, work at the mining camp, and finally, the word from "a man from Zacatecas" that María Rosalia had died. The progression mirrors Joseph's new life unfolding and, with the timely "news" of a wife's death, marriage (ca. 1765) puts the old life permanently to rest.

Women Adulterers

If male adultery had its place, female adultery was, to say the least, less acceptable. Husbands portrayed runaway wives as loose and immoral, adulteresses bent on going with other men. Such a construction put women on the defensive but, as can be seen from the way Lorenza de la Cruz defended her virtue (in her autobiographical statement of 1691), running away, even with another man, could still be seen as compatible with a conventional female identity. "The said Gerónimo [her husband] gave the witness a very bad life and abused her [and in 1683] after six years of marriage with him she could not stand it any more and ran away from him and went to the city of Guadalajara." As it happened, she ran away with a mulatto who happened to be at Temisco, the sugar estate where Lorenza and Gerónimo worked. Hence Gerónimo's charge. Lorenza's rebuttal, however, clarifies that he was the vehicle, not the cause, of her flight.

Lorenza and the women who used other men to flee their husbands should be differentiated from those who were abducted by force and raped. The former were women who abandoned their marriages by choosing other men as companions in flight, whether they were family, friends, lovers, or strangers. The only requirement was that they be near at hand; for once a woman determined to run away, she focused first on running from an old life, not to a new one.

Married men who abducted the wives and daughters of other men were engaging in a common behavior but one nevertheless irritating to inquisitors. In chapter 3, for example, we saw the prosecutor's sarcastic question put to the mulatto Francisco Gómez ("Is it your trade and custom to abduct married or single women?"), who in 1622 had allegedly abducted María de Figueroa. In truth the sarcasm was misdirected, for Francisco's flight with the Spaniard María de Figueroa came entirely at her initiative.

Here is how it happened. María had married the Spaniard Alonso Martín Cabello in 1621, but after six months of married life, he abandoned her, "abducted" another woman, and remained out of contact for two and a half years. At that point, in January 1624, he appeared before don Juan de Saldivar Maldonado, judge of the rural constabulary of León. He petitioned that María, "his legitimate wife," be arrested, noting that "a mulatto named Francisco at hacienda La Sieneguilla has her . . . and the said Francisco went to the estancia of his father-in-law, the Spaniard Pedro de Ortega . . . violently took her from him, and abducted her."

The complaint represents not what happened in a literal sense but the event euphemized to recount her leaving in legal and patriarchal terms. Another version can be pieced together from the testimony of María and Francisco. In her life apart from Alonso, María said she suffered a mala vida at the hands of her father and grandfather while living on her father's estancia. She reached a point of desperation one night [in December 1723?] when they threw her out of the house. From her testimony it seems that she then spoke directly to Francisco, but we do not know exactly how. Most likely, I think, she went straight to a lean-to or rough shelter where passing travelers were allowed to bed down for the night. He testified (a week or two after the event) that "one night about midnight María de Figueroa came to this witness and begged him to take her for 'the love of God' to Zacatecas or wherever he wanted, because her father Pedro de Ortega and grandfather Santiago give her the mala vida."[40] Gómez hesitated, saying that "she should excuse him so that her husband would not come out and kill him, for she was a Spaniard and a married woman. She answered that she was not married nor had she relatives who would be able to harm him and then she climbed up behind him on his mule."

We should not forget that María had not seen Gómez before that night. She was entrusting her person to a stranger, and a *casta* at that. In approaching a man in this way while denying that she was married, she was opening herself to his sexual advances (a calculated quid pro quo?). María's unconventional indifference about this and her heedlessness as to where she would be going (almost anything now seemed better than the mistreatment at the hacienda) show how single-mindedly she sought to escape. As a woman caught in and victimized by the conventions of her society (a husband's adulteries and abandonment, a patriarchal tyranny, and perhaps a mulatto stranger's lascivious expectations), she opportunistically chose the third to escape the first two.

What about Alonso's place in all this? Although he was living with another woman, he expected his wife to live modestly and chastely in his absence. Yet he himself had done exactly what he accused Francisco of doing. He judged the mulatto a violent abductor because males assumed the right to "steal" women but not to have their women stolen. And here, as Francisco had recognized at the time, a mulatto was adding insult to injury by running off with a Spanish woman. María eventually chose to ignore well-entrenched assumptions about male-female relations, for Alonso had forsaken married life and also abandoned her to mistreatment at the hands of her own family.

Men such as Alonso lived in fear that their honor would be impugned by the behavior, chosen or forced, past or present, of their wives. In this they shared a common anxiety, but not one that resulted in a fraternal bond. In fact just the opposite. They preyed on each other by coveting and abducting one another's wives and daughters. A man whose wife had been abducted likely abducted a woman in turn. And whether the woman he joined with was married or not mattered less than his chances of eluding or intimidating her "protector," if she had one. So men treated women as if they were property, possessing, protecting, and neglecting them, but also preying on them, abducting them, and pummeling them. But as we have already seen, it is more complicated than this. Women were not passive and victims, they also took matters into their own hands. They used intimidation, manipulation and guile to fend off despotic treatment or to control their own affairs. They stand out because in acquiescing in or inviting liaisons they harmed their husbands' reputations and put themselves at risk.

Marriages at Work: Roles and Expectations

We have seen that personality clashes, petty tyrannies, and loss of interest pushed men and women apart; that structures of law enforcement and economic organization pulled them apart.[41] These help to explain how married couples separated. Virtually every separation, however, was followed by a recoupling which, as formalized by marriage, of course became the crux of the bigamists' problem. What matters most here is the cycle, and its tendency to return to the same resting point. Couples, however unsuccessfully married, maintained an ideal of married life.

Occasionally husbands and wives managed to approximate an ideal of harmony, thriving together in a domestic division of labor in a life together as partners. In the 1570s, for example, Antonio Sánchez Navarro (born ca. 1533), a muleteer-storekeeper, complemented the work of his wife, Isabel Maldonado, in running an inn. A neighbor in Orizaba recalled that "all of their possessions were in common. She used to sell wine and other goods and he used to go with his mules to look for wheat and other things to sell and to stock in their house." Later they moved to San Juan de Ulúa (Veracruz), where another acquaintance described their partnership. "[Isabel] runs the inn and Antonio goes with his . . . mules and brings flour, biscuits, and supplies [including quinces and pomegranates from Veracruz] for the inn and other times he remains at home." The record of Antonio and Isabel's partnership runs for eighteen years. They have moved around and, according to one acquaintance, were thinking of moving again: "he is trying to go to Mexico City soon and thinks he can live there and earn a living by running a few mules on this highway." Their association in petty commerce complements their bond as husband and wife.

The partnership of work did not insure the permanence of a marriage, but it surely helped, because the failure of partners to carry their share of the day-to-day burdens of earning a living acted as a major source of discord. Consider a situation, for example, in which the husband no longer fulfilled his role as provider and protector. The Spaniard Juan de Lizarzaburo, by the time he faced the inquisitors in 1690, had for some time been so weak that he could no longer work as an itinerant peddler. Asked if he knew or could presume why he had been imprisoned, Juan could only think of the raucous quarrels that he had with Angela Muñoz, his wife of thirteen years. He recalled, for example, her "harsh temperament and . . . an argument last Easter when she said to him 'be gone Jewish dog'. And he does not know why she would have said such a foolish slur because he is a Christian and the son of Christians."

Three days later Juan again stressed the discord in his marriage when he asked the court to secure his property (five pigs, a horse, and a saddle) in the Indian pueblo of Copandaro (now in eastern Michoacán state). He had lived there for "many days," he explained, because "he could not live with his wife [any longer in Zitáquaro, four leagues away] because of her harsh temperament and the little or no attention that she paid to the person of this [witness]."

There can be little doubt that Angela had a strong personality and, well equipped with an earthy vocabulary, spoke forcefully enough to discomfit Juan. But because Juan's file does not include her testimony, we must infer why, perhaps more than usual in the rough and tumble of plebeian marriages, she insulted and neglected Juan. The answer lies in Juan's weakened condition which, in becoming more pronounced, provoked an ever more strident reaction from Angela. For years he had battled syphilis, having picked it up during a twenty-year career as a seaman traveling between Spain and the Indies with long stays on the isthmus of Panama. Although he had undergone the mercurial ointment treatment in Mexico City, his health continued to deteriorate and, at the time of his arrest, he suffered fevers, weakness, and loose bowels (*cursos*). Angela's dominance in conjunction with Juan's frailty inverted their domestic politics as she abused him actively with insults and passively with neglect. This culminated when Juan, suffering the mala vida, retreated to Copandaro.

The harshness of Angela's insults points to her strong dislike of and even contempt for Juan. It might also represent a bit of revenge for rough treatment handed out to her when he had been stronger. Now she could rail at Juan spontaneously and gratuitously without inhibition or fear of reprisal. And because this abuse was not connected with any particular grievance, at least not from Juan's point of view, he found it all the more upsetting. But Angela had a general grievance. Juan had ceased to contribute to their living. Angela's refusal to serve him constituted a retaliation in kind. In a society that expected men to dominate, Angela lost respect for Juan as she saw him increasingly unable to carry out his role of provider and household head. There is no reason to think that other women of Hispanic society would have behaved differently.

In the way she drove her husband away, the mulatto María Micaela can be compared with Angela. Her mother brought María (born ca. 1705) from Pachuca as a girl to Mexico City and placed her as a house servant with don Joseph de Abendaño, auditor of the tribunal of accounts. Two developments came from this: young María acquired a taste for expensive clothing and she became pregnant. Both probably link to don Joseph himself, for if we may trust Thomas Gage's observation, elite Spaniards of the capital flaunted elegantly dressed mulatto mistresses in the fashion of the day.[42]

After María married the mulatto shoemaker and coachman, Joseph Francisco de Chavarría (in 1721), the couple joined the household of María's parents. Joseph, summarizing their married life, testified that he

> supported her for about six years without any notable absences, working at his trade of shoemaker and other times serving various people. At the end of this period he left, fed up with his wife's impertinences and nagging, for she did not leave him in peace because she insisted on wearing clothing of the highest quality and other things that he was not able to acquire with only his work.

Elsewhere in his confession Joseph called his marriage a "mala vida . . . because his energies were insufficient to give [María] all that she wanted." Thus the mismatch between a humble man of limited means and a woman of humble origins whose tastes had been "artificially" elevated. Rather than lower her expectations she railed at Joseph.

Joseph may have exaggerated, but in outline his characterization of María seems accurate. Her own testimony, in fact, corroborates it in the way she spoke of a temporary reunion with Joseph.

> When the *sala [de crimen]* burned [at the stake] two men this
> last time, he appeared here serving as coachman to a priest of
> the said mine [Guanajuato]. . . . And running into her husband
> in the crowd gathered for the burnings she quarreled with
> him for running away and told him that she heard that he
> had married. He denied it, confessing only that he had had
> his weaknesses as a man with [various] women.

The answer satisfied rather than angered María, for she seemed more concerned with his failure to support her rather than with his adultery, complaining once again that "her husband came and went to her house but without helping her with anything although he had money." Perhaps hoping to keep Joseph at hand and squeeze some support from him, María and her mother searched out señor Miguel Castillo, Joseph's employer, and told him that Joseph should remain in Mexico City so he could live a married life with her, and Castillo should therefore discharge him.

They succeeded in getting Joseph fired, but he had no intention of hanging around. He again headed north and three years later (1735) in Guanajuato married Matiana, a slave. Why, when he had so recently seen María alive in Mexico City? And why a slave? Joseph, showing that his ideal of marriage survived the unhappy one with María, answered that he "married the second time to see if he could experience a better life than in the first one. He did not hear that [María] died, he just thought she must have because when he left [Mexico City] she was sick."

However weak this explanation to an inquisitorial court, it nevertheless is of interest for its now familiar pairing: the leaving of an old life and the attempt to make a new one, with the projection of a "probably" dead first wife to make it licit. Note, however, that Joseph did not have to marry Matiana. No one had threatened to whip, jail, or banish him for being in an illicit relationship with this slave. He proceeded because he wanted to, because he could not conceive of his projected "better life" as merely an illicit friendship. Rather he wanted it constituted as a fully authorized marriage. We know that Joseph thought his first wife too demanding. Perhaps the main characteristic he hoped for in his second one, symbolized by her slave status, was submissiveness. This would restore him to an orderly existence, reestablish the proper lines of authority in marriage, and affirm him as a man worthy of respect in his community.

In Joseph Francisco and Juan de Lizarzaburo we have the unusual circumstance of men claiming to be subjected to the mala vida by women. María Micaela demanded that Joseph support her at a level beyond his means because she had acquired expensive tastes. But surely she could not have indulged herself and so hounded Joseph without the support of her parents and don Joseph. Perhaps this is why he failed to oppose her with brute force, but instead adopted the "female" tactic of enduring for a time and then running away and starting over. María and Angela both expected more than their husbands could provide; Joseph and Juan, passively and defensively, only wanted a "peaceful" life, but lacked the forcefulness or allies to assert themselves within the traditional role. Flight rather than endurance or confrontation became the way to escape from so much unhappiness.

Another beleaguered male, on the defensive because he had failed to consummate his marriage, also shows us an inversion of the usual power relations between men and women. The Spaniard Baltasár Márquez Palomino had crossed to the Indies in 1613, married Agustina de Buitren six years later, and then was beset by impotence. Agustina and her mother Gerónima de Pálido, understandably upset, made matters worse by insults and threats of a lawsuit to annul the marriage. Shaken, Baltasár ran off to Guastepec where friar Natera at the Dominican monastery examined him and told him that Agustina "must have put a curse on him."

Baltasár returned to Mexico City several times but "every time he came to see his wife and mother-in-law they treated him so badly that [eventually] he was forced to agree to a separation and the three of them went to the house of a lawyer, Contreras, now dead, and he drew up a petition that they presented to the Vicar General of the city." On the vicar's order, two midwives examined Agustina and declared her a virgin, but Baltasár refused to submit to an examination and fled.

Five years later the marriage had neither been consummated nor had Baltasár returned a dowry of 3,000 pesos. After failing to do so once again,

Baltasár again went north where his problems disappeared. He recounted to the inquisitors that

> when he was absent from [Agustina] he had normal inter-
> course with many other women, fathered children with
> several of them, and twice impregnated the one he married
> in Agua del Venado [now in San Luis Potosí state]: the first
> a miscarriage and the second to be born, he has heard, in
> four or five months.

But there was a price to pay for this vindication of his manhood, for he had just confessed to bigamy. Why did it come to this? Might not Baltasár have continued with his itinerant life and the enjoyment of sexual relations with many women? His answer to this question shows that all along, through the unsatisfactory relationship with Agustina and compounded by her mother, he had clung to a more idealized notion of married life.

> From Zacatecas he went to the mines of Papagayo where
> he spent what little money he had. There fray Gerónimo
> Pangual asked him if he were married and whether he
> wanted to marry a young virgin who was poor but virtuous.
> And envious at seeing that other vecinos lived quietly with
> their wives he said he was not and, after a month, agreed to
> marry the girl.

Not an entrapment of passion, not the calculation of gain, not the threat of authorities, but the simple return to a quiet domestic conviviality drove Baltasár. The month that he took to decide must have been spent calculating the risk. And in human terms it was a risk he judged worth taking. To the inquisitors, Baltasár triumphantly stressed the detail that "the same night he consummated the marriage without any difficulty, even though he found her a virgin." But the precariousness of his newfound domestic contentment weighed heavily on Baltasár's mind when he confided his secret in Jusepe Ramos, his friend and former employer in Zacatecas. Jusepe testified (in 1632) that "Baltasar Márquez wrote him a letter telling him that he married a second time and asked that he keep it a secret because his honor was now in [Jusepe's] hands."

Baltasár's merging of his honor with his new life amounted to a personal affirmation, his entrusting it to his friend Jusepe a social one. It underscores that honor grew from the self-respect and personal contentment of an untroubled family base, the all-important platform from which one presented oneself to society. But why entrust a friend with such potentially damaging information? The answer, I think, has to do with Baltasár wanting his life to be not only a private reality but a public presence, legitimately constituted. To live as if only the former mattered was the incomplete outlaw life of the vagabond and outsider, without the substance of connections to locale and family.

Conclusion

In part, as we have seen, domestic life functioned as a self-contained system, where a gendered politics based on male authority and female subordination played itself out. Households became virtually the sole places where plebeian as well as other males in colonial Mexico became unquestionably dominant. They expressed that dominance by insisting on the subordination of women, and often they inflicted the mala vida on them. What we can learn of their words and behavior in this domestic context, therefore, stands as a relatively uninhibited expression of what they thought it meant to be a male, a husband, and a father in this society. Yet their authority was not unquestioned, nor was it absolute, for women sometimes found ways to return insult for insult, to fight back, to run away, and to seize the advantage when husbands could be put on the defensive. Domestic interactions more than any others, I think, defined, shaped, and expressed identity, for in a hierarchical world in which ordinary folk deferred, or pretended to defer, to those who dominated them, the household was where that domination ceased and one took charge.[43]

However self-contained married life, it nevertheless connected to society at every turn. Indeed, the very mentalities that people had internalized as their role models and expectations came from the larger culture. Married life can therefore serve as both a reference point and a vantage point for viewing the larger system. As a reference point domestic life acted as a kind of home base (a place of shelter, nourishment, companionship, and of work) from which people moved outward to make contact with groups, regions, and the formal institutions of their society. Our examples of such exchanges help to epitomize the patterns, workings, and rules concretely rather than abstractly. As a vantage point, and speaking now in interpretive terms, domestic life gives precedence to the informal associations of family, neighborhood, and clienteles more than to formal institutions of church and state to explain the movements and actions of people in society.

POSTSCRIPT

Social Control, Religion, and Individual Agency

IT IS IMPORTANT to step back and remember what proponents of the Inquisition thought they would achieve with a tribunal in Mexico. Writing from Taximaroa in September 1554, audiencia judge licenciado Lorenzo Lebrón de Quiñones expressed a representative view.

> The need for an Inquisition in this land is extremely great because crimes and acts of irreverence are so numerous . . . and neither the secular nor ecclesiastical justice metes out the appropriate punishments and [the problem] is going to increase because the ease or the dissembling of the penalty will give a new boldness and daring to sin.[1]

An Inquisition, then, would order and control crime, irreverence, and sin (there was not much to differentiate between them), in a way that existing institutions could or would not. In this light it is of interest to note what doctor Don Pedro Moya de Contreras, Mexico's first inquisitor, thought he had accomplished in the first auto de fe held on February 28, 1574. Writing to Juan de Ovando, president of the Council of the Indies about a month later (March 24, 1574), Moya mentions "an infinity of people" in attendance, "Spaniards as well as natives," whose presence "increased the authority of the act."[2] The size of the crowd gratified Moya because it was essential that the Inquisition tap into popular energies and sentiments. That could be done, he wrote in a letter of May 24, 1572, as people learned to "censor and denounce each other with very Christian zeal." Moya's model, then, envisioned a project of social control in which people controlled one another, but with inquisitorial direction through listings of suspect behaviors and opinions in the edicts of faith, the detailed error recounted in public readings of sentences, and exemplary punishments demonstrating the consequences of error.[3] Below I would like to explore the degree to which Moya's project was fulfilled as far as we can judge by bigamy cases.

Religious Practice

There can be no doubt, if one wants to put it this way, that the church transmitted its "ideology" to ordinary people.[4] But how completely and with what distortions? As might be expected, results varied in levels of piety and comprehension of doctrine as the transmitters (priests and friars in the parishes and *doctrinas*) contended less against outright disbelief or rejection than lethargy, doctrinal accretions, and daily preoccupations. We can see an example of the problem in the Spaniard Santiago Pantaleón, accused of being a "superstitious healer" and a bigamist. The prosecutor's arraignment in 1782 assumes an acceptable grounding in the faith, surmising that his "Catholic parents . . . would have given him a medium education, instruction in Christian doctrine . . . [and] sent him to primary school." Santiago did not confirm, deny, or clarify how well he had been indoctrinated, only that he had fallen away because of day-to-day concerns: "After giving himself to the work of cultivating the land, he forgot his Christian doctrine completely."

If Santiago had forgotten some sort of Christian formation, Eusebia Sánchez de los Santos claimed never to have had one. In her hearing before the inquisitors in 1789, she said that her "parents, poor rustics that they were, did not teach her to read or the Christian doctrine. Maybe they were ignorant themselves. But neither did her confessors or the priest's assistant who married her . . . This is why she is now so backward in the mysteries of our holy Catholic faith." Thus Eusebia traces her sin to her ignorance and also implicates the church in it, for the parish failed, given her parents' ignorance, to catechize her.

This was a good tactic, for the inquisitors had to assume the basic indoctrination of parishioners, "the principal prayers, the Articles of Faith, the Commandments of God, the sacraments, the works of mercy, the deadly sins," content that was common to Indian and Hispanic parishes alike.[5] We can see a typical list of the doctrine ordinary people were supposed to know in the questions the tribunal posed to the loba Bárbara Martina (January 1771): "Who is God? Who of the three divine persons became man? Who is in the holy sacrament? When will our Lord Jesus Christ come to judge the living and the dead? Where do those who die in grace go and where those who die in mortal sin?"

Following the usual pattern, the scribe did not record Bárbara's answers, only the inquisitors' assessment of them: "In substance correct in our common Spanish, although she left out or added one or another word." Satisfactory, then, but an exactly memorized recitation would have pleased them more.

The inquisitors also asked questions to elicit whether accused persons were practicing Christians as well as indoctrinated ones. A typical example would be, "Are you a baptized and confirmed Christian, do you hear mass, confess, and take communion at the times ordered by the Holy Mother Church?"

To build a picture of the religious practice of accused bigamists, inquisitors relied on the corroboration of third parties. In Oaxaca, for example, Juan López had come under review in 1561 because he married Ana Hernández, an alleged bigamist. Alonso Portuguese, who had known Juan for more than fourteen years and had lodged him in his house for a year and a half, appeared as a character witness, testifying that he

> takes Juan López for a good Christian although there would be some weakness in the said Ana Hernández in that she is a woman. He knows that [Juan] goes to hear mass every day to the cathedral, the churches of Santa Vera Cruz and Santo Domingo, and the hospital of Our Lady . . . He also gives alms, even leaving them at the house when he goes out so that they can be given to whomever comes to solicit them.

Others functioned at a lower level. The mestizo Pedro Mateo, for example, claimed in 1666 that he attended mass regularly but remained ignorant of Christian doctrine, "claiming that as a poor miserable he had no one to teach him." Francisco Macías had the usual religious rites of passage (baptism and confirmation in Aguascalientes) but in 1734, at age fifty, he testified that "he is too busy with his work" to manage more than a minimal once-a-year confession which would have been at Easter. José Francisco Ortiz also adhered to a minimal cultic practice, it seems, for in March of 1781 he stated that he had last confessed and taken Holy Communion about a year before, "last Easter in Guanajuato." He thought he had been baptized, but did not know if confirmed. Probably he had not, for the notary recorded that he showed "almost no understanding of Christian doctrine."

So levels of indoctrination ranged from virtually no understanding to "very good," and devotional practice, from rare attendance at Mass, not even the prescribed minimum of once per year, to daily attendance. Those who did not measure up to church standards voiced extenuating circumstances (they had forgotten, had been too busy working, had grown up as poor miserables without indoctrination) rather than doubts as to the truth and value of the faith itself. They sat well within the boundaries of the Christian fold and seemed to have a basic idea of heaven and hell, sin and salvation, this life and the next.

But this hardly qualified them to be the zealous guardians of faith and morals envisaged by Moya. Whatever piety they had, in fact, probably came to the fore most strongly when death appeared on the horizon and the church's monopoly of the means of grace, never doubted in the abstract, engaged them more urgently. Whether one's grasp of Christian teachings was rudimentary or developed, this was the time to put aside apathy or bravado. Diego de Villareal, for example, left his wife in Spain, and in New Spain he had lived for a time in concubinage with at least two women. His appropriately somber, if formulaic, reference to finding out that his first wife "was dead and had passed from this present life" prefaced his central concern, to put his own moral house in order, which in practical terms meant marrying Juana de Torres "in order to be in the service of Our Lord and not to be in mortal sin."[6]

The perilousness of mortal sin in popular discourse can be seen in the solemn counsel of Captain Olmeda, master of the muleteer Francisco Catalán, after Francisco asked what he should do after finding out that he was a bigamist. "He commended him to God and to the Virgin of Rosario to guide him in what he would have to do so that he would not lose his soul, and his master gave him letters to a priest named don Pedro de Esquivel who lives on the bridge of Santa Catalina Martir."[7]

Thus we can understand Manuel Domínguez's uneasy conscience about marrying a second time to free himself from the authorities who arrested him for having an "illicit friendship" with Petra Eugenia Velasco, a widow of Guadalajara. He fled immediately after the marriage. But his initial anxiety receded, and over a ten-year period, he resumed regular contact with Petra. On falling sick, Manuel confessed his bigamy to a friar who ordered him to denounce himself to the Holy Office. Yet as the sickness passed, so too did Manuel's sense of urgency to receive the absolution, penance, and reconciliation of the Inquisition, and he was actively evading the Inquisition when its agents arrested him in 1763. Like Manuel, Antonio Piñero suddenly became penitent on finding his life in danger. During a violent storm at sea, he determined to remove himself from a state of mortal sin by promising to marry his mistress Francisca Cabrera. Yet once safely in port, he returned to his procrastinating ways.

Antonio and Manuel both feared eternal damnation but tried to hedge their bets by carrying on with their lives once danger had passed. We can see that this could be a conscious calculation, as when the mestizo Pedro Manuel Galindo, five years after contracting an illicit marriage (in 1744) admitted that

> he kept silent to his confessors because he was afraid of the punishment of this Holy Office. Nevertheless he recognized the wrong he was doing and that he would not be able to save himself unless he got out of his illicit state, but the demon hobbled him and scared him so that he did not dare leave his illicit state for fear of the penalty referred to. He

knew that his confessions were sacrilegious, but even so he did not have a bad opinion of the holy sacrament of the penance of the Eucharist or of matrimony.

So Pedro Manuel tried to carry on as if all was normal but experienced a conflict that he did not or could not resolve. As long as a final accounting seemed distant, he lived with the tension, waiting, perhaps, until he was sick, old, or in danger to clear himself of mortal sin.

Unlike Pedro Manuel, Francisco Antonio García stopped going to confession after he married a second time in 1746. In a self-reflective statement before the inquisitors in May 1751 (just seven months before this thirty-year-old mestizo was to die), he explained how he had lived with an uneasy conscience. He said that even though "he knew and believed that with a first wife still alive one could not have a married life with a second, he [nevertheless] persuaded himself that this was licit." As an out, Francisco seized upon a bit of folk theology that "he had heard from some muleteers [that] if you do not have a nuptial blessing within seven years a wife becomes only a mistress." In fact this was a kind of fallback position, not an actual rejection of church teachings, a way to give himself a plausible excuse if required, for he had not tested it in the confessional.

Avoiding confession could be a telltale sign, in fact, as did the lobo Juan Lorenzo del Castillo, after abandoning his wife in 1702, also dropped his religious practices. In his first hearing before the inquisitors (in 1708), he said that he had "not heard mass, confessed, or taken communion at the times ordered by the Holy Mother Church since he left the said his wife, Teresa de la Cruz."[8] The sacrament of penitence, based on confession, required parishioners to reveal the truth. But confession meant punishment and sometimes the breakup of their new lives. At the same time, to conceal the truth amounted to a fearful sacrilege.[9]

The plea of ignorance, as we have already seen, was an argument for a mitigating circumstance, especially when used by people who presented themselves as rustics. We might be surprised, therefore, to see a wily Spaniard such as Miguel de Herrera (born 1695 in Havana) using it. Listen as he summarizes in 1722, with due contrition and yet with a certain aplomb, points he had covered earlier: "He did not realize that it [bigamy] was a great sin until his confessors told him. Once he realized its gravity, he tried to go to the tribunal for help . . . and although he did not succeed it is certain that this was his intention. And because he was not able to denounce himself he does it now in this confession."

The mulatto Laureano de la Cruz also pleaded ignorance and, once in custody, presented himself as penitent and because by then he had been properly instructed. His statement comes in response to a clause of the prosecutor's arraignment (March 31, 1788) that he married a second time "presenting himself as unmarried, maliciously believing that he was only committing a venial sin that he hoped to correct later with God's pardon." This portrayal has Laureano as ignorant (of the difference between venial and mortal sin), but also cynical and manipulative of the sacrament of penitence. Laureano replied that he "now knows the seriousness of the crime although, at the time he committed it, he did not know it was against our holy faith. In a way [*en cierto modo*], he has lived as a bad Christian in living incontinently with a woman." Thus Laureano paraphrases the formal charge but tries to remove the attribution of maliciousness in his motivation. He agrees in substance that he has "in a way" lived as a bad Christian but nonetheless a Christian.

So far, then, we have seen that bigamists accounted for their behavior in the language of penitents and no doubt genuinely dreaded the state of mortal sin. But not more so, perhaps, than they feared the punishments the Inquisition might impose. At the next stage, in custody and as they spoke in the dock, they had to make the best of it and this meant assuming the stance of sinners in the confessional. They admitted guilt, pleaded for mercy, and argued that extenuating circumstances (most commonly ignorance, false reports, or bedevilment) had caused their downfall. Such excuses, before the Inquisition became involved, stood people in good stead except, perhaps, when death seemed near.[10]

After all, as Pedro Pérez pointed out in 1621, disease and sickness were "given by God" and meant to be signs. The state of one's body often pushed people to confession and the sacrament of Holy Communion so as to be ready for the worst. The twenty-nine-year-old Spaniard Mariana

Monroy, whose first hearing before the inquisitors was in 1678, said (on March 3) that she "confessed [sacramentally] yesterday when she was gravely sick." The mention of her grave condition in conjunction with her religious observances charges these with a special intensity, but otherwise fits within her normal pattern of careful practice.[11] Don Manuel del Alamo, on the other hand, who had not been practicing his faith, had to make a complete turnabout. He testified (in 1788) that he had begun well,

> baptized in the parish of San Juan de Málaga and confirmed
> at a young age. In Spain he always heard mass on the days
> prescribed and on most of those that were not, confessing
> and taking communion each week, fortnight, and only rarely
> [as infrequently as] once a month because he lived an orderly
> and Christian life in fear of God.

Once don Manuel got to New Spain, however, his conduct changed as he fell in with "subjects of vicious conduct" and

> stopped hearing mass on some prescribed days, when
> he was gambling for example, so as not to leave the game,
> and other times when he did not bother to hear it because
> he was involved with some other diversion. But this was
> never out of contempt and he knew very well that he
> was sinning mortally. And in the same way his vicious
> passions dragged him down and he stopped confessing
> and taking communion.

Until his return to regular observance, don Manuel recalled, he had taken the sacrament only three times in the ten or eleven years he had been in New Spain:

> In Vera Cruz when he arrived from Spain; in this monastery
> of San Diego seven years ago; and last year in Apan [now in
> southeast Hidalgo state] with fray Joseph Manuel Arpide
> when he was bedridden and gravely ill. There he came to
> recognize his depraved life and tried to make amends with

a firm spirit, resolving to continue his confessions if God would take away his sickness.

Don Manuel's illness drove him back to the church, but his lapse in religious practice had not been a rejection of Christian faith. Being in mortal sin, he seemed to think, was temporary and correctable. The trick would be to pay attention to the signs (his illness, as it turned out) when they came. And he did, proving adept at "leaving the game" in good time.

So because one's accountability for this life determined one's fate in the next, bigamists could be at war with themselves, caught between their life instincts and their dread of eternal damnation. After a long struggle, Marcos de la Cruz surrendered to the authority of the church. He had fallen "into this misery," he said,

> dragged down and conquered by the love that he had for the said Juana Montaño . . . For fourteen years he received the Holy Sacrament sacrilegiously, because in hiding his second marriage from his confessors, he was aware that he had not confessed completely. He meant no disrespect for the Holy Sacrament but was afraid of being discovered. Even though his conscience accused him constantly, he could not leave Juana.

We do not know if Marcos and Manuel found peace, but their confessions suggest that they had run out of ways to evade the inevitable, which for most amounted to the same thing. In that sense they were fortunate, for one could not absolve oneself and few indeed were ready to pass from this life without absolution.

Yet the untimely death of the mulatto Pedro Domínguez reminds us that some missed their chance for a final reconciliation. Pedro, in the Holy Office's custody and known to be ill, was found dead, at thirty-one, on April 29, 1786. "I certify that in the house that was Colegio de San Juan [wrote the notary Diego de Cosío] and is now used as a hospital for sick prisoners, I found the body of Pedro Antonio Domínguez. I called his name several times, but he did not answer, so I knew that he was truly dead."

We may assume a better passing for the thirty-year-old mestizo Francisco Antonio García, who had sufficient time for the last rites. Francisco Antonio was apparently in good health when agents of the Inquisition arrested him in Izúcar in April 1750. But still incarcerated eighteen months later, his health was failing rapidly. Listen to the doctor's report of October 27, 1751, after his examination of Francisco Antonio in the prison in Mexico City: "Prisoner number 6 has become gravely ill of the sickness called diarrhea. He now is having frequent attacks and they're coming more and more frequently, and his condition is aggravated because it is so damp in the cell." Two days later the judges ordered Francisco hospitalized at San Juan de Dios. We have no further reports on his condition until December 8 when he died. Presumably the intervening weeks of inexorable decline allowed everyone to anticipate the end.

More difficult, but not less common, were the many prisoners who suffered mental illnesses and depression, as manifested in suicides, psychosomatic illnesses, and psychotic behavior that pointed to personality breakdown.[12] Consider, for example, the case of the twenty-nine-year-old mulatto Juan Lorenzo de Castillo whose manic-depressive mood swings baffled diagnosis. Dr. don Juan Joseph Brozuela, physician of the prisoners, filed a long report on Juan, dated August 12, 1709. In an assessment mixing certainty with tentativeness, he wrote that

> the prisoner in number eleven gives sufficient symptoms on which to base a probable judgment that he is truly demented. At the beginning of his imprisonment he suffered periods of great sadness accompanied by the silent refusal to take necessary nourishment. When the jailers punished him, wounding him in the head, he gave no indication that he felt it. And after the dementia, he became completely free of his former sadness . . . and instead of fear and silence, he became in equal measure daring and talkative, and from his old lack of appetite suddenly he is insatiably and extraordinarily voracious, gulping and devouring as much as is put in front of him. As a result the said prisoner is now not only healthy

but quite robust and in possession of all of his strength, except that he still is not directly in touch with his mind . . . [inferred] by the disposition and movements of his eyes and his [continued] insensitivity to the wound on his head . . . The witness judges, then, that the prisoner is unmistakably insane . . . and his madness will be difficult to cure because it does not admit or depend on natural principles but rather is an affliction of the spirit [*ánimo*].

Nothing more is known of Juan until he abjures his error publicly in September 1718, nine years later. Apparently because of his fragile mental condition, the judges excused him from the normal public flogging, and instead ordered him to confess on each of the next three Easters, to say the Rosary of Our Lady every Saturday for one year, and to resume married life with his first wife. Juan had been beaten by his jailer, examined by a perplexed doctor, and kept in the Holy Office's prison for ten years, but was reinstated to the fold and the sacraments and was therefore, at least for the time being, no longer in mortal sin. If all went well, he would die in a state of grace.

After a longer life and a shorter ordeal, the escaped slave and bigamist Sebastián de Loaysa managed to do the same, no mean feat given his circumstances. Ignacio de Villalobos, a muleteer of Teguantepec (now in southeast Oaxaca), was taking Sebastián from Guatemala to Mexico City in chains. En route Sebastián died. It was a quick death and, thanks to fray Juan de Saavedra, a Dominican who administered the last rites, most likely a peaceful one.

I certify on the word of a priest [wrote fray Juan] that today, June 23, 1675, Sebastián de Loaysa—mulatto, bald, branded, age sixty to seventy—died in this pueblo . . . I attest that he died wearing manacles and chains, which I had removed in order to bury him on consecrated ground, treatment he was worthy of because he died with all of the Holy Sacraments.

Individuals and Norms

Sebastián can stand for the complexity of the bigamists who came before the Inquisition, for none of the categories used to define him truly did: a slave, he passed as free; a skilled blacksmith, he practiced his trade sporadically and only at the behest of his owner; a mulatto, he was "very ladino"; a married man, he posed as unmarried to marry again; a renegade, he died in the arms of the same mother church that had chained him and ordered him to Mexico City for discipline. He represents, therefore, the disparity between society's labels and life. He, along with other bigamists, collaborated with efforts of church and state to impose an officially sanctioned ideology and range of behaviors, but selectively, imperfectly, and mostly on his own terms. There is little reason to think that he and the populace in general had an interest in morality in any abstract sense and equally little reason to think that they had an interest in church doctrine except, possibly, as it might have helped them avoid pain, suffering, and misery and to gain some measure of comfort, security, and well-being. In simple terms, that meant avoiding hell and getting to heaven.

As in all hierarchical societies, bigamists in New Spain deferred to those in authority over them—or at least they pretended to. Yet Moya's dream of incorporating them as active partners in their own control was too optimistic. More realistically, as we already saw, Lebrón de Quiñones thought that control came from giving out "the appropriate punishments." Sebastián would have understood. As a slave he knew his place at the bottom of society: the mark burned on his cheek by the branding iron served as a reminder and if he forgot, there was always the lash and the taunt. Yet he too carried on with his life and sidestepped attempts to control him as he entered into illicit liaisons, married twice, worked on the side to accumulate some property, ran away, and practiced his religion in a perfunctory way.

If identities are difficult to categorize, so too are behaviors. Even apparently simple acts involved a political calculation, which meant that what was said and done would change, depending on whether it was to or in the presence of an equal or a superior. This politics of dominance-subservience was a matter of degree and circumstance, not a simple polarity. It framed the content and tone of behavior, which was informed by the interplay of folk beliefs (the taken-for-granted web of everyday lore, rituals, ideas, and "popular religion" that accompanied daily life) and, however imperfectly grasped, the teachings of the church. In the main people concerned themselves with coupling, getting along, raising children, fitting into clienteles, finding work, and keeping track of each other. In this they were the agents and protagonists of their own lives. They worked like dogs, preyed on those they could victimize and, in a cut-throat world, in turn became victims of those more powerful than they; those who fell into debt, wandered near and far in search of a job or, better yet, easy money. They scrambled not only to make a living but to make a life, although they would not have differentiated between the two.

It is of course true that people flocked to see the spectacle of punishment and reconciliation of Mexico's first auto de fe, which Moya supposed had established the authority of the Inquisition. And they would continue to do so. They also collaborated with the Inquisition by denouncing each other and sometimes themselves. Yet attending a spectacle in early modern times did not necessarily imply support for or even understanding of the ideology it represented, as if endorsing the program of a political faction at a rally. To think this presumes that the event held the same significance for the mulatto shoemaker, the Spanish merchant, the Franciscan friar, the Indian pulque supplier, and the mestizo tamale vender, that it had for Moya and his colleagues. And neither should we think, ipso facto, that people who reported each other as fornicators, as bigamists, and as engaged in illicit friendships did so strictly or even mainly to eradicate scandal, immorality, and sin. That would again presume too simplistic a fit between official ideology and the behavior in question. It is true that denouncers used the language of official ideology, but that does not mean that this is what denunciations were about. Instead they should be seen as coming out of the complex interplay of in- and out-group dynamics, supporting one's own and distrusting outsiders. People kept track of each other, but conversations always worked their way back to networks and connections held in common. When these resulted in denunciations, they did so within the terms of reference of family, neighborhood, work, and clientele groupings.

We should remember that people primarily carried on with their own lives more than they observed those of their associates. And if forced to answer for their actions, they justified themselves with a mix of church teachings, folk wisdom, and common sense. Love, anger, lust, fear, pride, jealousy, friendship, concern for honor, ambition, opportunism, boredom, or depression cropped up in a thousand different ways and combinations, as people went about their business at home, in the streets, in the fields, and in distant places. These passions, emotions, and compulsions had a place amidst the most ordinary of daily routines. They also played their part in the complex event called "bigamy" which as marriage, moves us into the arena of private life; as sin and crime, to dynamics of social control by church and state; and, as "mistake," to the situational and fortuitous mix-ups and contingencies of everyday life.

With a sense of irony, perhaps, we should stress that bigamists complied with the norms of their church and society about as much as they avoided them. But in their own ways and, at least in part, on their own terms. Yes, they married a second time, but as part of the logic of their living rather than to defy the official model of comportment to which, in its details, they were largely oblivious anyway. In instances of a clash, they deferred to or worked around, but rarely defied directly the prescribed comportment. They appear as, in the main, conventionally religious, deferential to authority, and driven by the opinions of their peers. Their new worlds were quite a bit like their old ones. How they created or drifted into them provide a view of the circumstances, agency, and self-reflections of small people in colonial society.

Possibly the most extraordinary aspect of bigamists' lives was that they became entangled with a fearful, powerful, and often corrupt institution, the Holy Office of the Inquisition. We should not understate what this cost them. Bigamists suffered arrest, long confinements, confiscation of property, imprisonment, and terrible psychological stress; and in their trials and reconciliations, hardship, violence, humiliation, and stigmatization. We can only imagine the effects of a typical seventeenth-century punishment for bigamy: an agonizing and seemingly endless one or two hundred lashes, as one was paraded through the main streets of Mexico City jeered by spectators as a crier shouted out one's crime. Afterward came a long and brutalizing confinement of galley servitude for a term of five to seven years—if one survived.

Yet none of the bigamists ended up on a burning pyre; most were "reconciled" and returned to church and society; and many, perhaps more than we normally imagine, escaped the clutches of the Holy Office altogether. In the end the bigamists who constructed new worlds in the Indies should be seen not mainly as victims, heroes, or martyrs, but as ordinary folk making choices and carrying on day by day. In this they stand for countless others of their time and place, whose worlds have receded completely from our view.

APPENDIX

Sample of 216 Bigamy Files

Appendix: Sample of 216 Bigamy Files

Names	Birth date	Date of 1st Marr.	Date of 2nd Marr.	Sex	Length of 1st Marr. in Years	Length of 2nd Marr. in Years	Race	Race of 1st Spouse	Race of 2nd Spouse	Archival Citation[1]
Acosta, Miguel de, alias Sagualtipam	1745	1764	1774	Male	7	3	Creole	Mulatto	Indian	1156:13, folios 309ff.
Aguila, Francisco de	1498	1558	1558	Male	15	0.1	Spaniard	Spaniard	Creole	24, folios 13-16v; 27-28; 60-81.
Aguirre, María de	1517	1529	1550	Female		8.5	Spaniard	Spaniard	Spaniard	25: 4 and 5.
Alamo, don Manuel del, alias don Josef Tribaldo	1747	1772	1783	Male	4	4	Spaniard	Spaniard	Creole	1214: 11, folios 126-245.
Albertos, Francisco	1607	1631	1660	Male	26	1	European	European	Creole	580: 4, folios 486-734.
Alemán, Juan Bautista, alias Alegna	1700	1720	1735	Male	5	11	Slave	Slave	Mulatto	819: 8, folios 21-60.
Alexo, Francisco, alias Antonio	1658	1681		Male	4		Slave	Slave	Unknown	648: 7, folios 497-593.
Alonso, Miguel	1549	1572	1586	Male	7	3	Spaniard	Spaniard	Creole	137: 11.
Alvarado, Alonso de	1651	1664	1678	Male	14	8	Mulatto	Mulatto	Mulatto	524, folios 190-257.
Amador y Frias, Phelipe de		1679	1684	Male			Mulatto	Unknown	Unknown	526, folios 360-380.
Aranda, Juan de	1549	1566		Male	3		Spaniard	Spaniard	Unknown	108: 3.
Araus, Nicolás Antonio de	1711	1735	1737	Male	0.5	4	Mestizo	Indian	Indian	1139, folios 82-186.
Aspitia, Ana de	1547	1566		Female	8		Mulatto	Spaniard	Mulatto	135: 1.
Avila, Joana de				Female			Unknown	Unknown	Unknown	90: 31, folios 359.
Ayala, Christóbal de	1545			Male			Mulatto	Mulatto	Mulatto	26: 4, folios 83-114.
Azacar, Juan López de		1568	1573	Male	10		European	Mulatto	Creole	134: 6.
Azevedo, Antonio de		1571	1583	Male	7	1	Spaniard	Spaniard	Unknown	135: unnumbered
Balencuela, Juana María	1753	1768	1779	Female	5	6	Mestizo	Mulatto	Mestizo	1301: 4, folios 22-94.
Baraona, Antonio de	1676	1695	1704	Male	5	1.7	Mestizo	Mestizo	Unknown	547: 6.
Barrera, Juan de	1648	1672	1685	Male	5	0.1	Spaniard	Creole	Creole	523, folios 131-257.

1. All references (except two from the Huntington Library) refer first to the volume number in the Inquisition Section of Mexico's National Archive. File numbers within given volumes are preceded by a colon and folio references, sometimes including a r for recto or v for verso are preceded by the word folios. In some cases files are unnumbered and the citation lists only the volume and the folio pages, or vice versa.

Names	Birth date	Date of 1st Marr.	Date of 2nd Marr.	Sex	Length of 1st Marr in Years	Length of 2nd Marr in Years	Race	Race of 1st Spouse	Race of 2nd Spouse	Archival Citation[1]
Barrios Valderrama y Navera, Domingo	1746	1764	1766	Male	0.5	0.8	Spaniard	Creole	Creole	1066, unnumbered.
Benavides, Gerónimo de	1532	1543	1565	Male	0.1	12	Spaniard	Spaniard	Unknown	108: 2.
Berástegui y Cordillo, don Julian de	1733		1733	Male			Creole	Creole	Unknown	964, folios 376-405.
Biscarra, José Francisco	1751	1764	1776	Male	4	0.1	Mulatto	Indian	Mulatto	1104:7, folios 143-191.
Blasa de la Candelaria, María	1720	1736	1741	Female	2	8	Mestizo	Unknown	Mulatto	919: 1, and 918: 3, folios 41-50.
Buscarones, Ygnacio, alias don Ygnacio Bucareli	1718	1737	1744	Male		0.3	Creole	Unknown	Creole	918: 21, folios 330ff.
Bustinca, Pedro de	1540	1554	1567	Male	3	5	Spaniard	Spaniard	Unknown	91: 6.
Calderón, Marcos	1711	1734	1749	Male	2		Mestizo	Unknown	Unknown	933: 7.
Calderón, Sebastian, alias Andrade	1706	1734	1745	Male	5	1	Mulatto	Mulatto	Mulatto	1138, folios 211-341.
Campuzano Palazios, Manuel de	1694	1713	1732	Male	16	3	Spaniard	Spaniard	Creole	1234, unnumbered.
Cañada, Pedro	1535		1581	Male		4	Spaniard	Unknown	Unknown	136: 9.
Canto y Morales, don Salvador de	1714	1748	1751	Male	0.1	0.1	Spaniard	Spaniard	Spaniard	933: 8.
Castellón, Salvador	1741	1773	1778	Male	4	4	Mulatto	Indian	Unknown	1364:15, folios 370v-418.
Castillo, Isidro del	1688	1708	1725	Male	8	4	Mestizo	Mulatto	Mestizo	814: 4, folios 390-482.
Castroverde, Christóbal de	1576	1591	1611	Male	5	4	Mulatto	Mulatto	Unknown	310: 7.
Catalán, Francisco	1614	1652	1654	Male		13	Mestizo	Indian	Mestizo	606: 10 and 11, folios 578-613.
Cavallero y Basave, Joseph	1741	1758	1767	Male	7	9	Spaniard	Spaniard	Creole	1161, folios 1-141.
Cavallero, Juan Manuel, alias Manuel Castellano Alvarado	1701	1729	1736	Male	3	5	Creole	Mulatto	Mestizo	1387: 1, folios 1-121.
Cervantes, María Ignacia	1753	1767	1787	Female	16	1	Mulatto	Mestizo	Zambo	1214: unnumbered.
Chacón Gayon, Juan Antonio, alias Antonio Pérez Chacón	1661	1672	1697	Male	1.5	0.1	Spaniard	Unknown	Unknown	699: unnumbered.
Chamorro, Nicolás		1524	1537	Male		0.7	Spaniard	Spaniard	Spaniard	22: 11.
Chavarría, Joseph Francisco de	1706	1721	1735	Male	6	3	Mulatto	Mulatto	Slave	794: 24, folios 226-322.
Christóbal, Bernabé, alias Mavekp	1696	1715	1728	Male	3	1.5	Mulatto	Mulatto	Mulatto	834: 24, folios 410-491.
Contreras, Phelipe, alias Bartolomé de Peralta	1707	1720		Male			Mestizo	Creole	Unknown	969: 17, folios 210-294.
Cortés, Diego	1504	1521	1527	Male			Spaniard	Spaniard	Spaniard	22: 5.
Cortés, Mathias	1665	1691	1704	Male	7	2	Mestizo	Mestizo	Mestizo	547: 8.
Cruz Malagón, Gregorio de la	1710	1731	1734	Male	0.1	5	Slave	Mulatto	Mulatto	794: 1, folios 1-39.
Cruz, Andrés de la, alias Acevedo	1622	1647	1661	Male	6	4	Zambo	Indian	Mestizo	592: 3, folios 271-377.
Cruz, Antonio de	1706		1724	Male	0.5	2	Unknown	Creole	Unknown	814: 5 and 6, folios 289-389

Name				Sex						Reference
Cruz, Baltasár de la	1748	1761	1618	Male	3	6	Mulatto	Indian	Mulatto	347:3.
Cruz, Juan Laureano de la	1661	1678	1784	Male	4	2	Mulatto	Unknown	Indian	1277, folios 1-111.
Cruz, Lorenza de la	1625	1648	1691	Female	7	1	Mulatto	Mulatto	Mulatto	526:2, folios 37-151.
Cruz, Marcos de la, alias de Tobar	1627	1644	1657	Male	3	14	Creole	Unknown	Unknown	608:3, folios 216-99.
Cruz, Matheo de la	1609	1628	1660	Male	0.1	3	Indian	Mestizo	Indian	586:9, folios 502-72.
Cruz, Nicolás de la	1760	1772	1632	Female	1	2	Mulatto	Black	Black	381:7.
Delgadillo Hernández, María Guadalupe, alias Tres Palacios Hernández			1777	Female		1	Creole	Mestizo	Creole	1192, folios 1-85.
Díaz, Ana	1519	1554	1558	Female	1.5	12	Spaniard	Spaniard	Unknown	36:11, folios 500-75.
Díaz, Francisco	1549	1565	1587	Male	0.1	6	Spaniard	Spaniard	Mestizo	138:6.
Domínguez, Manuel Angel	1718	1737	1753	Male	9	0.1	Spaniard	Spaniard	Creole	1066:4, folios 168-176.
Domínguez, Pedro, alias Zacatecas	1750	1774	1784	Male	5	0.7	Mulatto	Mulatto	Mulatto	1277:10, folios 1-35.
Encarnación López, Juan Francisco de la	1743	1773	1785	Male	9	0.1	Mestizo	Mestizo	Mestizo	1277:11, folios 1-60.
Encarnación, María Jesús de la, alias María Filomena Tavares	1749	1768	1777	Female	7	4	Mulatto	Mulatto	Indian	1292:7, folios 1-101.
Espinosa, Inés de		1538	1579	Female	3	0.6	Unknown	Unknown	Unknown	134:7.
Figueroa, María de	1610	1621	1624	Female	0.5	0.1	Creole	Creole	Mulatto	370:3, folios 307-20.
Fragoso, Manuel		1562		Male		9	Spaniard	Spaniard	Mestizo	136:7.
Francisco, Juan	1588	1612	1615	Male	0.5	0.5	Spaniard	Spaniard	Creole	312:73, folios 428-93.
Gachupín, Joseph el		1671	1699	Male	12	3	Slave	Slave	Mulatto	544:23, folios 463-481.
Galdos, Don Juan de		1528		Male			Unknown	Unknown	Unknown	1371:9, folios 1-38.
Galindo, Pedro Manuel	1709	1726	1744	Male	6	3	Mestizo	Mestizo	Mulatto	921:29.
García Bullones, Pedro	1577	1584	1596	Male	0.1	0.4	Spaniard	Spaniard	Indian	22:2.
García de Hoyos, Diego	1523	1551	1577	Male			European	Spaniard	Unknown	250, folios 238-44.
García, Francisco				Male	3	2	Spaniard	Spaniard	Unknown	108:7.
García, Francisco Antonio	1720	1738	1746	Male	0.2	4	Mestizo	Mestizo	Mulatto	922:1.
García, Joseph Manuel Antonio, alias Joseph Manuel Marrufo, el cocoliste		1750	1760	Male	3	2	Mulatto	Slave	Mulatto	1231:6, folios 28-103.
García, Miguel	1522		1569	Male			Spaniard	Spaniard	Unknown	135:4.
Gómez Franco, don Juan	1700	1721		Male	7	4	Spaniard	Spaniard	Spaniard	972:1.
González Alvarez, Domínguez	1544	1751		Male			Spaniard	Spaniard	Unknown	136:3.
González Carmona, Diego	1556	1574	1607	Male	2	7	Spaniard	Spaniard	Unknown	Huntington Library

1. All references (except two from the Huntington Library) refer first to the volume number in the Inquisition Section of Mexico's National Archive. File numbers within given volumes are preceded by a colon and folio references, sometimes including a r for recto or v for verso are preceded by the word folios. In some cases files are unnumbered and the citation lists only the volume and the folio pages, or vice versa.

Names	Birth date	Date of 1st Marr.	Date of 2nd Marr.	Sex	Length of 1st Marr in Years	Length of 2nd Marr in Years	Race	Race of 1st Spouse	Race of 2nd Spouse	Archival Citation[1]
González, Antonio	1541	1570		Male		11		Spaniard	Unknown	Unknown 134: 12.
González, Beatriz			1536	Female		2	Spaniard	Spaniard	Spaniard	22: 12.
González, Joseph, alias Memela				Male	9		Mestizo	Unknown	Creole	524, folios 468-595.
González, Lucía				Female			Spaniard	Spaniard	Unknown	137: 5
Griego, Nicolás, alias Pérez	1539	1570	1585	Male	11		European	Black	Unknown	108: 1.
Guerra, Alonso	1544	1573	1585	Male	8	1	Spaniard	Spaniard	Spaniard	256: 5.
Guerra, Gerónimo	1554	1582		Male	3		European	Mestizo	Creole	135: 6.
Guizával, Alonso de	1654	1675	1681	Male	2		Mestizo	Indian	Zambo	642: 1, folios 1-97.
Gutiérrez de Estrada, Juan de	1568	1586	1597	Male	1	3	Spaniard	Mulatto	Mestizo	261: 3.
Gutierrez, Francisco	1520	1558	1559	Male		2	Creole	Unknown	Unknown	23: 8, folios 69-153.
Guzmán, Juan de	1576			Male	3	0.2	Spaniard	Spaniard	Unknown	308: folios 162r-162v.
Hermenegildo Hidalgo, Nicolás, alias Nicolás Cervantes		1754	1764	Male			Creole	Mestizo	Unknown	1073.
Hernández de Hermosilla, Gonzalo	1559	1582	1588	Male	3	1	Spaniard	Unknown	Unknown	138: 7.
Hernández, Ana, alias la serrana	1516			Female			Spaniard	Spaniard	Spaniard	24: 6, folios 157-249.
Hernández, Diego	1533	1571	1580	Male	6.5	2	Unknown	Mestizo	Unknown	134: 9.
Hernández, Gonzalo	1523	1550		Male	2	5	Mulatto	Unknown	Indian	137: 6.
Hernández, Pedro				Male			Spaniard	Spaniard	Unknown	24: 3, folios 109-126v, 143-155.
Hernández, Ynés, alias Florentina del Río		1524	1525	Female	0.4		Spaniard	Spaniard	Spaniard	22: 3.
Herrera, Miguel de	1695	1712	1721	Male	3	0.1	Creole	Creole	Creole	796: 52, folios 506-514.
Hojeda, Diego de	1558	1575	1579	Male	1	0.5	Mulatto	Indian	Black	134: 8.
Hortiz, Bartolomé, alias Manuel de Chanaquicia y Arteaga	1695	1717	1721	Male	0.5	0.3	Creole	Creole	Mestizo	790: 1, folios 1-200.
Hoz, Agustín de	1546	1561	1573	Male.	9	4	Spaniard	Spaniard	Spaniard	136: 10.
León, Gómez de	1542	1558	1571	Male	7	0.1	Spaniard	Spaniard	Unknown	91: 5.
Liçona, Manuel de, alias Manuel de los Reyes Hernández	1715	1727	1738	Male	10	8	Mestizo	Indian	Mulatto	1305: 2, folios 1-86.
Lizarzaburo, Juan de	1640	1674	1677	Male	16		Spaniard	Unknown	Unknown	657: 3, folios 300-23.
Loaysa, Sebastián de	1614	1641	1659	Male	9	12	Mulatto	Mulatto	Mestizo	595: 20, folios 456-538.
López de Utiel, Juan	1514			Male	3		Spaniard	Spaniard	Unknown	36: 10, folios 402ff.
López, Joseph Laureano	1743	1759	1765	Male		3	Mestizo	Mestizo	Unknown	1062.

Name				Sex						Reference
Lorenzo del Castillo, Juan	1680	1693	1706	Male	5	0.1	Mulatto	Mestizo	Mestizo	548: 4.
Lorenzo, Juan, alias Lorenzo Ramírez, alias Phelipe de Santiago	1677	1694	1704	Male	10	0.2	Slave	Slave	Indian	548: 5.
Luis, Juan	1585			Male				Unknown	Indian	310: 3.
Luis, Juan, alias Ruíz, alias de la Cruz	1656	1641		Male	1.5	6	Mulatto	Indian	Mestizo	594: 9, folios 534-619.
Luis, Martín, alias Nicolás Rico	1561	1585		Male	2	2	Mestizo	Spaniard	Mestizo	138: 5.
Macías, Francisco, alias el flaco	1714	1718		Male	1	3	Spaniard	Spaniard	Zambo	1246.
Maldonado, Rosa, alias Rosalía del Carmen Maldonado	1742	1759		Female		6	Mulatto	Mulatto	Mulatto	1180, folios 14-98
Mallón, Alexandro	1557	1583		Male	1	1	European	Spaniard	Unknown	138: 2.
Márquez Palomino, Baltasár	1587	1619		Male	0.1	2	Spaniard	Unknown	Mulatto	374: 11, folios 146ff.
Martín, Fulano, alias Flamenco	1587	1601		Male	1		European	Mestizo	Unknown	308.
Martín, Juan	1519	1544		Male	10	5	Spaniard	Spaniard	Mestizo	136: 1.
Martina, Barbara, alias María Estephanía	1745	1760		Female	5	3	Mulatto	Unknown	Mestizo	1089: 1, folios 1-108.
Mascarenas, Juan Antonio, alias Juan Antonio de Armenta	1700	1718		Male	12	2	Mestizo	Unknown	Unknown	824: 12, folios 74-197.
Matheo, Pedro, alias Pedro de Moya	1642	1660		Male	1	0.3	Mestizo	Indian	Mestizo	605: 2, folios 189-278.
Mayorga, Nicolás	1692	1727		Male	1	2	Creole	Mulatto	Mulatto	1139, folios 187-287.
Meléndez, Hieronimo	1585			Male			Spaniard	Unknown	Unknown	308, folios 140-140v.
Méndez, Juan				Male		0.1	Mestizo	Indian	Mestizo	26: 2, folios 12-27.
Mendiola, Manuel de	1640	1662		Male	15		Spaniard	Spaniard	Unknown	526: 7, folios 380-398.
Miguel, Joseph, alias Miguel Antonio	1713	1738		Male	6	3	Black	Slave	Indian	978, folios 59-188.
Molina, Joseph de	1560	1586		Male	0.2	7	Mestizo	Indian	Mestizo	262: 3.
Molina, Joseph Manuel	1725	1743		Male	17	10	Zambo	Zambo	Mulatto	1102: 1, folios 1-130.
Monroy, Mariana	1649	1663		Female	2	2	Creole	Spaniard	Spaniard	441: 2, folios 356-411v.
Monterroso, Diego de	1656			Male		7	Mestizo	Indian	Mestizo	526: 1, folios 1-36.
Mora y Arellano, José de	1720	1750		Male	5	0.8	Creole	Spaniard	Mulatto	1145: 19, folios 192-282.
Morales, Domingo, alias Hernández, alias Santos	1677	1705		Male	2	1.3	Mulatto	Mulatto	Slave	796: 1, folios 1-101.
Moxica, Sebastián de, alias Domingo Moxica	1667	1693		Male	2	7	Mulatto	Mulatto	Mulatto	1258, folios 1-89.
Muca, Pedro de la	1586			Male		2	Spaniard	Spaniard	Unknown	138: 1.
mungía, Sebastián Domingo de	1587	1624		Male			Slave	Slave	Slave	399: 2.
Muñoz de Sanabria, Joseph	1686	1705		Male	3	6	Mestizo	Mestizo	Unknown	815: 1, folios 1-133.

1. All references (except two from the Huntington Library) refer first to the volume number in the Inquisition Section of Mexico's National Archive. File numbers within given volumes are preceded by a colon and folio references, sometimes including a r for recto or v for verso are preceded by the word folios. In some cases files are unnumbered and the citation lists only the volume and the folio pages, or vice versa.

Names	Birth date	Date of 1st Marr.	Date of 2nd Marr.	Sex	Length of 1st Marr in Years	Length of 2nd Marr in Years	Race	Race of 1st Spouse	Race of 2nd Spouse	Archival Citation[1]
Muñoz Palomir, Pedro	1568	1707	1718	Male	0.1		Spaniard	Spaniard	Unknown	797, folios 234-354.
Muñoz, Isabel	1512	1585	1532	Female		3	Mestizo	Mestizo	Unknown	137: 10.
Muñoz, Ysavel, alias la muñoza	1532	1522	1532	Female			Spaniard	Spaniard	Spaniard	22: 4.
Ortega, Melchior, alias Melchior de León Ortega	1532	1560	1573	Male	2.5	14	Spaniard	Spaniard	Creole	
Ortíz, José Francisco, alias Charco de la piedra	1740	1773	1778	Male	5	3	Indian	Indian	Indian	
Ortíz, Pedro, alias Martín Ortiz	1533	1569	1573	Male	1	4	Spaniard	Mestizo	Unknown	1194: 1, folios 1-102.
Orvel, Favian	1726	1748	1764	Male	2	23	Creole	Creole	Mestizo	134: 13.
Otalora Carvajal, Lorenzo de	1626	1653	1659	Male	1	4	Slave	Indian	Mestizo	1231: 9, folios 171-287.
Ovando, Christoval	1735	1752	1780	Male	16	14	Spaniard	Spaniard	Creole	610: 11, folios 233-384.
Pabón, Juan Antonio	1680	1701	1711	Male	1.5	0.3	Mestizo	Mestizo	Indian	1199: 29, folios 214-62.
Pacheco, Juan Estebán	1721	1734	1758	Male		1	Zambo	Unknown	Unknown	815, folios 456-573.
Palomino Arias, Nicolás, alias García Espinosa	1672	1713	1720	Male	2	2	Mulatto	Mulatto	Mestizo	1088, folios 211-74.
Pan y Agua, Joseph María	1716	1736	1740	Male	0.8	6	Creole	Creole	Unknown	796: 53, folios 515-523.
Panizal, Pedro de, alias Pedro Cortés	1548	1768	1576	Male		3	Spaniard	Spaniard	Unknown	816: 35, folios 315-90.
Pantaleón, Santiago	1742	1750	1779	Male	5	0.2	Creole	Mestizo	Mulatto	136: 4.
Pérez de Gardea, Joseph	1731	1562	1751	Male	2	4	Mestizo	Mestizo	Mulatto	1242: 19, folios 262-316.
Pérez de Othaeugui, Joan		1752	1581	Male		5	Spaniard	Spaniard	Unknown	137: 3.
Pérez Escandon, Joseph Antonio			1763	Male		1.5	Zambo	Indian	Indian	1145: 27, folios 377ff.
Pérez, Ana				Female	9		Spaniard	Spaniard	Spaniard	22: 8.
Pinero, Antonio	1544	1564	1608	Male	7	3	Spaniard	Spaniard	Mestizo	317: 1.
Pinto Maldonado, Antonio	1705	1726	1581	Male	11	2	Spaniard	Spaniard	Mestizo	136: 5.
Pisa, Antonio de	1747	1764	1742	Male	5	3	Mulatto	Mestizo	Mulatto	1336: 14, folios 1-70.
Pisano, María Manuela	1670	1692	1781	Female		5	Zambo	Unknown	Mulatto	1234: 1, folios 1-37.
Puerto y Arriola, Francisco del	1711	1746	1702	Male	6.5		Spaniard	Spaniard	Creole	548: 3.
Quesada, Agustín de	1577	1595	1746	Male	5	1.4	Spaniard	Spaniard	Creole	820: 1, folios 1-52.
Quiñones, don Francisco del, alias don Alvaro de Quiñones			1607	Male		8	Spaniard	Spaniard	Creole	308, folios 99rff.
Quintero de los Sanctos, Joan	1539	1582	1586	Male	0.3	3	Spaniard	Spaniard	Mestizo	138: 4.
Quintero Pastor, Joan		1569	1583	Male	2	6	Spaniard	Spaniard	Mulatto	138: 3.
Quintero, Christobal				Male			Black	Spaniard	Unknown	23: 5, folios 23-29
Rabelo, Manuel	1551			Male			Spaniard	Spaniard	Unknown	135: 2.

Name			Sex						Reference
Ramírez, Andrés	1712	1735	Male	2	5	Mestizo	Indian	Mulatto	964: 4, folios 211-302.
Ramírez, Beatriz	1549	1560	Female	2	6	Mulatto	Indian	Black	134: 3.
Ramírez, Juan Antonio	1716	1733	Male	0.5	3	Creole	Mulatto	Creole	1341.
Rangel, Francisco	1630	1730	Male	1	0.5	Mestizo	Unknown	Mestizo	606: 4, folios 381-414.
Reyes, Joseph Miguel	1750	1757	Male	2	6	Mestizo	Indian	Mestizo	1013.
Reyes, Mariana de los	1565	1585	Female			Mulatto	Black	Mestizo	137: 2.
Reyes, Pascual de los	1712	1730	Male		1	Slave	Slave	Indian	918: 19, folios 247-313.
Riberos, Francisco de	1576	1606	Male	0.4	1	Spaniard	Spaniard	Spaniard	325: 6.
Rivera, Gerónimo de	1570	1591	Male		3	Spaniard	Spaniard	Unknown	Huntington Library-12-HM35106-Pt. 2.
Robles Quiñones, Cosme de	1586	1604	Male	1	0.1	Creole	Mulatto	Unknown	508: 1, folios 1-76.
Rodríguez, Antonio Bezerra	1555		Male		5	Spaniard	Spaniard	Unknown	308, folios 110-111.
Rodríguez, Domingo	1597	1619	Male	0.5	0.5	Mestizo	Indian	Mulatto	332, 7.
Rodríguez, Felipe, alias Joseph González	1725	1741	Male	25	1	Mulatto	Mulatto	Indian	1156.
Rodríguez, Francisco	1541	1556	Male	2	7	Mulatto	Spaniard	Indian	108: 4, folios 291-92.
Rodríguez, Jhoan	1553	1575	Male	0.3	10	Spaniard	European	Indian	272: 1, and 262: 6.
Rodríguez, Luis, alias Luis Ramírez	1556	1576	Male	0.3		Spaniard	Spaniard	Spaniard	137: 4.
Rodríguez, Manuel de la Trinidad, alias Chauca	1714	1734	Male	7	9	Mestizo	Indian	Mulatto	942, folios 1-100.
Rodríguez, Pedro Pablo	1721	1742	Male	4	20	Mulatto	Mulatto	Mulatto	1166: 7, folios 172ff.
Romano, Manuel	1559	1577	Male	0.3	1.5	Spaniard	Indian	Mulatto	108: 5.
Rosas, Hernández de	1575	1599	Male	18	2	Spaniard	Unknown	Unknown	333: 29.
Ruíz, Catalina			Female			Spaniard	Unknown	Unknown	134: 1.
Ruíz, Petronila	1555	1572	Female	0.1		Mulatto	Unknown	Mulatto	134: 10.
Sánchez de los Santos, Eusebia	1752	1765	Female	3	2	Mulatto	Unknown	Mulatto	1266: 8, folios 246r-311v.
Sánchez Matheus, Pedro	1545	1558	Male	24	3	Spaniard	Spaniard	Spaniard	137: 1.
Sánchez Navarro, Alonso, alias Pedro Navarro	1533	1563	Male	12	18	Spaniard	Spaniard	Spaniard	135: 3.
Sánchez, Martín	1529	1556	Male	6	11	Spaniard	Spaniard	Spaniard	134: 11.
Sanctabaya, Alonso de	1549	1567	Male	5		Spaniard	Spaniard	Unknown	136: 8.
Santana Izquierdo, Juan de	1743	1775	Male	6	1.3	Mulatto	Spaniard	Mulatto	1279: 13, folios 1-99.
Sebastián, Nicolás, alias Sebastián López	1651	1671	Male	0.1	20	Mulatto	Slave	Unknown	525: 51.
Serna, Alonso de la	1511	1530	Male			Spaniard	Spaniard	Unknown	22: 6 and 10.
Serrano y Mora, don Joseph	1730	1760	Male	0.3	1	Spaniard	Spaniard	Creole	1128

1. All references (except two from the Huntington Library) refer first to the volume number in the Inquisition Section of Mexico's National Archive. File numbers within given volumes are preceded by a colon and folio references, sometimes including a r for recto or v for verso are preceded by the word folios. In some cases files are unnumbered and the citation lists only the volume and the folio pages, or vice versa.

Names	Birth date	Date of 1st Marr.	Date of 2nd Marr.	Sex	Length of 1st Marr in Years	Length of 2nd Marr in Years	Race	Race of 1st Spouse	Race of 2nd Spouse	Archival Citation[1]
Soriano y Galbes, Joseph Antonio, alias Joseph Antonio Roquete	1733	1752	1763	Male	1	5	Mestizo	Indian	Mulatto	1062: 2.
Sotomayor, María de			1537	Female	10	1.3	Spaniard	Spaniard	Spaniard	36: 6, folios 199-311.
Ulloa, don Juan Antonio	1649	1667	1680	Male	11	1.5	Spaniard	Spaniard	Spaniard	657: 1, folios 125-75.
Valencuela, Pedro de, alias Pedro de Pineda, alias don Pedro de Valencuela, alias don Pedro Ponce	1581	1600	1604	Male	2	0.1	Spaniard	Spaniard	Unknown	466: 14, folios 329-82.
Valle, Francisco del	1616	1647	1654	Male	7	0	Creole	Creole	Creole	563: 16, folios 413-633.
Valles, Vincente del	1727	1748	1759	Male	11	0.3	Spaniard	Spaniard	Creole	1066.
Vargas, Gerónimo de	1518	1537	1547	Male	2	0.5	Spaniard	Spaniard	Unknown	134: 5.
Vargas, Luisa de	1545	1556	1569	Female			Unknown	Unknown	Unknown	29: 11, folios 102-412.
Vázquez Borrego, Manuel Antonio	1729	1762	1776	Male	7	7	Spaniard	Creole	Creole	1207: 6, folios 118-257.
Vázquez, Juana	1505	1522	1530	Female	10	8	Spaniard	Spaniard	Spaniard	22: 16, folios 235-276.
Vega, Catalina de	1550	1562	1563	Female	0.1	10	Spaniard	Unknown	Unknown	91: 9.
Velásquez, Francisco	1706		1742	Male			Indian	Indian	Unknown	919: 8.
Villagrán, María de	1552	1566	1582	Female	6	4	Mestizo	Mulatto	Indian	137: 5.
Villar, Anna María de, alias la Xixona, alias buen rostro	1713	1726	1746	Female	5	7	Indian	Unknown	Unknown	964, folios 1-168.
Villareal, Diego de	1523	1540	1547	Male	1		Spaniard	Black	Unknown	23: 10, folios 166-226
Zapata, María Ignacia	1765	1777	1786	Female	1.5	1	Creole	Mestizo	Mulatto	1275: 16, folios 1-110.
Zavala, Joseph Eugenio	1740	1758	1768	Male	5	2	Creole	Creole	Slave	1102: 3, folios 135-190.
Zúñiga, Bartolomé de	1663	1677		Male	4		Spaniard	Creole	Unknown	543: 11, folios 141-75.

1. All references (except two from the Huntington Library) refer first to the volume number in the Inquisition Section of Mexico's National Archive. File numbers within given volumes are preceded by a colon and folio references, sometimes including a r for recto or v for verso are preceded by the word folios. In some cases files are unnumbered and the citation lists only the volume and the folio pages, or vice versa.

Glossary

adulterino (a): person born of an adulterous union

alcalde: member of a municipal council and judge of first instance

audiencia: high court and advisory council to viceroys

barragana: common-law partner

barraganía: cohabitation of a man and a woman outside the bonds of matrimony

cacao: chocolate

calidad: judgment of worth in Spanish colonial society with reference to race, wealth, culture, and connections

casta: person of mixed race

compadrazgo: kinship through godparentage

compadre (plural compadres): godfather; friend; a ritual kin through sponsorship of a child at baptism or a bride or groom at marriage

converso: converted Jew, a "new" Christian

doctrina: Indian parish

don, doña: honorific reserved for men and women of noble birth but increasingly debased from the seventeenth century

encomendero: holder of an encomienda

encomienda: grant of Indians by the crown to a private individual who gains tribute payments or labor from them

escuela de amigas: girls school

espurio: person fathered by a priest

estancia (plural estancias): farm or ranch

estanciero: owner of an estancia

gachupín (plural gachupines): derogative term for Spaniard

hacendado: owner of an hacienda

hacienda: large rural estate

hidalgo: person of the lower nobility

labrador: farmer or farm worker

ladino, a: mestizo or Indian person who functions in Spanish culture and language

lobo (a): person of African and Indian descent

luterano (a): Protestant

madrina: godmother

maestro (a): teacher

mala vida: bad life

Merlina: nickname from Merlin of the Arthurian Legend

mestizo (a): person of Indian and Spanish descent

milpa: plot of land used for growing maize

morisco (a): in Spain a Muslim convert to Christianity; in Mexico, a light-skinned mulatto

novena: nine consecutive days of prayers and devotions

padrino: godfather

patrón (plural patrones): patron

pícaro: rogue, rascal

posada: inn, lodging house

presidio: frontier fort in which soldiers were permanently garrisoned

proceso: trial

pueblo: town

rancho (plural ranchos): farm smaller than an hacienda

real (plural reales): Spanish coin

tierra: land, but in the sense of "his tierra" the meaning his homeland

vaquero: cowboy

vecindad (plural vecindades): collective residence

vecino (plural vecinos): citizen

zambo: person of Indian and African descent. See also lobo.

Notes

Introduction

1. John Bossy, "The Mass as a Social Institution," *Past and Present* 100 (August 1983): 39.

2. Ibid.

3. John Tutino, *From Insurrection to Revolution in Mexico: Social Bases of Agrarian Violence, 1750–1940* (Princeton: Princeton University Press, 1988), 61.

4. E. P. Thompson, "Patrician Society, Plebeian Culture," *Journal of Social History* 7(1) (fall 1973): 383.

5. Cited in Edward Muir and Guido Ruggiero, eds., *Microhistory and the Lost Peoples of Europe*, trans. Eren Branch (Baltimore and London: The Johns Hopkins University Press, 1991), xii.

6. Emmanuel Le Roy Ladurie, *Montaillou: The Promised Land of Error,* trans. Barbara Bray (New York: George Braziller, 1978); Carlo Ginzburg, *The Cheese and the Worms: The Cosmos of a Sixteenth-Century Miller,* trans. John Tedeschi and Anne Tedeschi (Baltimore: Johns Hopkins University Press, 1980).

7. As opposed to indirectly, in labor drafts vetted by native leaders. Charles Gibson, *Tlaxcala in the Sixteenth Century* (Stanford: Stanford University Press, 1967 [1952]), 192–94; Charles Gibson, *The Aztecs Under Spanish Rule: A History of the Indians of the Valley of Mexico, 1519–1810* (Stanford: Stanford University Press, 1964), 380; Juan Javier Pescador, *De bautizados a fieles difuntos: Familia y mentalidades en una parroquia urbana: Santa Catarina de México, 1568–1820* (México: El Colegio de México, 1992), 202.

8. Peter Laslett, *The World We Have Lost* (London: Methuen and Company, 1965 [1970]), 53.

9. Pierre Chaunu, "Inquisition et vie quotidienne dans l'Amérique espagnole au XVIIe siècle," *Annales E.S.C.* 11(2) (1956): 230. See also Jean-Pierre Dedieu, "The Archives of the Holy Office of Toledo as a Source for Historical Anthropology," trans. E. W. Monter, in Gustav Henningsen and John Tedeschi, eds., *The Inquisition in Early Modern Europe: Studies on Sources and Methods* (DeKalb, Ill.: Northern Illinois University Press, 1986).

10. Julio Caro Baroja, *Los judíos en la España moderna y contemporánea,* 3 vols. (Madrid: Alianza Editorial, 1961).

11. Richard E. Greenleaf, *The Mexican Inquisition of the Sixteenth Century* (Albuquerque: University of New Mexico Press, 1969), 1–2.

12. James Lockhart, review of *Reliving the Past: The Worlds of Social History,* ed. Olivier Zunz, *Hispanic American Historical Review* (hereafter HAHR) 67(3) (August 1987): 500.

13. See the appendix for all known birth and marriage dates for the entire sample.

14. Enciso Rojas, "El delito de bigamia," 80–81, 104; Solange Alberro, *La actividad del Santo Oficio de la Inquisición en Nueva España 1571–1700* (México: Instituto Nacional de Antropología e Historia, 1981), 233–34.

15. Alberro, *La actividad,* 15–17.

16. Enciso Rojas, "El delito de bigamia," 96.

17. Alberro, *La Actividad,* 257.

18. Enciso Rojas, "El delito de bigamia," 112–13.

19. I borrow the term "pointillism" from Emmanuel Le Roy Ladurie, *Montaillou, village occitan de 1294 à 1324* (Paris: Gallimard, 1982[1975]), 10.

20. In Boyer, *Lives of the Bigamists,* 252 n28, I discuss the issue in more detail and give examples of how other historians have handled the question.

21. Archivo General de la Nación, Mexico (hereafter AGN), Inquisición tomo 642, exp. 1, f. 75v.

Chapter One

1. AGN, Inquisición, t. 1038, fs. 1–78. This paragraph is drawn from various sections of the file: the first *audiencia de oficio* of the inquisitors with Andrés, the description made of him when he was put in the inquisitorial jail, and the certified copy of the record of this marriage in the parish register of Escuintla. Archival references to all other cases in this study, together with other vital data, can be found in the appendix.

2. Ignacio was a cousin of Paula's mother.

3. Today Salamá, ten miles or so east of Rabinal.

4. Jaime Contreras and Jean-Pierre Dedieu, "Geografía de la Inquisición española: La formación de los distritos, 1470–1820," *Hispania* 40 (1980): 40–42.

5. Edward Peters, *Inquisition* (Berkeley and Los Angeles: University of California Press, 1989), 84.

6. Jaime Contreras, "Aldermen and Judaizers: Cryptojudaism, Counter-Reformation, and Local Power," in Anne J. Cruz and Mary Elizabeth Perry, eds., *Culture and Control in Counter-Reformation Spain* (Minneapolis: University of Minnesota Press, 1992), 93–123.

7. Contreras and Dedieu, "Geografía de la Inquisición española," 40–42.
8. Jaime Contreras and Gustav Henningsen, "Forty-four Thousand Cases of the Spanish Inquisition (1540–1700): Analysis of a Historical Data Bank," in Henningsen and Tedeschi, eds., *The Inquisition*, 113–14. The attempt to quantify Inquisition activity provided scholars with a picture of broad trends, but one that has proved to be statistically unreliable; Henry Kamen, *The Spanish Inquisition: A Historical Revision* (New Haven and London: Yale University Press, 1998), 198–99, 341 n12.
9. Richard E. Greenleaf, *Zumárraga and the Mexican Inquisition, 1536–1543* (Washington, D.C.: Academy of American Franciscan History, 1962), 3–25; Greenleaf, *The Mexican Inquisition*, 7–8.
10. Contreras and Henningsen, "Forty-four Thousand Cases," 115.
11. Charles V's cedula of 1538 placed Indians under the jurisdiction of the viceroy rather than the Inquisition but became effective only on December 30, 1571, as decreed by Philip II. Greenleaf, *Zumárraga,* 74 and 68–74.
12. Greenleaf, *Zumárraga,* 17–18, 68, 74; Solange Alberro, *Inquisición y sociedad en México, 1571—1700* (México: Fondo de Cultura Económica, 1988), 21–22; Robert Ricard, *The Spiritual Conquest of Mexico*, trans. Lesley Byrd Simpson (Berkeley, Los Angeles, London: University of California Press, 1966), 272–73; Serge Gruzinski, *Man-Gods in the Mexican Highlands*, trans. Eileen Corrigan (Stanford: Stanford University Press, 1989), 197n.
13. After a chart prepared by Yolanda Mariel de Ibáñez reproduced as appendix 31 in M. Ballesteros Gaibrois, "Los fondos inquisitoriales americanísticos," in *Historia de la Inquisición en España y América*, vol. I, directed by Joaquin Pérez Villanueva and Bartolomé Escandell Bonet (Madrid, 1984), 132. Don Pedro Moya de Contreras arrived in Mexico City on September 12, 1571.
14. Bartolomé Bennassar, *L'inquisition espagnole du XVe au XIXe* (Paris: Hatchette, 1979), 326–36 and cited in Dedieu, "The Archives," 59; Gustav Henningsen, "The Archives and the Historiography of the Spanish Inquisition," in Henningsen and Tedeschi, eds., *The Inquisition*, 67. In Mexico, diocesan courts handled most of the concubinage cases whereas in Europe, the Holy Office was strongly concerned with it. Ibid., and Alberro, *La actividad,* 68.
15. Alberro, *Inquisición y sociedad*, 26.
16. "Instrucciones del Ilustrísimo Señor don Diego de Spinoso, Inquisidor general, para la plantación de esta Inquisición," Madrid, 18 August 1570, in Archivo General de la Nación, México, *Catálogo del Ramo Inquisición (1)*, revisado y corregido por Guillermina Ramírez Montes (México: Departamento de Publicaciones del Archivo General de la Nación, 1979), 12–21; Alberro, *Inquisición y sociedad*, 199–202. The directives pay close attention to record keeping.

17. Alberro, *La actividad*, 18.

18. María Paz Alonso Romero, *El proceso penal en Castilla (siglos XIII-XVIII)* (Salamanca: Ediciones de la Universidad de Salamanca, 1982), *passim*; Jean Pierre Dedieu, "L'inquisition et le droit: Analyse formelle de la procédure inquisitoriale en cause de foi," *Mélanges de la Casa de Velázquez* 23 (1987): 250.

19. Alonso Romero, *Proceso penal*, 208; Jean Delumeau, *Sin and Fear: The Emergence of a Western Guilt Culture, 13th–18th Centuries*, trans. Eric Nicholson (New York: St. Martin's Press, 1990), 191–92.

20. L. Suárez Fernández, "Los antecedentes medievales de la Institución," in *Historia de la Inquisición en España y América*, vol. 1, 266–67; J. Contreras, "Las adecuaciones estructurales en la Península," ibid., 754–59.

21. Jaime Contreras, quoting from a "Juramento que ha de leer el pueblo antes de que se lea el Edicto de fe," [undated but most likely from the second half of the sixteenth century] in "Las adecuaciones estructurales en la Península," in *Historia de la Inquisición en España y América,* 755. To date, 281 edicts of faith promulgated in Mexico between 1576 and 1819 have been located in the Mexican archives, all but twenty of which originated in Mexico. Alberro, *Inquisición y sociedad*, 75n, 76n.

22. Kamen, *The Spanish Inquisition*, 175–76.

23. Cited in Julio Jiménez Rueda, *Don Pedro Moya de Contreras: Primer Inquisidor de México* (México, 1944), 49, and in Medina, *Historia del Tribunal*, 47, 52. The first edict, authored by Moya, was published November 4, 1571. Alberro, *Inquisición y sociedad*, 128.

24. Defined by the Council of Trent as contrition, confession, and satisfaction. Rev. J. Donovan, trans., *The Catechism of the Council of Trent* (Dublin: Keating and Browne, 1829), 262–72.

25. Medina, *Historia del Tribunal*, 47.

26. Alberro, *Inquisición y sociedad*, 75–77.

27. Cited in Ruth Behar, "Sex and Sin, Witchcraft and the Devil in Late-colonial Mexico," *American Ethnologist* 14(1) (February 1987): 50.

28. Medina, *Historia del Tribunal,* 65–66. The high fascination focused on the English corsairs of John Hawkins who were captured off Veracruz in 1568.

29. Peters, *Inquisition,* 1–74. This paragraph is based on ibid., 75–104.

30. Henry Charles Lea, *A History of the Inquisition of Spain*, vol. III (New York: AMS Press, 1966), 37; Kamen, *The Spanish Inquisition,* 205.

31. Alberro, *Inquisición y sociedad,* 30–79; 223–80 (on prison life), 379–413 (on frontier zones).

32. Donovan, trans., *The Catechism of the Council of Trent,* 278.

33. Peters, *Inquisition,* 87; Le Roy Ladurie, *Montaillou,* xiii; Jacques Le Goff, *The Birth of Purgatory,* trans. Arthur Goldhammer (Chicago: University of Chicago Press, 1981), 214, and 213–17.

34. Pierre Goubert, *The Ancien Régime: French Society, 1600–1750,* trans. Steve Cox (New York: Harper and Row, 1973), 267.

35. For similar conventions in seventeenth-century Florence, see Giulia Calvi, *Histories of a Plague Year: The Social and the Imaginary in Baroque Florence,* trans. Dario Biocca and Bryant T. Ragan, Jr. (Berkeley and Los Angeles: University of California Press, 1989), 56. My thanks to Jacqueline Holler for pointing me to this work.

36. The notary inserts that don Juan was "gravely ill and close to death," which may account for the five-week delay between Andrés's arrest and hearing.

37. For a detailed treatment of the problems involved in collecting the evidence against Andrés, see the first edition of Boyer, *Lives of the Bigamists,* (1995), 22–29.

38. Regulations called for the completion of the three hearings within ten days of formal incarceration. Gustav Henningsen, *The Witches' Advocate: Basque Witchcraft and the Spanish Inquisition, 1609–1614* (Reno: University of Nevada Press, 1980), 40, 456–57n.

39. Revisions crop up in second and third hearings, but usually only small ones. Yet slight emendations and rephrasings can provide significant clarifications of prisoners' stories and reveal glimpses of their states of mind as imprisonment drags on.

40. Hiding the identity of witnesses protected them from possible retaliation. Summaries omitted identifying detail, not what a notary might have thought was irrelevant detail. Note, however, that at the very outset of this case the deputy alcalde mayor failed to hide the identity of a denouncer by sending Andrés and Ignacio to Guatemala together.

41. Representing the bishop within whose jurisdiction the crime took place.

42. Don Francisco Xavier Gamboa and don Francisco Leandro de Viana, judges of the criminal chamber.

43. In this case a *sentencia con méritos,* which was a summary of the trial together with the verdict. Rarely were such judgments read behind closed doors.

44. Northrup Frye, *Anatomy of Criticism: Four Essays* (Princeton: Princeton University Press, 1957), 43–52.

45. Peters, *Inquisition,* 87.

46. Dedieu, "The Archives," 168.

47. Ida Altman, *Emigrants and Society: Extremadura and Spanish America in the Sixteenth Century* (Berkeley, Los Angeles, London: University of California Press, 1989), 92.

48. Asunción Lavrin, "Sexuality in Colonial Mexico," in Lavrin, ed., *Sexuality and Marriage in Colonial Latin America* (Lincoln: University of Nebraska Press, 1989), 47–92.

49. Alberro, *La actividad,* 233–34.

50. Patricia Seed, *To Love, Honor, and Obey in Colonial Mexico: Conflicts Over Marriage Choice, 1574–1821* (Stanford: Stanford University Press, 1988), 63, 266–67n.

51. Robert McCaa, "Marriageways: Courtship, Coupling, Cohabitation and Matrimony in Mexico and Spain, 1500–1900" (Paper prepared for a conference on "Familia y Vida Privada: América, siglos XVI a XIX, May 3–4, 1993, Mexico City), 13; Thomas Calvo, "The Warmth of the Hearth: Seventeenth-Century Guadalajara Families," in Lavrin, ed., *Sexuality and Marriage,* 292–93, 297; Pescador, *De bautizados,* 147, 149, 201. Illegitimacy rates for Indians is far lower than for Spaniards, castas, and blacks, and lower in rural than urban places. Claude Morin, *Santa Inés Zacatelco, 1646–1812* (México: Instituto Nacional de Antropología e Historia, 1973), 73–74.

52. Woodrow Borah and Sherburne F. Cook, "Marriage and Legitimacy in Mexican Culture: Mexico and California," *California Law Review* 54 (1966): 950–51. As a formal contract in writing, barraganía seems to have died out in the fifteenth century (McCaa, "Marriageways," 7) but stable forms of cohabitation informally embedded in the culture continued to be a commonplace as we shall see. Pilar Gonzalbo Aizpuru, *Las mujeres en la Nueva España: Educación y vida cotidiana* (México: El Colegio de Mexico, 1987), 44–47.

53. Michael C. Scardaville, "Crime and the Urban Poor: Mexico City in the Late Colonial Period" (Ph.D. diss., University of Florida, 1977), 167, 164–74. The census of 1811 records that no fewer than 70 percent of all women were living in households without men in the parish of Santa Catarina in Mexico City (Pescador, *De bautizados,* 222, 243–44).

Chapter Two

1. Elsa Malvido, "Algunos aportes de los estudios de demografía histórica al estudio de la familia en la época colonial de México," in Seminario de historia de las mentalidades, *Familia y sexualidad,* 92–94.

2. Pescador, *De bautizados,* 210 and 202–12 *passim.*

3. Ibid., 210; see also Josefina Muriel, "La transmisión cultural en la familia criolla novohispana," in Pilar Gonzalbo Aizpuru, *Familias novohispanas: Siglos XVI al XIX,* (México: El Colegio de México, 1991), 113–22.

4. Carlo Ginzburg, "Clues: Roots of an Evidential Paradigm," in Carlo Ginzburg, *Clues, Myths, and the Historical Method,* trans. John and Anne C. Tedeschi (Baltimore and London: Johns Hopkins University Press, 1989), 114–15.

5. Martín spent his first six or seven years in Colmenar del Arroyo (province of Madrid), the next eight years in San Martín de Valdeiglesias (province of Madrid), and then moved to Cebreros. Martín's mother was from San Martín and his father from nearby Hoyos [del Espino].

6. By now Martín most likely held the title of master, for aside from examiners being more lenient with the sons of colleagues, the assumption was that daily contact with a father resulted in sufficient knowledge of the father's trade. Felipe Castro Gutiérrez, *La extinción de la artesanía gremial* (México: UNAM, 1986), 75–76.

7. By his first wife, Martín had six children. Three survived; two went to the Indies. He also had three children by his second wife, but it is not clear whether in Seville or in Mexico. In the second marriage, Gerónimo Sánchez a co-worker in the mint (and possibly a relative?), acted as padrino, a point that shows us once again Martín's linkages to other men of his trade.

8. He mentions only the "pull" factors of Seville and then the Indies as destinations, but not debt or an unhappy marriage, which might have "pushed" him.

9. Also known because Joanna the Mad, daughter of Ferdinand and Isabella and technically joint ruler of Spain with her son Charles V (Holy Roman Emperor from 1519), had been locked up in the Tordesillas castle for nearly fifty years (1506–1555). Geoffrey Parker, *Philip II* (Boston, Toronto, 1978), 87.

10. Later, in New Spain, he commented expertly on different handwriting in letters sent from home.

11. For some patterns and variations see Altman, *Emigrants and Society,* 150–53.

12. Cosme was an *hijo natural,* the offspring of unmarried parents and the least serious of the illegitimate categories, for had his parents ever married, he automatically would have become legitimate. Ann Twinam, "Honor, Sexuality, and Illegitimacy in Colonial Spanish America," in Lavrin, ed., *Sexuality and Marriage,* 118–49, esp. 119.

13. On the logic of avoiding interracial marriage, the Spanish jurist Juan Solórzano Pereira noted that "few Spaniards of honour . . . would marry an Indian or Negro woman." A young man who petitioned to do so in nineteenth-century Cuba cited his "misfortune of being one of those men . . . cut off from society and in constant contact with the pardos." Verena Martínez-Alier, *Marriage, Class and Colour in Nineteenth-Century Cuba: A Study of Racial Attitudes and Sexual Values in a Slave Society* 2d ed., (Ann Arbor: University of Michigan Press, 1989), 64–65, 161n.

14. On the marginality of "non-encomendero farmers and stock growers," see Lockhart's comments in "Spaniards Among Indians: Toluca in the Later Sixteenth Century," in James Lockhart, *Nahuas and Spaniards: Postconquest*

Central Mexican History and Philology (Stanford: Stanford University Press, 1991), 209.

15. In Puebla Cosme worked at his trade for less than half of the four-year period following the marriage, and for a year and a half in Mexico City after he left Juana. Possibly he collaborated in some way with his brother Pedro Muñoz (who used his mother's surname), apparently a journeyman tailor.

16. They too were probably married to Indian women from the town although Joseph does not specify this. He does say that one sister was married to a French pharmacist (*chímico*) in Tezcuco and another to Vicente [?] Alvarez, a weaver in Calpulalpan.

17. As a guess, he might have gambled away some of his wife's possessions, which did happen. For literary treatment of the vice of gambling within the context of Counter-Reformation Spain, see Anne J. Cruz, "La bella malmaridada: Lessons for the Good Wife," in Cruz and Perry, eds., *Culture and Control,* 160.

18. Felipe could say the Lord's Prayer, Ave Maria, Salve, and Credo well and could name the sacraments correctly, but he crossed himself incorrectly and stumbled on the ten commandments. He did not learn to read or to write. Rural types, as we shall see in other cases, seemed to fare less well in their knowledge of religious doctrine.

19. A hint of the cost of such an end comes from his request, ten months before he died, to be allowed some time in the sun to relieve the pain in his feet caused by the dampness of his cell. Juan's linkage of dampness and problems with the feet suggests poor circulation, possibly gout, a form of arthritis. Juan died with his request denied.

20. Jean Pierre Dedieu, "'Christianization' in New Castile: Catechism, Communion, Mass, and Confirmation in the Toledo Archbishopric, 1540–1650," in Cruz and Perry, eds., *Culture and Control,* 3–6; Adriaan C. Van Oss, *Catholic Colonialism: A Parish History of Guatemala, 1524–1821* (Cambridge: Cambridge University Press, 1986), 143–46, 162. Parental rejection of schools once again underlines their supplementary place in raising children.

21. Pilar Gonzálbo Aizpuru, *Las mujeres en La Nueva España: Educación y vida cotidiana* (México, 1987), 129.

22. Dedieu, "'Christianization' in New Castile," 3–6; Gonzalbo, 92, 104–5, 127–47.

23. The quotation is from María's hearing of May 6, 1788.

24. Gonzalbo, *Las mujeres,* 129. On comparative literacy rates from a sample of 659 marriage applications from the archdiocese of Mexico City, Seed, counting the ability "to put even a few letters together," found only 16 percent of women literate as opposed to 46 percent of men. Patricia Seed, "Marriage Promises

and the Value of a Woman's Testimony in Colonial Mexico," in *Signs* 13 (2) (winter 1988): 272.

25. From 1542, Perpignan was under siege by French troops in the fourth in a series of wars (1542–1545) between Spain and France. Don Francisco de Paula Mellado, et al., *Diccionario universal de historia y de geografía,* 7 vols. (Madrid, 1846), II, 180; VI, 72; Antonio Domínguez Ortiz, *The Golden Age of Spain, 1516–1659* (New York: Basic Books, 1971), 59.

26. Lockhart, *Nahuas and Spaniards,* 93.

27. The laws of the Indies specified three general categories of *escribanos*: public, royal, and enumerated. A royal scribe could work anywhere in the king's domain except in towns where enumerated scribes had been granted a monopoly. Bernardo Pérez Fernández del Castillo, *Historia de la escribanía en la Nueva España y del notariado en México* (México: Editorial Porrúa, 1988), 55.

28. Not officially the capital until 1561.

29. Louisa Schell Hoberman, *Mexico's Merchant Elite, 1590–1660: Silver, State, and Society* (Durham and London: Duke University Press, 1991), 65, 64–68; Muriel Nazarri, "Parents and Daughters: Change in the Practice of Dowry in São Paulo (1600–1770)," *Hispanic American Historical Review* 70: 4 (November 1990), 639–65.

30. *Chalupas* are small two-masted boats fitted with six or eight oars on each side.

31. Among them, archbishop designate and future Viceroy of New Spain doctor don Juan Antonio de Vizarrón y Eguiarreta (1734–1740), like Manuel a Basque, and as well several inquisition judges.

32. For influential Basques in Chihuahua see Phillip L. Hadley, *Minería y sociedad en el centro minero de Santa Eulalia, Chihuahua (1709–1750)* (México: Fondo de Cultura Económica, 1979), 42–43, 46–47.

33. Cosihuiriáchic had "200 vecinos ca 1745"; at roughly the same time San Felipe reportedly had a population of "2000 families of 'Spaniards' . . . in addition to an undisclosed number of mestizos and mulattoes." Peter Gerhard, *The North Frontier of New Spain* (Princeton: Princeton University Press, 1982), 190, 200. There were other settlements as well within the district. The main centers, Santa Eulalia and San Felipe, counted 214 and 292 vecinos, respectively, in 1725. Hadley, *Minería y sociedad,* 33.

34. On the care with which the Jesuits looked after the spiritual life of their workers on haciendas, see Gonzalbo, "Ortodoxia imposible," 862.

35. So Mateo said in his autobiographical statement, nearly twenty years later (November 23, 1666). Mateo also claimed that his father-in-law later sent a letter reporting that María had died.

36. Mateo, claiming to be "sickly" (*achacoso*) and suffering from the cold of his cell, asked for a blanket after his first hearing. His discomfort, however, lasted but a short time, as the judges decided that he was an Indian and remanded him to the jurisdiction of "the ordinary of the Indians of this archbishopric."

37. Miguel de Cervantes, "Rinconeta y Cortadillo," in *Six Exemplary Novels,* trans. Harriet de Onís (New York: Barron's Educational Series, 1961), 166.

38. The family had consisted of both of Juan's parents, a maternal uncle, and paternal aunt. The aunt had two sons and two daughters: one son was still single and the other was a priest; the daughters were both married to bakers, one with three children, the other he did not know about. In addition Juan's brothers, Joseph, Casimiro, and Miguel (all apparently older than Juan and therefore having benefited from longer parental contact) also based themselves in or near Puebla. Joseph followed the trade of his maternal uncle, gunsmithing, and married a woman of Puebla; Casimiro moved to nearby Acacingo, probably to farm, and to marry (Juan didn't know with whom); Miguel married a woman from Puebla but later moved to Mexico City. Because Juan moved between Alvarado, Veracruz, and Mexico City, he maintained regular contact with Miguel (the only brother whose children, three in this case, he knew about) in Mexico City but apparently not with Casimiro and Joseph.

39. In this he would have been a typical product of a parish school, where the object was to teach reading by means of printed prayers and catechisms. These would have been partly memorized anyway, so the "reading" must have been a quasimnemonic aid. Probably the ability to read cursive writing depended on learning to write.

40. The first comes from his "confession," a statement taken on January 23, 1731, when he was arrested, the second from Bernabé's autobiography, in his hearing of September 3, 1731.

41. In his midthirties he knew that his parents were dead and could say that he had known his maternal grandmother (Juana la Bautista, "Indian") and two maternal aunts ("Thomasa, married to Pedro, a slave; María, married to an *indio chino* tailor"). "He only had one sister, María de la Candelaria; he left her in Querétaro and knows nothing about her."

42. For this series I include Baltasar, who at seven ran away from his uncle; "ten" could be ten to twelve, assuming that Pedro Mateo's "pretty big" might mean twelve or so.

43. Tezontepec was an Augustinian doctrina from 1554, but by the middle of the eighteenth century it had been secularized. It was in the far south of the Pachuca jurisdiction. Peter Gerhard, *A Guide to the Historical Geography of New*

Spain (Cambridge: Cambridge University Press, 1972), 209–11. Bárbara mentions San Mateo Yxtlahuaca as her place of birth; Bustamante said it was Rancho Santa María.

44. In this Pedro was not alone, for a parish census of Xalostotitlan in 1650 has more than a third of the pueblo's Indians not registered because they were on haciendas. Gerhard, *North Frontier,* 107.

45. On early modern mortality rates see, for example, Robert Wheaton, "Introduction: Recent Trends in the Historical Study of the French Family," in Robert Wheaton and Tamara K. Hareven, eds., *Family and Sexuality in French History* (Philadelphia: University of Pennsylvania Press, 1980), 13.

46. Silvia Marina Arrom, *The Women of Mexico City, 1790–1857,* (Stanford: Stanford University Press, 1985), 62.

Chapter Three

1. Nancy F. Cott, "Divorce and the Changing Status of Women in Eighteenth-Century Massachusetts," *William and Mary Quarterly,* 3d ser., 33 (1976): 611–12; Arrom, *The Women,* 65–79.

2. On dowries see Thomas Calvo, "Matrimonio, iglesia y sociedad en el occidente de México: Zamora (siglos XVII a XIX)," in Gonzalbo, *Familias novohispanas,* 107n; Asunción Lavrin and Edith Couturier, "Dowries and Wills: A View of Women's Socioeconomic Role in Colonial Guadalajara and Puebla, 1640–1790," *Hispanic American Historical Review* 59 (2) (May 1979): 282; Altman, *Emigrants and Society,* 70–72, 96, 98.

3. Arrom, *The Women,* 62, 67–68; Lavrin and Couturier, "Dowries and Wills," 282.

4. Muriel, "La transmisión cultural en la familia criolla novohispana," in Gonzalbo, *Familias novohispanas,* 109.

5. Ibid., 51; Robert Wheaton, "Introduction: Recent Trends in the Historical Study of the French Family," in Wheaton and Hareven, eds., *Family and Sexuality,* 11. The *información matrimonial,* or marriage application, preceded Trent and, after the Confesionario of fray Alonso de Molina (1569), consisted of the petition, the authorization to proceed by the vicar general, the testimony attesting to the unmarried status of the petitioners, the statement by the petitioners that it is their will to marry, and the granting of a license to marry. María de Lourdes Villafuerte García, "Casar y compadrar cada uno con su igual: Casos de oposición al matrimonio de la ciudad de México, 1628–1634," in Seminario de Historia de las Mentalidades, *Del dicho al hecho . . . : Transgresiones y pautas culturales en la Nueva España,* (México: Instituto Nacional de Antropología e Historia, 1989) 66–67.

6. Ramón Gutierrez, *When Jesus Came, the Corn Mothers Went Away: Marriage, Sexuality, and Power in New Mexico, 1500–1846,* (Stanford: Stanford University Press, 1991), 241–70 *passim,* but especially 267–68 for the sacramental rite in the church setting. This is a kind of ideal version. Often there was no nuptial mass; often the marriage took place out of sight of the priest or, with him present, but in a private home; often there was a long gap between marriage and the *velación,* or priestly blessing. Calvo, finding the marriage and blessing increasingly fused into one event from 1727, suggests that this represents a culmination of the church's long campaign to transform marriage from mainly a social to a sacramental occasion. Calvo, "Matrimonio, Iglesia y sociedad," 105–6; see also his *Poder, religión y sociedad en la Guadalajara del siglo XVII* (México: Centre d'études Mexicaines et Centramericaines, 1992), 169.

7. Gutierrez, *When Jesus Came,* 254, 227–29; Beatrice Gottlieb, "The Meaning of Clandestine Marriage," in Wheaton and Hareven, eds., *Family and Sexuality,* 70; Robert McCaa, "Gustos de los padres, inclinaciones de los novios y reglas de una feria nupcial colonial: Parral, 1770–1814," *Historia Mexicana* 40 (4) (1991): 586–91.

8. But, as Seed has shown, for church officials to annul a marriage on grounds of clandestinity would normally require a woman to testify that "she had [not] willingly participated in the sexual act . . ." Thus, the existence of the impediment seemed directed more to protect the consent of contracting parties than to alter procedures as such. In French law clandestinity equates with abduction rather than elopement because *clandestinité* meant "without parental consent" rather than "without proper formalities." Patricia Seed, *To Love, Honor, and Obey,* 255 n9, 32–34, 89–90, 275 n49. See also Charles Donahue, Jr., "The Canon Law on the Formation of Marriage and Social Practice in the Later Middle Ages," *Journal of Family History* 8 (2) (summer 1983), 144–45.

9. Seed, *To Love, Honor, and Obey,* 34–35, 254 n6; G. L. Mosse, "Changes in Religious Thought," in *The New Cambridge Modern History,* IV, 185–87.

10. John Lynch, *Spain under the Habsburgs* (Oxford: Basil Blackwell, 1964), I, 258 and 236–70 *passim.*

11. J. H. Elliott, *Europe Divided 1559–1598* (Glasgow: Fontana/Collins, 1968), 162.

12. Seed, *To Love, Honor, and Obey,* 35–40.

13. Martínez-Alier, *Marriage, Class and Colour,* 104.

14. Elsewhere he said eight days. Note that this adds precision to his bold statement quoted above that he had fled after the nuptial.

15. The brothers were in San Lucar for final embarkation when, at the last minute, Francisco fell ill and remained behind. For a year he stayed in Seville, avoiding contact with anybody in Lepe while awaiting the next year's sailing

and a reunion with Pedro in New Spain.

16. As we shall see in chapter 4, Mariana later regretted the marriage, ran away from Manuel, and remarried.

17. She was therefore an *espurio*, the most despised category of illegitimates in Hispanic society. Borah and Cook, "Marriage and Legitimacy," 950–51; Ann Twinam, "Honor, Sexuality, and Illegitimacy in Colonial Spanish America," in Lavrin, ed., *Sexuality and Marriage,* 119.

18. Gutiérrez, *When Jesus Came,* 190 and 176–226 *passim.*

19. But nothing is said of a *marriage,* the mutual pledge to be man and wife, which apparently did not happen.

20. Lavrin, "Introduction," 6; "Sexuality," 62–63; Seed, "Marriage Promises."

21. On the contractual basis of marriage as drawn from Roman law see James A. Brundage, "Sexual Equality in Medieval Canon Law," in Joel T. Rosenthal, ed., *Medieval Women and the Sources of Medieval History* (Athens and London: University of Georgia Press, 1990), 68; Lavrin, "Introduction," 6.

22. Cott, "Divorce," 599.

23. Gutiérrez, *When Jesus Came,* 255; McCaa, "Gustos," 593; Pescador, *De bautizados,* 150–75.

24. Gutiérrez, *When Jesus Came,* 231.

25. On don Bernardino see Guillermo Porras Muñoz, *El gobierno de la ciudad de México en el siglo XVI* (México: Universidad Nacional Autónoma de México, 1982), 391–94.

26. Vega must have been a notary attached to the local Spanish governor because Indian notaries writing in Nahuatl handled wills, deeds, and other legal instruments and they also wrote out the documents that recorded matters of town government. The governor (*corregidor*) would have adjudicated "petty squabbles over lands, debts, thefts, and women" and dealt with blacks, castas, and Spaniards as well as Indians. Gibson, *Aztecs,* 91; S. L. Cline, *Colonial Culhuacan, 1580–1600: A Social History of an Aztec Town* (Albuquerque: University of New Mexico Press, 1986), p, 37 and for Indian notaries, 43–47 and *passim;* Rebecca Horn, "Spaniards in the Nahua Countryside: Dr. Diego de León Plaza and Nahuatl Land Sale Documents," in Richard Boyer and Geoffrey Spurling, *Colonial Lives: Documents on Latin American History, 1550–1850* (New York: Oxford University Press, 2000), 101–11.

27. Porras Muñoz, *El gobierno,* 205, 268.

28. Martínez-Alier, *Marriage, Class and Colour,* 111; Twinam, "Honor," 127. We shall return to this theme below.

29. Lesley Byrd Simpson, *Many Mexicos,* 4th ed., (Berkeley and Los Angeles: University of California Press, 1966), 133.

30. The marriage to Alonso might not have been entirely satisfactory, to judge from a long-standing liaison Catalina had with Blas Mexía while married to Alonso. Blas, a vecino of Mexico City seventeen years older than Catalina (age forty when he testified in 1573) said that he "had Catalina de Vega as his mistress (*concubina*) for four or five years but left her two years ago out of fear of his conscience." This may have been possible only because Alonso had abandoned Catalina for long periods.

31. For additional discussion of clerics as brokers see Boyer, *Lives of the Bigamists,* (1995), 79–81.

32. As well the age discrepancy between the bride and groom may have been a reason to keep the wedding out of public view—thus eliminating two of the public announcements of it—to avoid the disorderly outbursts of ridicule that sometimes accompanied such matches. For the French case, see Natalie Zemon Davis, *Society and Culture in Early Modern France* (Stanford: Stanford University Press, 1975), 105, 301 n35.

33. The petition appears as direct speech as indicated by my translation.

34. When a similar report surfaced in Zultepec before the marriage, Carreño extracted such strong denials from Pedro that he allowed the marriage to proceed.

35. Gottlieb, "Meaning of Clandestine Marriage," 69.

36. Martínez-Alier, *Marriage, Class and Colour,* 122 and 103–19 *passim.*

37. For an instance of the "alliance-making" between servant and mistress to facilitate the latter's love affair—"a potent, if unreliable weapon in women's campaigns to blunt male power"—see Elizabeth S. Cohen and Thomas V. Cohen, "Camilla the Go-between: The Politics of Gender in a Roman Household (1559)," *Continuity and Change* 4 (1) (1989): 53–77. I'm grateful to Asunción Lavrin for this reference.

38. Richard Boyer, "Juan Vázquez, Muleteer of Seventeenth-Century Mexico," *The Americas* 37 (1981), 436–40.

39. See appendix, Matheo de la Cruz.

40. Seed speaks of a "semantic drift" in the meaning of love late in the eighteenth century from "attachment or will" based on reason to "uncontrollable sexual passion." Seed, *To Love, Honor, and Obey,* 118–20.

41. Under Spanish law a "*miserable*" was considered "weak and wretched" and therefore granted special procedures reserved for people without the resources to defend themselves. See, for example, Borah, *Justice by Insurance: The General Indian Court of Colonial Mexico and the Legal Aides of the Half-Real* (Berkeley: University of California Press, 1983), 11–12.

42. Martínez-Alier, *Marriage, Class and Colour,* 122.

43. Richard Boyer, "Negotiating Calidad: The Everyday Struggle for Status in Mexico," *Historical Archaeology* 31 (1) (1997): 64–73.
44. Gutiérrez, *When Jesus Came,* 213–14.
45. This account comes from the denunciation of the Spaniard don Manuel Francisco de la Torre of Querétaro. The notary kept don Manuel's account in the first person, as is reflected in my translation.
46. Manuel and Josepha settled into a married life that in eleven years produced four children. Then about 1738, Manuel went to San Luis Potosí, "deflowered" an eighteen-year-old servant in his supposed half-brother's household, and eloped with her.
47. Cervantes fictionally contrived to "solve" the problem of rape in his "La fuerza de la sangre," in *Spanish Stories/Cuentos Españoles,* ed. Angel Flores (New York: Bantam, 1960), 64–91.
48. Don Francisco's sister was doña Ana del Valle y Ávila, widow of don Pedro de Candinas, a former magistrate and [wheat?] farmer in nearby Tepeaca and Guaxoçingo."
49. On the attribution *muger del mundo* as a male tactic to counter a woman's claim that betrothal had preceded seduction see Lavrin, "Sexuality," 59; McCaa, "Gustos," 599, 601, and 602; François Giraud, "La reacción social ante la violación: del discurso a la práctica (Nueva España, siglo XVIII)," in Seminario de Historia de las Mentalidades, *El placer de pecar y el afán de normar* (México: Editorial Joaquín Mortiz, 1987), 330.
50. Inns, taverns, and private houses dispensed large quantities of pulque or wine. Laws attempting to limit the number of such outlets in Mexico City date from 1579, 1585, and 1586. William B. Taylor, *Drinking, Homicide and Rebellion in Colonial Mexican Villages* (Stanford: Stanford University Press, 1979), 37. In the sixteenth century towns in the valley of Mexico began to shift production from maize to pulque to supply "taverns with pulque along the entire route to Mexico City by 1590." Gibson, *Aztecs,* 318. For the eighteenth century see, in addition to Taylor, Juan Pedro Viqueira Albán, *Propriety and Permissiveness in Bourbon Mexico,* trans. Sonya Lipsett-Rivera and Sergio Rivera Ayala (Wilmington: Scholarly Resources, 1999), 129–63; and Michael C. Scardaville, "Alcohol Abuse and Tavern Reform in Late Colonial Mexico City," *Hispanic American Historical Review* 60 (4) (November 1980): 643–71.
51. Not apparently, because she needed one, for she no doubt spoke Spanish, but likely "in the name of juridical unimpeachability." Lockhart, *Nahuas and Spaniards,* 106. Nevertheless it may mean that Nahuatl was Leonor's mother tongue in spite of her designation as mulatto.
52. The distinction can be seen, for example, in Corella's seventeenth-century

manual for confessors. P Fr. Iayme de Corella, *Práctica de el confessonario y explicación de las 65 Proposiciones condenadas por la santidad de N.S.P. Inocencio XI: Su materia los casos más selectos de la theología moral: Su forma un diálogo entre el confesor y penitente* [Valencia: Imprenta de Iaume de Bordazar, 1689], 105–6. I am grateful to Asunción Lavrin for calling my attention to this work.

53. Lavrin, "Introduction," 6. For Blas López, another example of the type, who was "notorious for wooing women with promises of marriage," see Gutiérrez, *When Jesus Came,* 237–38. The behavior may have become more frequent during the eighteenth century (Seed, "Marriage Promises").

54. Martínez-Alier, after legislation by the Council of the Indies in 1780, also distinguishes between "elopements for reasons of marriage" and "elopement with a view to premarital concubinage." Martínez-Alier, *Marriage, Class and Colour,* 103–19.

55. Edward Shorter, *The Making of the Modern Family* (New York: Basic Books, 1975), 73.

56. Gutiérrez, *When Jesus Came,* 231. The exception, as we have seen, might be foundlings or illegitimate daughters that parents expected to remain permanently in the household as "servants."

57. This paragraph comes from Isabel's autobiographical statement (October 29, 1588).

58. Corella, *Práctica de el confessonario,* 60.

59. The distinction failed to impress the judges who found him guilty and sentenced him to two hundred lashes and six years rowing in the galleys.

60. Cited in Borah and Cook, "Marriage and Legitimacy," 950 (emphasis added).

61. Pierre Bourdieu, "Marriage Strategies as Strategies of Social Reproduction," in Robert Forster and Orest Ranum, eds., *Family and Society: Selections from the Annales: Économies, Sociétés, Civilisations,* trans. Elborg Forster and Patricia M. Ranum (Baltimore: The Johns Hopkins University Press, 1976), 140.

62. Gottlieb, "Meaning of Clandestine Marriage," 67.

63. Seed has shown how arguments within parental oppositions stressed the *future* contentment of their children. Seed, *To Love, Honor, and Obey,* 120–21, my emphasis.

Chapter Four

1. John Bossy, "The Counter-Reformation and the People of Catholic Europe," *Past and Present* 47 (May 1970): 60.

2. Ibid., 15; André Burguière, "Le rituel du mariage en France: Pratiques ecclésiastiques et pratiques populaires (XVIII siècle)," *Annales: Économies, Sociétés, Civilisations* 33, 3 (May–June 1978): 644; Sara Tilghman Nalle, "Religion and Reform in a Spanish Diocese: Cuenca, 1545–1650," (Ph.D. diss.,

The Johns Hopkins University, 1983), 228–32, and Sara Nalle, "Popular Religion in Cuenca on the Eve of the Catholic Reformation," in Stephen Haliczer, ed. and trans., *Inquisition and Society in Early Modern Europe* (London and Sydney: Croom Helm, 1987), 67–87; and Dedieu, "The Inquisition and Popular Culture," in Haliczer, ed. and trans., *Inquisition and Society,* 129–46.

3. As the model applies, see François Giraud, "De las problemáticas europeas al caso novohispano: Apuntes para una historia de la familia mexicana," in *Familia y sexualidad en Nueva España: Familia, matrimonio y sexualidad en Nueva España, Memoria del primer Simposio de Historia de las Mentalidades* (México: Fondo de Cultura Económica, 1982), 58–59. I also deal with this connection in Boyer, "Women, La Mala Vida, and the Politics of Marriage," in Lavrin, *Sexuality and Marriage,* 252–55.

4. Giraud, "La reacción social," 340.

5. Shorter, *Making of the Modern Family,* 222 and 218–27 *passim* provides a general orientation to the rest of the paragraph. See also Davis, *Society and Culture,* 97–123.

6. Bossy, "Counter-Reformation and the People of Catholic Europe," 54.

7. The notary's recording of Petronila's testimony as direct speech is reflected in the translation below.

8. Ruiz Gaytán reminds us that "adultery and seduction" as well as rape, were "middle and upper class moral dramas" but never much of an issue when working class or servant women were so violated. Beatriz Ruiz Gaytán F., "Un grupo trabajador importante no incluido en la historia laboral mexicana (trabajadoras domésticas)," in Elsa Cecilia Frost, Michael C. Meyer and Josefina Zoraida Vázquez (compiladores), *El trabajo y los trabajadores en la historia de México* (México and Tucson: El Colegio de México and University of Arizona Press, 1979), 433. See also Giraud, "La reacción social."

9. Killing one's spouse to marry a lover was obviously an invalidating impediment. Corella, *Práctica de el confesonario,* 120–21.

10. I take Campomayor to be El Campo "in Trujillo's tierra," which at that time had ninety-seven vecinos. Both villages were in the province of Cáceres. Altman, *Emigrants and Society,* 103.

11. Remembered by Francisco López, the shoemaker, from a conversation he had with Violante after she returned to El Campo.

12. Cited in Mary Elizabeth Perry, *Gender and Disorder in Early Modern Seville* (Princeton: Princeton University Press, 1990), 14.

13. She wrote from Tordehumos, in the diocese of Palencia.

14. The quotations come from Beatriz's testimony, recorded as direct speech, in 1538.

15. For a discussion of how abandoned women might have supported themselves, see Perry, *Gender and Disorder,* 14–32.

16. Appendix: don Salvador de Caoto y Morales.

17. Diego was not among the conquistadores who made representations to the first viceroys (1540–1550) for rewards for services. This is probably because he had shifted his base to Peru. Francisco A. de Icaza, compiler, *Conquistadores y pobladores de Nueva España: Diccionario autobiográfico sacado de los textos originales,* 2 vols., (Guadalajara: Edmundo Aviña Levy, 1969 [Madrid, 1923]).

18. Juan Núñez de Prado left Potosí late in 1549 with seventy soldiers—one of them must have been Diego—and arrived in the Tucumán area in the early 1550s. In 1552 he moved the original foundation of Tucumán, El Barco, fifty leagues to the south where Santiago del Estero is located. Roberto Levillier, *Nueva Crónica de la Conquista del Tucumán,* 3 vols., (Madrid: Sucesores de Rivadeneyra, 1927–1931), I, 183.

19. This testimony, dated 1562, is part of Diego's proof of service collected by his son Pedro in Lima.

20. Huntington Library, HM 35159.

21. The fleet left Spain in the last two weeks of May, 1600, and on arrival at Veracruz (the exact date is unknown), fourteen ships were lost, because they failed to navigate the sandbar. Diego was therefore lucky to arrive unscathed. Huguette et Pierre Chaunu, *Séville et l'Atlantique, 1504–1650* (Paris: Librairie Colin, 1955–56), 4: 92, 99n.

22. Emphasis added.

23. Possibly Valle de San Francisco where the Alamos mining camp was located (now in San Luis Potosí state).

24. Jan Bazant, *Cinco haciendas mexicanas: Tres siglos de vida rural en San Luis Potosí (1600–1910)* (México: El Colegio de México, 1975), 30–34.

25. For a more detailed discussion of beating as part of the mala vida see Boyer, *Lives of the Bigamists,* (1995), 132–40.

26. Cited in Glen Caudill Dealy, *The Latin Americans: Spirit and Ethos* (Boulder: Westview Press, 1992), 36 35n.

27. Manuel probably devised the plan that brought Mariana from safety. He enlisted the help of Mariana's friend, Francisca de Garibay, who (as Mariana recounted it) went to the convent and "told [Mariana] to go back to her house and she would give her whatever she needed. She was not to be afraid because Manuel had fled after [Francisca] complained to the Viceroy, the marqués de Manzera, telling him that Manuel Figueroa had given her the mala vida and abusive treatment [because] he was going to send Manuel to China [that is, the Philippines]."

28. Cott, "Divorce," 611–12; Arrom, *The Women,* 247–49; and appendix C.
29. Although María was born of Spanish parents, she was orphaned at four months and raised in the convent of Santa Clara in Mexico City. At fourteen she went to live with a sister and in 1772, a year later, married the mestizo José Antonio Santos. José was from San Juan Teotihuacán and a farmer (*labrador*) in nearby Tepexpan. As José was a man of humble standing, María had not gained much by marrying him. As an orphan, however, she lacked the economic leverage to do better.
30. María ran away to Mexico City and served sister Gertrudis Gil in the convent of San Lorenzo. Five months later, however, three aunts of her husband, José Antonio Santos, saw María on the street, took her to the priest of Santa Catalina, and notified José. José came and brought María back to Tepexpan to resume married life.
31. Her mother was probably a widow, for nothing is said of her father.
32. In Mexico don Joseph married a second time, in 1772, and the Inquisition arrested and tried him for bigamy. To the inquisitors in 1774 he told a more embellished story than my brief summary suggests. He apparently hoped they would accept it as justification for the abandonment of doña Francisca. The day of the wedding, he said, "a *compañero* and friend said, 'what have you done, man? This woman is a descendant of Jews.'" For good measure, don Joseph added, the same friend "after some years" told him that doña Francisca had died. The inquisitors were not impressed. They found don Joseph guilty and sentenced him to abjure a light suspicion of heresy (abjure de levi), to receive two hundred lashes, and to serve in an African presidio (to be determined by the Supreme Council of the Inquisition in Madrid) for six years.
33. The quotation comes from his autobiographical statement.
34. In the same statement he points more directly to his reason for separating from Ignacia after a six-year marriage (1764–1770). "At the end of 1770 he separated from her because of the 'annoyances of imprisonment' because his brother-in-law Marcos de la Cruz had him arrested for 20 pesos that he owed him."
35. Ruth Behar, "Sexual Witchcraft, Colonialism, and Women's Powers," in Lavrin, ed., *Sexuality and Marriage,* 183.
36. She described his visits as follows: "The first time he came with his brother and stayed a few days. The second and third times were last May when she was sick. He came by and she complained to him with tears that she was poor and destitute. But he had only come to pick up a hat that he had left the last time he was in Mexico City. She didn't see him again until last Thursday afternoon [June 1722] when he came with his uncle, both on horseback, and

stayed until Saturday. He slept at the house every night but took his meals outside and then the Inquisition arrested him."

37. He had sponsored the child of Gómez and Francisca at baptism.
38. H. Parry, *The Sale of Public Office in the Spanish Indies under the Hapsburgs* (Ibero-Americana: 37; Berkeley and Los Angeles: University of California Press, 1953), 6.
39. Quoted in María de Lourdes Villafuerte García, "Casar y compadrar cada uno con su igual: Casos de oposición al matrimonio de la ciudad de México, 1628–1634," in Seminario de las Mentalidades, *Del dicho,* 66.
40. Francisco was returning to the Jesuit hacienda La Sieneguilla from Mexico City on an errand for Father Pedro Sánchez.
41. For a discussion of the pressures on married life caused by debt, crime, and punishments, see Boyer, *Lives of the Bigamists,* (1995), 152–56.
42. J. Eric S. Thompson, ed., *Thomas Gage's Travels in the New World* (Norman: University of Oklahoma Press, 1958) 68–69.
43. James C. Scott, *Domination and the Arts of Resistance: Hidden Transcripts* (New Haven and London: Yale University Press, 1990), 1–16.

Postscript

1. Francisco del Paso y Troncoso, compiler, *Epistolario de Nueva España, 1505–1818* (México: Antigua Librería Robredo de José Porrúa e Hijos), 7: 248.
2. Paso y Troncoso, *Epistolario,* 11: 144.
3. Jiménez Rueda, *Don Pedro Moya de Contreras,* 49.
4. The Seminar on the History of Mentalities and Religion in Colonial Mexico goes further. After Althusser, they hypothesize "the church as the ideological apparatus of the dominant state." They seem to mean by this that church teachings meshed with the interests of the dominant classes who controlled the state, a supposed connection I have commented on elsewhere (Richard Boyer, "Escribiendo la historia de la religión y mentalidades en Nueva España," in Seminario de Historia de las Mentalidades, *Familia y sexualidad,* 119–37.) My concern here is the more modest one of showing some examples of the mentality of ordinary people, or, in different terms, some results of the so-called imposition of church ideology.
5. Ricard, *Spiritual Conquest,* 102–3.
6. Also the clear sequence serves to underscore his good faith in not marrying a second time until *after* hearing of his wife's death.
7. Surprisingly, Esquival himself seemed unsure of what to do, and referred Francisco to another priest named Soriano, who told Francisco to go to the Holy Office and confess his sin "because [as Pedro remembered] if your first

wife is still alive clearly you cannot marry a second time when you are a faithful Christian Catholic."

8. Which he dated as "the year that the fleet of the black vomit, as it was called because so many were sick, arrived at Vera Cruz."

9. Pastoral theology distinguished between contrition (sincere remorse) and attrition (fear of punishment), the latter ruining "the efficacy of the sacrament." Donald J. Wilcox, *In Search of God and Self: Renaissance and Reformation Thought* (Boston: Houghton Mifflin, 1975), 259.

10. In fact death always lay close at hand, ready to strike with or without warning. Almost any sickness or injury could prove fatal and the afflicted often seemed more likely to die than to survive.

11. Before she became sick "she heard mass every day at Santa Teresa, and for the past two years she has always confessed; the last time that she took communion was in her house while she was sick in bed."

12. For more on these tragic results of confinement by the Inquisition (a product of boredom, isolation, interminable imprisonments, and unbearable psychological pressure) see Alberro, *Inquisición y sociedad*, 252–60.

Index